Imagine being in an agricultural village near a city of well over a million people and you're one of maybe six Americans you interact with. You don't speak the local language and you're there to teach English to some college students whose entire life will be irrevocably influenced by how well they do on their tests. Either they will do well and go on to some form of higher education or they will do poorly and end up in some dark factory room counting ball bearings day after endless day.

Your tiny on-campus apartment has a chair that falls over unless you sit in it just so. You do have a computer that can even get on the Internet. Sometimes. Washing clothes in the "washing machine" is a man-vs-machine contest and drying takes two to three days, even for the lightest garments. For much of the year you wear two sets of thermal underwear under your clothes plus an overcoat if you want to stay warm. And that's inside.

Most of your classrooms do have functioning electricity, and the college library does have some books, but few that anyone would want to read. There are a few tall buildings in the village but not one of them, save the fancy hotel, has an elevator. Supermarkets? Forget it. The sky is mostly gray, television is government controlled and predominantly in Chinese, and you're there for a year and a half.

How do you handle all of this? If you're Susan and Robert McKee, you handle it very well, thank you.

Days Like Floating Water provides a full-immersion plunge into twenty first century China. You see real life, not tourist life. You do not meet the Chinese people, you meet actual Chinese people dealing with human challenges that sound achingly familiar in the midst of an incredibly alien culture.

There's King Lake (you just have to love a boy with a name like that) who wants to marry Barbara but is concerned that her family has more money than his so they will not find him suitable. Besides, the couple are in their early 20's and romance is usually reserved for those closer to 30 or so. Chris is a young girl who is so stressed out by her upcoming tests that she can't eat or sleep for weeks and has to go to the hospital for her endless stomachaches. Lucy is born to music, though she has access to no musical instrument until Susan buys a keyboard and teaches her, of all things, Chopsticks.

The stories are fascinating, the people are charming, the most mundane activities are adventures. These are folks, the McKees and their Chinese friends, you want to know better and experiences you will want to keep exploring. This is a book you simply don't want to end.

DAYS LIKE FLOATING WATER

DAYS LIKE FLOATING WATER

A Story of Modern China

SUSAN EDWARDS MCKEE

oak leaf
impressions
press

San Luis Obispo, CA

Oak Leaf Impressions Press
1241 Johnson Ave. #207
San Luis Obispo, CA 93401
www.dayslikefloatingwater.com

Publisher's Cataloging-In-Publication

McKee, Susan Edwards.

    Days like floating water : a story of modern China / Susan Edwards McKee. -- San Luis Obispo, CA : Oak Leaf Impressions Press, c2008.

       p. ; cm.

     ISBN: 978- 0- 9799306- 0- 7

     1. China-- Description and travel-- 21st century. 2. China-- Social life and customs-- 21st century. 3. Americans-- China--Biography. 4. Humanitarian volunteers--China. I. Title.

DS712 .M424 2008   2007939299
951.06/088372-- dc22   0801

LCCN 2007939299

ISBN-10: 0-9799306-0-X

Cover and Book Design: Patricia Bacall
Cover Art: Susan E. McKee
Book Consultant: Ellen Reid

Printed in the United States of America on acid-free paper.

*For Robert, my everlasting love and best friend, and
for our two one-of-a-kind daughters Robin and Bonnie,
along with our number one son Wes. They have enriched our
lives and hearts further now with their own cherished families.*

Contents

I gratefully acknowledge the invaluable guidance of my "book shepherd" Ellen Reid, as well as the graceful graphics work by Patricia Bacall and just the right words by Laren Bright.

I'm also indebted to my best friend and artistic wizard Judy Carroll.

From the Author

China looms large in the world as it emerges from hibernation. Of course this lumbering dragon has not actually been sleeping. Those of us outside the Great Wall have only recently been able to peek between the stones at this ancient culture. Fear quivers on both sides of the wall.

Then why did Rob and I volunteer to spend a year and a half living next to a grumpy water buffalo outside our apartment window? This was Communist China! The college students at the small teacher's school were desperate to improve their English because they saw this as a path to a better life. But they were terrified of us, their new English teachers. We'd just unpacked our books when NATO bombs mistakenly crushed the Chinese Embassy in Yugoslavia killing several people. We huddled in our dark apartment seeing TV footage of the weeping father of one of the dead women at the embassy clutching a blood-soaked blanket, and of shrieking Chinese crowds burning the American flag.

Slowly though we were accepted, insofar as foreigners ever can be, into the swirling current of life inside this proud culture as it tossed its fire-breathing nostrils and warily eyed the Outside World. Our students stumbled over our language at first. Their village, primary English teachers were Chinese who had never heard English spoken. We laughed together at our mistakes, ours as we bumbled into their lives, and theirs as they relaxed and quizzed us about life in the United States. This story is true. I've changed some names, but they're real people who, hesitantly at first, stepped into our lives. We could not have dreamed those first days and months that one of our students would struggle and succeed in expressing his so-Chinese thoughts in writing, more than a year later:

> *"Time is precious; we should master it, not the slave of it. And we must keep it in our own hand. It is a big treasure; we should do and must do something for both ourselves and the society. We must study hard and learn more so we will not regret it that we've spent the meanless time and floated. The days, like floating water, will never come back again."*

But maybe they will! Here. In these pages.

GRAY IS THE COLOR

G ray is the color, so much gray. Concrete buildings with little thought of ornament, utilitarian, barred windows, winding streets awash with two and three-wheeled bicycles hauling people, rusted propane bottles, sugar cane, chunks of cement or rocks, absolutely anything. People are in gray, with dashes of color here and there. The sky is often gray too. It's winter here in Chuga, a small village on the edges of the ancient city of Ningbo, China, a city of 1.2 million souls lurching into the twenty-first century, anxious to be rid of its past of crumbling buildings, wearing its adolescence in tall towers and taxicabs rather self-consciously. In the cold rain, and it seems to rain often here, umbrellas bloom in colors, but the heavy gray seems to mute even those.

Curious eyes follow my husband and me as we wind through the crowd searching for scallions, bok choy and snow peas at the large, new cement-covered market. I'm new at this, going from stall to stall, squinting at the vegetables and muttering in probably incomprehensible Chinese that the peas do not look fresh today, hoping to bargain for a lower price. (Chen Je Jun—Jenny—who quickly became our advisor, instructor and friend the day we arrived in

China, has coached me on exactly what to say.) I wonder if the vendors, their fabric sleeve protectors pulled over their coat sleeves, can sense my apprehension. I've read that animals can smell fear. What about people? I wonder if I'm sending out signals as my heart thumps and beads of sweat gather even under my winter coat.

The meat-sellers call out and wave their wares to attract our business. I'm not used to the hunks of fat and meat with hooves and hair still attached or the whole pigs' heads or ears just lopped off the bleeding animal. My tender American supermarket sensibilities have provided antiseptic separation from the realities of what we eat. Now I'm faced with animals, either quite dead or live chickens, or plumed, exotic birds which I'm expected to dispatch myself.

Vegetarianism becomes more and more appealing. Eggs! I see piles of eggs! But there are many sizes and shapes of them. Here are small speckled ones, here eggs coated with mud and straw, here dappled eggs. There! These look like chicken eggs. One by one, we select six eggs, which the giggling stall proprietress carefully weighs in a hand-held scale. We negotiate the price, which comes to 2.8 yuan today, about thirty cents. Carefully she puts them in a thin blue plastic bag, and now I'm expected to take them home on the bus. Intact.

With our string bag and backpacks full, we wait in the rain for the small bus, probably built in the Ming Dynasty, and flag it down as it careens around the corner. Rob in his Raiders-of-the-Lost-Ark hat and I in my knitted lavender beret (no Chinese seem to wear hats, no matter how cold it gets) are real traffic stoppers anyway. Even babies gape at us. We don't think we look so different from everyone else, but apparently we do. We climb aboard the bus, announcing that we want to go to Nong Shaw. Again Jenny taught us the magic words that tell the bus driver where to let us off. The bus monitor —there must be an official name for the men or women whose job it is to stand at every bus door and impatiently wave and push passengers into the bus—doesn't understand us at first. The bus seats only about twenty passengers, but standees usually double that number. The wonder is that the engines actually continue to function through the gear grinding and the jackrabbit gait the drivers maintain. The monitor comes around to collect our one yuan apiece fare (about twelve cents), and we repeat, Nong Shaw.

"Eh?" Then comprehension, "Ah, ah a-a-ah." She gets it now, the old name of the college where we teach English. It's been called Zhejiang (our province) Rural Teachers College for fifty years, but the locals still know it by its old name. At any rate, after a few days most of the folks around know that the two foreigners with white hair and peculiar clothing need to get off the bus at the college, no matter how they slaughter the Mandarin language.

Rob and I've been in mainland China for two weeks, the start of a year-and-a-half contract to teach English. We're in our sixties, and have been cautioned by the people who sponsor us not to discuss politics or religion in China. That's the deal the Chinese government made so we and others could come and China would get native English-speakers to meet the huge hunger for English teachers here.

China's disenchantment with Russia years ago and their dashed hopes that Russia would lift them into the modern world led them to look to economic competition in the world market to bring prosperity home. So all the schools in China that had been teaching Russian as a second language turned to English, the language of world commerce. The difficulty was that so few Chinese actually spoke English. Chinese teachers struggled with books and a few poorly made tapes to teach a language they'd never heard spoken. That meant students finished high school able to read English at a basic level but terrified at the prospect of actually trying to understand or, worse yet, speak with a native English speaker. Into this setting stepped the two of us one frigid February morning two weeks ago as the students returned to college after the Chinese New Year's holiday. We were all equally apprehensive.

So what skills do we bring with us to these icy classrooms in eastern China (no heat or hot water in any of the buildings on the campus except our on-campus apartment and a few administrative offices)? Are we trained language teachers? No. Robert's Army officer career did include a fair amount of teaching. He later worked in a university administrative position, then as a private consultant overseeing some planning, remodeling and building at the university. Along the way he earned a master's degree in business, hardly an English teacher's background. As it turned out, his business degree earned him downright reverence among our Chinese students.

My background's a bit more pedestrian: a bachelor's degree in English, some substitute teaching over the years, mostly in elementary and junior high schools, while I was "nesting" from Georgia to Germany for my military husband and our three kids. If laying kitchen tiles, scrubbing walls, stretching beef Stroganoff to feed Rob's company officers and their wives, racing from tent to tent at a Girl Scout camp to make sure all the girls were okay during a freak hailstorm, providing taxi service for our son's T-ball team, or dancing the cancan for a charity fundraiser qualify me to teach English as a second language, then I'm in.

In preparation for this volunteer service we had only six full weeks of ESL (English as a Second Language) training and Mandarin Chinese. On our fortieth wedding anniversary we lugged our suitcases to the airport wearing our conservative clothes, me in a dark skirt and jacket, Rob in a suit and tie. Fortunately, we'd e-mailed the couple we were to replace in China, who warned us there was no heat in the buildings and told us they wore two layers of thermal underwear, wool slacks and coats indoors. Our luggage reflected that suggestion, and we carried a suitcase of language workbooks as well. Our predecessors told us that good books were non-existent in China, so we shipped high heels and dressy clothes home to our kids and used our precious suitcase space for warm clothes and books. Summer clothes we shipped via surface mail.

We also decided to take the very calculated risk of packing vitamins, medications and even some sterile syringes. As I packed I imagined the ugly scene of a Beijing customs official opening our suitcases and finding the syringes. We could have been arrested as drug addicts. The people training us, however, advised us to provide our own needles should we ever need an injection in China. They knew of cases where unscrupulous but creative Chinese entrepreneurs recycled syringes, rinsing hospital discards in a murky river, then selling them admirably packaged as new back to the hospital. We decided to take our chances with the customs officials.

We both learned empathy for voodoo dolls after many trips to the hospital for shots to shield us from diseases we recognized and some we'd never heard of. We were cautioned that handwashing was our best friend, to be wary of drinking water and of eating anything unpeeled or uncooked. We got clean bills of health from doctors and dentists. All the instruction, protection, cautions were over. We were a couple of overaged, graying baby birds about to slide to the end of the branch and launch ourselves into the unknown.

We're old hands at flying, but the seventeen-hour flight—a stopover in Tokyo before Beijing—was achingly long. Day and night blurred. We finally stepped off the plane at the Beijing airport at 3:00 a.m. Deserted. Where were the glowering police with rifles slung across their shoulders? This was Communist China! In fact, where was anybody? If there were customs people checking, I don't recall it. I remember only that we had four monstrous suitcases and two smaller ones to manhandle. We grunted and hauled them along echoing, empty corridors and finally found an attendant asleep at a luggage storage area. I truly understood for the first time why the early American pioneers tossed precious heirlooms off the covered wagons. The grumpy attendant thrust a claim ticket at us so we could retrieve our things in the morning for the final leg of our trip, then flopped her head back onto the counter to continue her nap. A cab took us to a hotel where we crawled into very modern beds. Even my fear of the future slept briefly.

Chuga, the village where we shopped for food.

2

WE ARRIVE
IN NINGBO

The gray of China surrounded us that morning in Beijing two weeks ago. In and out of Los Angeles many times, I'm no stranger to smog. Rob and I settled in California up the coast from L.A. long ago, in a small university town that still bristles with ranches, cattle and vineyards. But the smog in Beijing is palpable. The taxi ride back to the airport rambled past unending blocks of unadorned cement apartment buildings and weary businesses. Of course it was February, but we'd come from California with its unrelenting flowers, so my eyes kept hoping for a bit of cheer, maybe a brave potted palm or a tired geranium in a window. But no. Rob and I decided then we'd have to inhale deeply sooner or later, and while the gluey air might shorten our lives, we might as well savor every minute of the unique adventure we were about to leap into.

A much shorter flight took us from Beijing to Ningbo, our final destination—or Ningpo on some maps—a huge city about two hundred miles south of Shanghai at the confluence of three rivers, a bit inland from the South China Sea. It still amazes me that the Western world knows nothing of so populous a city.

Jittery about coming face-to-face with the university people who would meet us at the Ningbo airport, I glimpsed a group of children scrambling over rubble at the end of the runway as our plane taxied in. Some looked up from their play to wave at the plane, a tiny gesture that briefly pulled our worlds together for me. I could still taste the apple I'd had for breakfast though. We were fearful of the hotel restaurant's hygiene and opted for the last two apples we brought with us from the States. Could it have been the taste of fear of the unknown in my mouth as well?

At least half a dozen people met us, first Chen Je Jun—Jenny—whose job at the Zhejiang Rural Teachers College was to take care of and act as liaison for the school's foreign teachers whose ranks we swelled to three. Jenny was about my height, around 5'7", probably in her early forties. Short hair capped a round smiling face, and I noticed she had a habit of tucking her head to one side shyly and lowering her eyes when she was complimented. Her English was very good, and she quickly became our mentor and friend. Zeng Jia Men—James—a young man so slim it seemed his belt could run twice around his waist, was also there to meet us. We learned that he worked with the city of Ningbo recruiting foreign teachers and business people to the area. His English was rapid and eccentric but very understandable. There were others: James' boss, who spoke not one word of English but bowed and welcomed us; the driver of the official car brought to transport us back to the college, no English, only smiles and handshakes; and the Walls, tall Elwood "Woody" Wall and his wife Sandra, also volunteers teaching English at Ningbo College in the city itself. They were old-timers, there for a year already, but were at the airport to greet us, welcome us and offer to e-mail our family to tell them we'd arrived safely. Our suitcases were hoisted into the car. We waved goodbye to the Walls, who returned to their school, and to James and company, and began the drive out of the city to the college that would be our home for a year and a half. Jenny instructed the driver to stop at a hotel, where we had our first Chinese lunch.

The horror that both Rob and I had dreadful colds punctuates my memory of that lunch. We sat at a large table with the traditional lazy susan in the center, covered with the many dishes Jenny ordered. Each of us had a small saucer and a pair of chopsticks, and it became obvious that we were to select tidbits from each serving dish, put the morsel into our mouths, and then dip again into the common bowls. I have always been wary of food poisoning, but that first day Rob and I were painfully aware that our own mouths were a form of germ warfare. We could find no other way, however, to seem polite and feed ourselves but to dip and eat and dip again.

I've never been a fan of seafood. My parents never put it on our table when I was growing up, so when faintly fishy things kept appearing, I began an eighteen-month love affair with peanuts. Dishes of flavored peanuts often appear on the Chinese table.

One disadvantage of the Western style of dining, loading your plate with food and then eating it, is that everyone can see what you leave behind untouched. In China, eating peanuts with chopsticks consumes time and lets you avoid the heaps of tiny shrimp with their little heads and feelers intact or the eel cooked in an odiferous brine. Unless someone is watching what you select, the grazing technique, with no telltale dinner plate in front of you, lets you eat as much or as little as you like.

I was in awe of the young driver, stuffing huge quantities of the tiny, whole shrimp into his mouth with apparent enjoyment. I tried to peel the little rascals and squeeze the heads off before I swallowed one or two, which amused our Chinese hosts. I did taste everything, though I was surprised to see no rice on the table. At the end of the meal we were asked if we would like some rice. We ignorantly chose the right answer and said, "No, thank you." Later we learned that in this area of China, the host offers the best dishes he has. If you ask for rice, he assumes he did not provide enough superior food. I don't know if we gave our new friends and hosts our colds that day, but we feel pangs of guilt about it.

3

THE SWAMP

The drive from Ningbo took us past row after row of apartment buildings and electrical parts stores set among grim office buildings. The view tapered to smaller, square cement buildings, most with iron bedsteads in front displaying rubber products, plastic kitchen bowls or what looked like motor parts. At night we supposed the wares would be packed up and the bed frame withdrawn into the family's living quarters. As the miles rolled away, even those buildings thinned to fenced areas littered with chunks of marble and rock piled near shabby warehouses or heaps of rusted metal beside broken sidewalks. That and the jerry-rigged electrical wires overhead made the scene a safety inspector's worst nightmare! Then came fields with green sprouts. Rice? No, I don't think so. I craned my neck, hoping to see my first water buffalo. Traffic became lighter outside the city, but the pace, noise, and often death-defying choices drivers made left us wondering where all the broken bodies of unwary pedestrians were. Countless bicycles, with their own set of eye-contact rules, added to the confusion. It seemed that if a driver or cyclist refused to make eye contact with an oncoming driver at an intersection, he got to go first. Everyone seemed okay with the "No peekie rule," so Rob and I decided independently to dump the idea of getting bikes for local transportation.

By the time we arrived at the college and our new home, we were not even startled when the driver pulled through a pedestrian gate and drove much too quickly along the path where students were walking and pulled up at our apartment. The apartment was a long—did I mention that it was gray?—concrete building with fifteen units. We were in the first floor end unit. Jenny scurried out of the car, embarrassed because the apartment was locked and no one seemed to have the key. The driver, Robert and I grunted and pushed our behemoth suitcases to the door while Jenny disappeared in search of a key. The driver spoke no English, and the Chinese we'd struggled to learn didn't get us much past exchanging names, weather pleasantries and counting to twenty, which was hard to work into a conversation, so we were left to survey our new surroundings.

All along the building's decaying front, concrete clothesline poles leaned drunkenly between broken, tangled wires, yes wires, not lines. Weeds grew greedily at their feet, and farther down clothes hung limply on the sagging wire.

Jenny reappeared with a key, and we stepped into our apartment. Jenny was obviously pleased with the offering, and we smiled in appreciation. A small sitting room with three chairs opened into a kitchen/eating area. (Later we learned to sit squarely on the sitting room "easy chairs" since a slight sideward twitch caused the chair, along with its occupant, to roll over onto its side.) She was proud to point out all the modern equipment: a two-burner electric cook top, an electric rice cooker, a five-gallon water bottle, a sink with running water (non-potable, I'd been warned), a refrigerator—small by American standards but huge by Chinese—a table and four chairs. The small cupboards were furnished with dishes, pots and pans, even Western silverware. We followed her down a short hallway to our bedroom with a large bed and a much-used free-standing wooden clothes closet, then into the bathroom. Jenny tried to conceal her pride at the Western style toilet, bathtub with shower and small sink. There was even a square automatic washing machine pushed to one side. The drain at the center of the bathroom floor caught my eye, but I said nothing.

Finally everyone left us to unpack, and we sank onto the bed with its bright Oriental red and gold silk flounces. "Uhff!" It looked like a bed but felt like something slightly softer than a sidewalk. Now, we like a firm bed, but this was a cruel joke! The ancient, spotted dark green indoor-outdoor carpeting throughout was worn in spots completely through to the concrete floor. I knew I'd soon be a slave to my compulsive cleaning gene. The apartment was what we learned to call "China clean," but my Swedish background called for a bristle brush and disinfectant. Too, that bathroom drain haunted me. We met our predecessors briefly in America, an American couple, also in their sixties, who were the first humanitarian volunteers to come to this college, and who lived in this apartment. Their message to us was, "Please don't worry. The Chinese will love you!" Comforting, but hard to believe. She also told me she'd found that rats liked to poke their way up into the bathroom through that drain, so she kept a bottle of bleach over it.

We slept well that night, even on our "concrete" bed.

Gradually I learned to shop for food and to cook it. Jenny took us once on the bus to show us where and how to shop in Chuga. My predecessor warned me to scrub all fruits and vegetables with soap and water (remembering that the tap water is not for drinking), then put them in a tub of potable water with a spoonful of bleach, then in a clean wash of potable water—a bit of drudgery I was willing to undergo for a healthy time in China.

Now that we're settled in and learning to live here, a swoosh of water sailing past my kitchen window occasionally startles me. It seems the upstairs neighbors don't always use their sinks to dispose of dishwater or refuse, because the puddles of mud outside the building always hold bits of rice and dinner remnants. I gingerly asked Jenny that first day we arrived where we take our kitchen garbage for disposal. She took Robert to show him, and when I asked to see too, he shook his head. "You don't wanna know." Well, I do need to know, and now we vie so the other one takes the trash to the spot a little way from our building, between two classroom buildings. It's not a bin or a receptacle, just a spot in the ground where everyone deposits whatever they have no use for. Rats and bugs make it their home, and the only reason it isn't an unholy mountain of filth is that an old man comes with a push cart and an ancient twig broom and sweeps it up and carries it away from time to time. (We discovered that it goes over the walls between the school and the busy street that runs past the college.)

But back to the apartment. At night we often hear peculiar gurgling sounds coming from the bathroom. An occasional belch and watery burp usually mean that the next person who goes to the bathroom in the dark (sixty-year-old bladders don't make it through the night) may well step onto a seeping floor or into a puddle, which is more than disconcerting. I announce to Robert,

"We've got to do something!" which he knows means that he must do something. He mutters something like, "I feel like Humphrey Bogart in *The African Queen*. All I need are leeches." Water is bubbling up from that wretched drain in the middle of the bathroom floor. It is necessary for the washing machine (more about that later), so it can't be permanently plugged up. We stumble over the bottle of bleach meant to plug up the drain. Just where and what the water is coming from is a question I don't want an answer for. My knees are raw from scrubbing the floor, I use huge quantities of bleach. Though we call the bathroom The Swamp, I still needle Rob to do something. We know the building will be demolished in a few months to make room for a new dormitory, so repairs and updates are unlikely.

Robert's been enthralled watching the building going on all over campus—all over China, in fact. Tall dormitories and classroom buildings are going up without heavy equipment. The sole tools here are wheeled carts, sledgehammers with long flexible handles, muscle, and thousands of workers. No cement trucks, only small cement mixers endlessly churning at the job site. Rob's past experience supervising building and his awe at what sheer manpower is doing have drawn him to have smiling, nodding acquaintance with many workmen. One day his inventive mind sends his fingers rummaging through my kitchen shelves looking for just the right jar lid. Finally he finds a peanut butter lid that satisfies him. Out at the cement mixer, he asks with gestures and Chinglish if he might have a dollop of cement. The workmen laugh and give him enough to fill the lid. They shake their heads, convinced the silly foreigner has very peculiar tastes.

The cement hardens. He slips the lid into the bathroom drain, and we have a drain cover that stays in place, maybe thwarts The

Rat, can be removed at will, and sometimes even keeps the swamp reasonably dry.

We've scrubbed, scraped and cleaned the apartment's seeping walls and feel quite comfortable. The building, that houses other college staff members who nod to us as we pass outside, is scheduled for demolition next summer. The young father at the other end of the first floor seems especially friendly. His plump wife and baby girl, maybe about eight months old, smile at us too when we stop to beam and coo at the child on our way to classes. If it's not too icy the granddad holds the baby outside. The Chinese language, I'm learning, has different names for each of the four grandparents showing which are the parents of the father or mother. This grandpa is the dad's father, and he's the chief babysitter, which is the usual arrangement. While Mama and Papa go to work, grandparents take care of the babies. They all live in an apartment the size of ours. We note, though, that ours and Jacques', the Canadian teacher next door, are the only ones with an air-conditioning unit at one window.

Air-conditioning seems eons away right now. We have one small, portable heater which oozes heat, then jealously hugs it to itself. We try to crouch near, but beyond the two feet or so it generally warms, the apartment is frigid.

Electricity is very limited, and we need to be cautious about how many things are plugged in at once. Last night the lights flickered and died. Rob got the emergency light and went outside. It wasn't difficult to locate the fuse box, because it was on fire! The young neighbor dad and a neighbor from upstairs came rushing outside too. Somehow they quashed the fire. Then they all scratched their heads, gazing together into the jerry-rigged wooden fuse box. Pretty soon, they'd dragged chairs up to the fuse box, all the better to peer into it, Rob commenting in English (which the men clearly didn't understand) and the two Chinese men, along with other bystanders, keeping up a steady stream of animated Mandarin. After some fiddling, everyone's lights came back on, and the baby's dad promised to come fix it more permanently tomorrow. We think.

Our first apartment, ground floor

4

WHY VOLUNTEER

I am hiding my apprehension under a thin veneer of cheerful-
ness. Maybe it's too soon yet to separate and identify my
reasons for stepping out to volunteer, to leave everything
behind me. My parents, friends and our church nourished and set
cherished patterns of community service for me. Our American
sensibilities encourage charitable service which might mean leaving
our comfortable homes and giving perhaps two years of service in,
for example, the Peace Corps. I've witnessed and marveled the way
people return more mature and understanding of others' points of
view from such times. I've wondered about this unique chance in a
lifetime to step outside self-interest and devote oneself completely to
serving others. But what are *my* reasons? I'm not entirely sure myself.

They're a lot like elusive trout in a still mountain lake, leaping and
glistening in the sun until you spin around to see them. They leave only
the echo of their splash and the vanishing concentric circles in the water.
I feel sure I can scoop them up, my "fish," but *look*! Isn't that another one
way over there? So, what *are* my reasons for coming to China?

My great-grandparents in Sweden, Denmark, and Wales changed
profoundly when they ripped themselves from their homelands and

became pioneers in America, responding not just to a new country and its possibilities, but to the message of religious freedom. This raw, brawling young country offered tantalizing freedoms especially to people from the old countries who couldn't even imagine ever owning their homes or land there. As immigrants streamed west in America, self-sufficiency was vital as isolated farms and towns were born in the vast, sometimes free spaces. But that isolation also nourished compassion in many, and the realization that a neighboring pioneer offering help would tip the odds toward survival for some. Folks helped one another when they could. Even when it pinched. This bubbling cauldron of nationalities, religious and ethnic backgrounds didn't always get along, but for the most part, they learned to offer a hand when it was needed. Maybe this urge to help was embedded in me by my pioneer ancestors.

Recently two friends, a couple we've loved for many years, returned from humanitarian service in Laos. They were in a communist country and could not speak of politics or religion. They told us of riding rusty bicycles through the countryside and teaching English to doctors and physical therapists. Jeanann, who was struck by lightning in her native Canada when she was a girl, is herself a spinning bolt of energy. Lee, a quieter, wiry man, a retired physical therapist and health and fitness enthusiast, was amazed when he was diagnosed a few years ago with lymphoma. They both thought he had a remission, after surviving a near-death cure at UCLA, possibly because they needed to serve that time in Laos. Rob and I figured we could do as much. He and I talked late into many nights, and the seed of possibility embedded in my heart. The first "fish" perhaps?

Our three kids are grown, launched, two with spouses. Our one eight-year-old grandchild Jordan is a wiry, bouncy girl with a mane of golden-brown hair, and we adore her. Do I need to feel needed now? I've feathered my empty nest quite nicely and have enjoyed it. I honor my nascent urge to paint with some satisfaction and recognition. I have delightful friends, a fine life, but is that enough? With all the getting and embracing of stuff and blessings, do I need to be giving? Yes, I think so. I'm on the local symphony board, help feed the homeless once a month, go with the Music Van to all of the county elementary schools, giving kids a chance to try various musical instruments. I pay a generous tithe. Is that fair coin for taking up my space on earth? Nope, not enough. Another "fish" or two?

Could the wanderlust of my childhood as an Army brat and the wife of an Army officer be a factor? I've been planted in the charming soil of San Luis Obispo for almost twenty-five years. Buried maybe? Another "fish"? All during my growing-up years our family would move to the area of my father's military assignment. We'd circle a new environment like an old dog into its blanket, making friends, settling into new schools, routines, only for Dad to receive yet another assignment. One year, two, three. It was often wrenching, but I learned from my mother to place value not on things, but on the constants, family and valued friends. I came to savor the anticipation, sometimes wondering just where we'd be going next. Then, even though I promised myself that my adult years would find me rooted in one community, I married an Army officer and began the cycle all over again! Our family retired here in this delightful west coast city, and I love it, but am I feeling a bit of atrophy settling in?

Do I just need to feel alive, a dancer at the powwow, not just a spectator? Am I a wee bit fearful of being old and useless? Having spent a lifetime of dodging and weaving to meet challenges in new communities, making new friends, starting new careers, does "retirement" feel like a four-letter word to me? Do I want to pack up and go plunge into a new experience just to prove I can still do it? Or to put a more positive spin on it, can I feel worthwhile, useful and serve in a unique way so my experience can help people I've never even met? Does the clang of the fire bell still make this ol' engine want to rev up and go? More "fishes"? More rings in the lake.

Here's an interesting thought. After more than forty years of marriage, yoked mostly happily, rearing a family of pretty extraordinary kids, I see that Rob and I have concentrated on different jobs in the past: Army career, home, child-rearing, teaching. We chat comfortably in the evenings as we come together. Can we pull together now, do one job, live and teach together twenty-four hours a day? Do I want to find out? OK. That brings me face to face with my fears, the downside of going.

"I don't want to leave my family for a year and a half!" I wailed to Rob as we discussed the possibility a year ago. "A year and a half away would be excruciating."

He countered with, "We love our kids, but let's try not to smother them. They're perfectly capable of living happy, productive lives all on their own."

I remember muttering, "I would miss them terribly." I know that our son is on the cusp of marrying a marvelous girl. We've been dreadfully adult and told him that when the time is right for them to get married, they shouldn't postpone their plans to wait for our return from China; but my heart screams that I want to be there. Generally, on long, overseas, volunteer contracts, folks do not return home for family events. Complete immersion in the volunteers' environment and day-to-day goals, as well as the financial cost of returning are the most obvious reasons.

China. Why China? We actually asked if there were an opening in the Orient, even China. There was, so my gnawing fear about stepping off into this particular end of the world makes no sense. We asked to come here. Maybe I've read too much about the Cultural Revolution, the disappearance of thousands of political prisoners, the absolutely closed society controlled by the Chinese Communist Party, and in more recent history the Tiananmen Square massacre. I'm willing to shrug off my comfort zone, but my brother Dick, my only sibling and my ally and pal from the days when he made the neighborhood kids let me play ball with them, is not. As kids, he saw to it that his gangly teenage sister knew how to dance and didn't have to stand against the church gym wall, pretending I didn't care if no one asked me onto the dance floor. While we had our tussles growing up, he was always my defender and ultimately my best friend. (He even took the heat when our mother discovered tiny ink circles all over the wall behind the toilet in our bathroom. Since I was only three at the time, she was sure my six-year-old brother must have been the culprit. He still tells me I owe him on that one.) He worries about us going to China. His two one-year tours with the Army in Viet Nam soured his outlook on communists and the Far East in general. We two are all that's left of our nuclear family. We live with most of the US separating us, but the glue of our shared memories and deep tenderness for one another keep us in close touch. He doesn't like the idea that Rob and I are going to China. Further, a new cancer has been discovered in his kidney, and the kidney had been removed just before we left.

There are our own health issues. We're both in excellent health, but I have read of primitive, even filthy practices in medicine in modern China that seem hard to believe except that—well, I do.

Should two people in their sixties take themselves so far from modern, Western medical care?

Finally, there is the fear that I just wouldn't measure up, couldn't do a competent job of teaching English. I've had only brief training in teaching English as a second language. I've been a classroom teacher for young children, occasionally substituting in a junior high school class. (Once I was called to sub for a seventh grade shop class. My husband couldn't stop laughing at the picture in his mind of me trying to direct adolescent boys in using a jigsaw. As it turned out, I just kept them away from all those puzzling power tools, and asked the smartest, most co-operative-looking boy for his opinion on something. It worked.) I don't yet have any kind of mastery over the Mandarin language. Can I represent our nation well? As a person? An American? A woman? A wife? A Christian?

I look directly into the scowling face of each fear and decide that "I wish I had — " are some of the saddest words in life. I can't claim that I left all those fears behind. My reasons for coming here, those "fish," are many, complicated, even self-serving, but I'm here.

Our arrival at the Ningbo airport

5

FINALLY WE
MEET THEM

e've met our next door neighbor, Jacques, a pleasant young man from Canada and the only other foreign teacher here at the college. French is his first language, but he speaks passable English. He's probably in his mid to late twenties and has come as an "expert" in cultivating grapes for wine. The Chinese overwork the term "expert." Rob and I are proudly introduced as "foreign experts," which makes us squirm.

We've scrubbed our apartment, arranged and rearranged the books and workbooks, both those we brought and the ones left behind for our use. Rob and I try not to appear nervous about meeting our first students, but we have so many unanswered questions. Jenny brings our schedule. We see that we'll be team-teaching our first Monday morning class, then split up for individual classes through the week. We're amazed to see that we meet each class only once a week. A language class, only once a week! We thought we made it clear to Jenny that we could handle no more than thirty students in a class. She admires the goal but says that classes of fifty to sixty students are normal. "No," we insist, "if the students are to

learn to speak and understand oral English, the ratio must be lower."
Have we won or lost this round? We'll see Monday. Students will
soon be streaming back to campus from the month-long Chinese
New Year holiday.

It's time. Robert and I gather some props and make the short walk
down our cracked sidewalk, over the arched bridge, past the muddy
soccer field on one side and the busy construction workers on the
other. The circular gathering area in front of the one four-story
classroom building boasts a tall flagpole. The large red flag with five
gold stars flutters as we pass, making us feel very far from home.
Students rush past us but turn with curious stares. Some smile and
wave, some say hello and giggle at the foreign word on their tongues.
My nervousness fades a bit as I smile back and try to give a friendly
impression to kids who have *never* seen a foreigner before! It's difficult for us to conceive of a whole nation so sheltered, so cut off, that
a huge portion of its people have never seen an outsider.

Rob and I have already wandered through the empty classroom
building so we know where our first class is. The building is old,
and the odor from the bathrooms seeps into the halls. Since there
is no running water in the troughs that serve as toilets, I wonder
what it will be like when the winter cold no longer masks the
stench. Instead of the quiet echo of our feet on the hard floor
during our solo, reconnoitering visit, now the sound of chattering
students fills the narrow hallways. We note the sudden still of
happy conversation as we pass. I'm getting a sense of what it
must've felt like to be the first American Indian brought before
Spanish royalty by a triumphant Columbus.

We see again what we noted on our first visit: the wooden floors
scuffed by several generations of feet; the raised teacher's platform at

the front of each classroom, some with chunks of flooring missing. Standing immobile behind the tall teacher's desk while droning a lesson might offer safety. Taking up a piece of chalk and going to the green chalkboard on the front wall presents its own challenges. Chalk dust infests every surface in the room and rises from the trough at the base of each ancient chalkboard like tender ghosts from the past. The sharp edges of that trough hide their teeth behind years of accumulated dirt and dust but wait to bite nonetheless. The step down from the height of the podium can catch a too enthusiastic teacher mid-stride and send her sprawling. The walls have been painted. Once. Long ago.

We noted that if there is an electrical outlet in the room, there's about a fifty-fifty chance that it works. Lighting is good on bright days, because the outside wall is a bank of windows. On cold days, however, we quickly learn to appreciate our long underwear, since it shields us from the biting winds whistling into the room through broken panes. On gray days the few overhead fluorescent lights barely lift the gloom.

Each classroom is furnished with a twig broom and a dustpan. The broom's rather like a prop for the witch in *Hansel and Gretel*, except that the short handles require the user to bend almost double. The dustpan also has a rustic short handle attached to a triangular basket.

The students' desks are firmly bolted to the floor, one desk for two students, neatly set out in rows all dutifully facing the teacher's platform. Both Rob and I wonder during our pioneer visit how we can modify the stark atmosphere to encourage a more relaxed approach.

We both breathe deeply and open the door for our first class. The seats are filled and all eyes turn to stare at us. Then *applause*! Amazing! Maybe we've even won a round with Chinese inscrutability since there are exactly thirty students beaming up at us. We grin and plunge in. "Hello. I'm Mrs. McKee."

"Hi! I'm Mr. McKee," Robert follows, "so now you know something about us. We're married. To each other." Laughter. I print our names on the board with the dustless chalk we were coached to bring with us, since it's not available in China. We pull out the photos of our three grown children and show them, telling something about them and ourselves. They reverently repeat our kids' names: Robin. I tell them, "She is a director of plays in the theater in America, mostly in California but occasionally in other states. She also lives in California, not too far from our home." Then "Bonnie. She designs computer programs for companies and individuals." We watch to see if they understand, trying not to speak *too* slowly, choosing our words carefully. They study the pictures and pass them from hand to hand. "Wes is our youngest and our only son." Nods of approval. "He works for a TV station in Fresno, California, directing the news programs." More discussion and appreciative noises. "We've flown here to China, a very long flight, but we're excited about helping you improve your oral English. Now will you please introduce yourselves to *us*." That is clearly a novelty to them.

We've been given printed class rolls with the Chinese characters and the names also in Pinyin, Chinese spelled phonetically in our alphabet. I read a first name aloud and look up expectantly. A pause. Then a boy springs to his feet, almost at attention, "Chen Jun!" he barks, a far cry from my attempt at his name.

"Tell me a little about yourself," I say. I see the terror in his eyes as they roll to his classmates for help. His chin quivers. He reminds me of a terrified, cornered animal. "Where is your hometown?" I'm hoping to give him a cue. Again, confusion. "Thank you. Please sit down."

Then his desk mate stands, "Zhang Yachu" He doesn't seem quite so afraid. He says he's from a village not far from here.

"Huang Ying Xue," a girl stands. I note it's rare to see a boy seated next to a girl. Socially, they seem like American junior high students.

"You Ni Na." I hear the four Mandarin tones we've been trying to emulate, but they go by so quickly I almost despair of reproducing them.

We decide to nip the formal standing to report in the bud. "Please, you do not need to stand when you speak. This is a language class, and we *hope* we can speak informally and comfortably together." That, obviously, is a strange concept because conversation erupts immediately—in Chinese.

Two things become quickly obvious: first, their years of English language training in elementary and high school may have taught them to read English fairly well, but they can barely understand spoken English or speak it; second, *we're* going to have to scramble to learn *their* names, which seem to us like unrelated syllables strung together.

We have our camera and decide to take their photos in sets of two. The forty-five minutes go by quickly with a much more relaxed atmosphere settling into the chilly room. Remember that the temperature outside hovers around freezing with absolutely no heat in the building. There simply is no provision for heating or cooling in a part of the country with stark winter and summer extremes.

A bell jangles in the hall, and the students say it's time for "*Xiuxi*" —to have a rest. Robert tries to replicate the word, "*Xiuxi*" (Shiew–shee), and the room bubbles with laughter. It's a good teaching moment to point out that when we make mistakes trying out strange words, we can laugh and learn together. A few dash for the bathrooms, some cluster in the room in conversation, shyly glancing up to see what we're doing. Another bell after ten minutes and we resume for the remaining forty-five minutes. Since we meet this group only once each week, we encourage them to speak English with one another during lunch or in their dorm rooms for a half hour every evening. They have no textbook, however. Books are at a premium here. That's why we brought paperback workbooks with us. There aren't enough for everyone and no storage space in the building. We teach about three hundred students, so we must haul armloads of books to each class. In the Chinese system, students are assigned to a class group and remain together throughout their college years, all in one classroom where all the teachers meet them unless they have a specialty class like computer science. That means we haul those books from class to class instead of setting up a room of our own, conducive to language study.

The bell to end the class rings too soon, and Rob and I feel exhilarated but suddenly drained. A trio of students comes and asks if they may carry the books back to our apartment. Terrific! They dance alongside us as we walk, telling us we're the very first foreigners they've seen, that the class was "very different and very lovely." We invite them to come visit us in our apartment in the evening some time and step inside. We dump the books on the kitchen table and collapse into an easy chair, having learned from hilarious but sometimes painful experience *not* to lean sideways. We don't have another class until after lunch, but we're finally launched. It's obvious the students are wary and fearful of their first contact with Americans, but we feel that we can convince them that we're humans too and that we want to know and appreciate them as individual persons while we help them learn our language.

Me with two deskmates in class

6

TAKING PICTURES

At our request Jenny leads us through winding streets to show us the shop where we can get photos developed. (This happened before the advent of digital cameras.) We feel a little like Hansel and Gretel, glancing over our shoulders as we turn among lookalike vendors' stalls and concrete shops. Finally we follow a narrow path that runs beside a sluggish canal into a dark shop with a faded Kodak poster on one wall. We hear a child in the back before a young woman emerges and looks startled to find us there. Jenny explains that we have film to be developed. The young woman ducks her head beneath the bare counter and brings out a form and an envelope, and our film is whisked away. We're told to return in two or three days. Business concluded. It all seems so incongruous: the tiny shop with fish drying on lines outside; sampans tied up along the canal; a man who looks to be about 150 years old cooking vile-smelling *Dou-fu* (tofu) on a brazier and offering it for sale to children; and a Kodak shop. Robert and I figure we have about a fifty-fifty chance of ever seeing the students' pictures in hard copy, but we think we have the trail to the shop memorized, just in case. (The photos *were* ready days later, and that surprisingly consistent service continued the whole time we were in China.)

Our plan is to glue each picture of a set of deskmates to a manila folder and put their names below the photo to help us learn their names and address them informally as soon as possible. Jenny tells me that to be polite I really should use all three given names for each student. No American shortcuts or first names only, so a lot of new sounds and tones are my homework.

We've heard and read that many Chinese students also use English names. Robert thinks that's an excellent idea. I'm not so sure. Why should they have to take an English name to make my life easier when their families gave them beautiful names? The fact that my tongue doesn't wrap around them easily is no reason for them to adopt pseudonyms. "But," Rob argues,"I've heard they *like* to have English names." Here we diverge. I decide that if they already have an English name and want to use it, I'll be happy to, but if they don't volunteer the information, I assume they prefer their Chinese names. Robert passes two sheets around his classes, one with girls' names, one with boys' and asks them to select one that appeals to them. We both learn that some kids got names from former Chinese English teachers: Bonnie, Dick, Judy. Some, however, have chosen more flamboyant titles: King Lake, Stone, Cash, Peony, Sunshine. Do those names mean something particular to them? Do they even know what they mean?

Today I ask my class of Ornamental Horticulture majors, "What would you like to know more about?" Their responses, after they're sure I really want to know, are varied: basketball, Michael Jordan, what Americans eat, the Back Street Boys, American films, what American college students do.

Uh oh! I'm already out of my league. Basketball and Michael Jordan will require some research. The Back Street Boys ring a vague bell. A musical group? Okay, I'll create some lessons around their interests and slip in conjugating irregular verbs and subject-verb agreement around the Back Street Boys. I'm beginning to peek into the interests of some of the kids. The photos that we took the first week to help us learn their names are working.

Stone, (*why* did she select this English name for herself?) has laughing eyes and eager questions. Her English is quite good, and I sense she'd like to be "cool" and American, if only she knew how. It hits me that the students are forming their impressions of what an American teacher wears by me! I brought wool skirts, but the bitter temperatures inside and out quickly chased me back to two layers of long undies, wool sweaters, warm slacks, a parka, and hiking boots, my only defense against the chill seeping up from the floors. I'm acutely aware that the students wear flimsy clothing worn in layers. Stone, for example, has two or three nice sweaters and a jacket she usually wears. She's one of the few girls who customarily sport slacks. Many of the girls wear graceful dresses under their jackets or coats. No blue jeans. The high platform shoes amaze us. Chinese girls are not especially tiny, but the current rage has them tottering to and from class on grotesque shoes that add three to five inches to their stature. And they carry it off without looking foolish. Stone hasn't adopted the shoe craze, but I see her eyes assess my ensemble, and I yearn for warmer weather when I can shed the snow bunny look. Maybe then I can give her a glimpse of a reasonably well turned-out American lady.

Magazines are almost non-existent, so we plead with friends and family to send us colorful magazine photos. Our students *love* the game we play giving each a picture, a little time, and then a chance to tell a story about what they see in the picture and what they think is happening. American food is always a hot topic of conversation. They want to know what we eat! So today Rob arms himself with some magazine pictures, including some mouth-watering ones of good old sandwiches. Sandwiches are one of his favorite foods, so he tenderly displays a photo of a huge sandwich, maybe a mayonnaise ad, and they squint at it and pepper him with questions. He begins by extolling the virtues of bread. "What is that?" they want to know. In the parts of China where wheat is grown, a version of yeast bread is well known, but around Ningbo, it's a rare commodity. He thinks he explains bread pretty well, pointing out that you use two slices and then put various things between them.

Cheese. Puzzled faces. No one here has ever tasted cheese. "It's made from milk." Another rare commodity. Now that I think of it, we haven't seen a cow since we arrived! Milk in non-refrigerated boxes for babies is on the grocery shelves, but a Chinese adult would never consider drinking it. Rob plunges ahead, trying to explain the way milk ages into cheese. Incredulous looks on the students' faces. Milk, and curdled at that! And we actually *eat* it?

A slice of meat. A whole chunk of meat at once may seem extravagant, but they let him proceed.

Apparently catsup figures in the picture, so he mentions tomatoes, which they are familiar with, and makes squishing motions. Exhausted, he wishes he'd chosen an easier topic for discussion.

Hoping to go on to another picture, he pauses when one girl points to the alfalfa sprouts. "What is that?" He tries to extricate himself and finish the discussion. He started the morning trying to describe American dry, cold cereal, and got puzzled looks, so he just looks at her and mutters, "Grass."

He tells me that she got a peculiar look on her face but accepted his answer, obviously thinking that Americans eat prodigious amounts of some puffy grain product wrapped around smashed tomatoes, a congealed cow product, meat and grass.

In Chuga, near the photo shop

7

NO MORE WOK TOAST!

No more wok toast! Well, you can make toast in a wok. I've been doing it for the past month, but we decide to spring for a real toaster. If we can locate one. Of course, the real challenge is to find bread. In this part of China it's tough to find. Jenny took us by bus across town one day to a huge store, which she explained is a joint venture with the Germans, a Wal-Mart wannabe with clothing, toys, appliances and food. Now we make the journey every week or ten days. Our backpacks groan with the weight of bread, milk, cheese (!) and meat sealed in clean cellophane. At least I don't see flies crawling over the slabs of meat. We fill our backpacks and large plastic bags with our cherished purchases, then hail one of the many hovering taxis for a luxurious ride home.

Since electrical power is scarce and unreliable throughout China, and the prices of appliances are beyond the reach of most, a toaster is a luxury. Robert, however, is nothing if not single-minded, so we plod through department stores with untouchable goods displayed and sales clerks who have no idea and no interest in how the things work, and we find a toaster! I'm reminded of those tiny flies that cluster around your face in swamps, because a cloud of sales clerks comes from nowhere to observe and nod approval. It must be the first such sale they've made, maybe ever.

That inspires us to invent a game to help our students stretch their imaginations and feel more comfortable with English. We quickly discovered that their textbooks, even the ones we brought from America, are geared far beyond their abilities and comprehension. And they are *dull*. Our own children were the *Sesame Street* generation, used to songs, flashing colors, puppets and entertainment to make learning *fun*. A certain amount of drudgery and hard work *are* necessary to learn the times tables and spelling, but innovative and creative teachers in America challenge young minds with humor and spice. Chinese students have never been exposed to that. They're expected to absorb the information teachers pour into them by droning the required lessons. At the end of each elementary and junior high school session, students who are unusually good at squeezing the information back onto impossibly difficult written tests may be selected to go on to high school. So much rides on the results of those exams that students often have stomach problems, excruciating headaches, and suicidal anxiety. For perhaps five percent of high school graduates, yet more difficult exams decide the opportunity to go to college or university. The shorthand for all that is that regurgitating information on written exams spells the difference between tending pigs in the village or a job paying real money in a big city. Education is important business in China, though in the villages teachers often have little more education than their students.

Our students can parrot or read from a text, but generating a conversation or understanding the spoken word frightens them. In the first weeks we urge them gently to tell us about their hometowns (many glowing reports and invitations to visit them in their homes), their families, their hopes for the future. That last one is almost universal: "I want to be in *business*, earn much money and maybe one day travel to America." (Giggles. Are they trying to impress us?)

After the toaster adventure, Rob and I decide to explain the word *gadget* and ask the kids to dream of a new tool of any kind they would like to invent. Cost is no object. I take a can opener to class and describe its use. Most of the students *have never* seen one! Cans are pretty rare here and expensive. I pass around a potato peeler, a ball-point pen (also fairly new in China) and a tape recorder (very familiar). We talk about the items and explore their uses. Then all I see is the tops of their earnest heads as they set to work writing. We make it a homework assignment as well since they aren't ready to speak up and need to write out their ideas.

Here are some samples of the results of their dreaming, clearly an unusual assignment for them.

If I have lots money, I want to buy a strong pen. It can help me to do some difficult problem, for example, when my hand is tired for writing too long, it will make my hand comfortable. When I'm working some mistakens on doing my homework, it will tell me by writing in red ink. When I'm having my examination in a poor subject, it will help me by telling me how to do or do excise by itself. I want to have that kind of pen. Because I think it will make me more self-confidente and it will lead me to the success.

I want a coat that like a common coat. Of course, it is very beautiful. If I am in it, and turn on the switch, I can fly in the sky. It's speed is very quickly, so if I am late for the school I can turn on the switch. For it, I won't be late for the school. This is a good idea, I think. What do you think?

My grandfather is a seventy years old man. His eyes are so bad that he can hardly read books. However reading is only one hobby of him. So, if I have very, very much money, I will buy a gadget which can read to us if we touch the words. Thus, my grandfather can read again.

I am an average student with average intelligence. I often play myself and am not contacted with others. Whatmore I don't tell my advice when talking about something, because I am afraid that others will laugh at me if my advice is error. So my life has not too joy. I wish a gadget can encourage me everytime so that I enough courage to accomplish everything. If it were true, I would talk with others freely and I more a top and happy student.

Composition. During my study, I have to remember something that the techer had taught us, but it is too much for me to remember it, especially history and English words. So I expect to have a kind of food. Its figure like the bread. If I put a piece of bread above the page. After a while there is some information in the bread. When I hungry, I will eat the bread. In this way, I will remember these information easily. I named it remembrance bread.

I want have a pair of wings. When I put on the wings, I can go where I want. It fly as if birds winging their way across the sky. I can often fly between home and college. Don't worry about keep up with bus or train. I can fly to the top of a mountain that no one come.

If I were a president, so I would have much money, then I'll buy a gadget. It's very little, but very beautiful, and it like a heart. If you put on it, when you stay with others, you will know so who is really good to you, and so who is making use of you. Then you can protect yourself from being cheated and you will get more happy.

I want a type of perfume. It can drive the fly. When I spurt it on my body, the fly won't bite me. So I can sleep and felt at east in the summer.

These give us a glimpse into those gentle hearts. Asking them to dream seemed outrageous to them at first, but some of them really warmed to the task. Some even honor us by sharing some very private thoughts. I doubt that the shy girl who "has not too joy" and would like to "talk with others freely . . . (and be) a top and happy student" has expressed her yearning to many. And wouldn't it be a breakthrough if we all had a gadget—"it like a heart"—to sort out those who are sincere.

Rob returned to our apartment a little later than I did one afternoon, smiles and doubts were struggling in his mind. "What happened in class?" I asked.

"Well, I've been reading simple fables to them and using the pictures we created to give them a clue to what they're about, you know. They love stories and myths and it's great for their listening comprehension, right?"

"Yeah, so?"

We were also fighting an uphill battle to get the kids to raise their hands if they needed an explanation or didn't understand something. To question the teacher goes against everything they've been taught. We *beg* them to raise their hands if they're befuddled or need clarification, but usually we have to search their faces to see whether or not they understand. So Rob said he reminded them to raise their hands if they have questions and went over vocabulary words that might be a mystery. Then he launched into reading *Jack and the Beanstalk*. They'd been swimming in a sea of complex English texts far beyond their abilities and interests, but they succeeded with short, illustrated fairytales. It's a place to begin. At the end of the story, he asked, "Anyone need to know what any of these words mean?" Nope. He paced up and down between the rows of desks, unusual behavior in a

Chinese classroom; the teacher is expected to stay up on the raised platform. "Let's discuss this silly story." Then he noticed a girl desperately flipping through her English-Chinese dictionary. Discouraged that she wouldn't raise her hand to ask for clarification, he paused beside her desk. "Can I help you? What word are you looking up?"

Tears came to her eyes as she blurted, "Fee Fi Fo Fum."

He laughs when he tells me the story. It hadn't occurred to him how impossible those nonsense words would be. We both have a lot to learn!

8

OUR PHYSICAL EXAM

Months before we left America we began the tedium of getting complete physical exams, numerous shots to protect us from unpronounceable diseases, dental cleanings, probings, old fillings replaced—the works. Our sixty-something- year-old bodies had a complete lube and oil change and were in about as good a shape as duct tape and medical science could produce. Our suitcases rattled with vitamins, mouthwash and deodorant, items we were warned would be unavailable in China. We were *ready!*

Now that we're finally on the ground in our new environment, we're beginning to absorb and to comprehend the new life we have here. We both feel healthy and up for the challenge each day offers. My earlier fears recede farther, almost forgotten, until one dreary day when Jenny comes to our apartment. We can tell there is something she doesn't want to broach. She smiles and ducks her head when she's embarrassed, and all the signs tell us she has a bit of information she's sure will displease us. She's right." The Chinese government," she reveals, "insists that you have a physical examination before they will issue a foreigner's work permit."

"But, *Jenny!* We've *had* physicals! You have all the records, our shot records and TB test results, everything. What more could they possibly want?"

"I'm sorry. It's the law. You must get physical examinations. I will pick you up tomorrow morning in the school car, and we will go to the hospital together."

All the stories of unsanitary conditions in this nation's hospitals, the warnings that we carry our own syringes since there's no guarantee of clean ones, and the sheer nuisance of trailing into Ningbo to spend a day redoing what we'd spent plenty of time and money doing in the United States are upsetting. Our warm friendship with Jenny faces its first real test. We send an emergency e-mail to our daughter Bonnie at home in California. Please go to our doctor's office and get all the recent medical records and scan them to us. After she scurries around dealing with a very cooperative medical secretary, we present the volumes to Jenny. She is unmoved. "*Chinese* doctors must give you a physical examination. I'm so sorry."

So we bundle into our coats and reluctantly climb into the car college officials use. Jenny, as always in a neat dress, high heels and a warm coat, tells the driver where we need to go. The cold, drab day reflects my mood as we swing through the always crowded streets. I have to admire the driver's insouciance as he dodges bicycles, pedestrians and innumerable taxis with aplomb before we pull into the courtyard of an ominous building in a street of equally oppressive, concrete structures. Maybe my overactive imagination is at work, but the "hospital" seems to glower as we approach the door. Only a few people are in sight, poorly dressed and wary. We enter a drab waiting room, and Jenny goes to the bored clerk to begin our immersion into Chinese medicine. The clerk is a caricature of communist officialdom. He leans back in his wooden chair studying his newspaper, insisting that Jenny wait until he notices her, then makes a ceremony of putting the paper down and consulting a roster. His irritation at being disturbed evident, he makes it very clear that he is in charge and can make us wait as long as he likes. Dirty wooden benches line the walls, and we're obliged to take seats there to await the clerk's call. We are alone in the waiting room, so crowds can't be the cause for delay.

After a wait, my mood a match for the gloom outside, Jenny indicates that we can start the first stage of our exam. We three get up to enter a cubicle, and our driver starts to join us. I ask Jenny to ask him to stay in the waiting room.

Another bare room. Another bored, annoyed bureaucrat reading the newspaper, wearing what was once a white lab coat, looks up. She asks Jenny for information, never really looking at us. Then, satisfied that the forms are properly filled out, she waves us on to the next cubicle.

They test our eyes there. The charts are simple forms facing various directions, so we can respond with hand gestures. I begin to relax. Maybe this won't be so traumatic Then we're ushered into a small room with a woman armed with a syringe. "She must draw some blood for testing," Jenny explains.

"No," we insist, "if she must take blood, we will provide our own syringes."

The nurse is obviously startled when I produce a syringe from my purse. Then she's triumphant. "Too small!"

Jenny translates. "The hospital uses larger needles. You must use theirs."

"Then she may use two of ours," I counter, glaring at the nurse. I'm amazed that I make her look away first, and she waves her hand impatiently and takes my syringes. She fills two vials with my blood, then two more with Robert's. I stare into the deep crimson fluid filling the syringes.

The next room is the blood pressure room. The lady puts the cuff around my arm and pumps it up. I watch her worried conversation with Jenny, so it's no surprise when Jenny turns to me and says, "She says your blood pressure is quite high." Humor often doesn't translate well into another language, so I don't think Jenny knows why the comment strikes me as funny after the test of wills in the other cubicle. Apparently the Blood Pressure Lady decides not to make an issue of my numbers.

We move into another room dominated by a Rube Goldberg machine. My mind conjures up one of Jim Henson's Muppets. The creaky machine looks especially like one particular puppet, a huge furry mammoth that must've been inspired by the drive-through car washes in America with the flubbery tentacles that shlurp across the car's surface.

We're instructed to remove our coats. As I eye the contraption warily I have no idea what it is supposed to be checking, but my relief at getting through the syringe battle unscathed bubbles out in gulping laughter. I offend the official who tends the unbelievable machine. He indicates that it's a sort of chest X-ray, and thrusts me up against the moving tentacles. I can't imagine that it serves any useful purpose, but both Rob and I take a turn at hugging the Dr. Seuss creation.

As we step into another bare room our young driver, obviously bored with the waiting room, wanders in to join us. The attendant doesn't seem to mind. I do, especially when the attendant tells me (through Jenny) that this is an ultrasound machine and I'm to lie down on the table. I worked at one time for a physical therapist and have used the ultrasound wand on patients myself. The portion of the body to be treated is bared and special cream is spread on the area to make a good connection. First, it was cold, and, second, I'm not about to expose any part of my shivering body to a crowd of semi-bored walk-ins. When I complain, the attendant says that I need remove only my coat. He can work through the other layers. I can't imagine any kind of reading is possible, but I agree to pretend.

Time crawls as we're led from room to room, but we begin to relax when we realize the exercise is a face-saving device for Chinese bureaucracy, not a puncturing of our bodies by unknown, unclean objects. Apparently we pass the physical exam because we get very official-looking Chinese foreigner work permits.

9

SUNDAYS

Sundays bring a taste of home to us in this bewildering foreign world. Is it the isolation from all things American, or are we especially blessed to have four wonderful American English teachers nearby?

Sandra and Elwood "Woody" Wall from Portland, Oregon, have been teaching English at Ningbo College for a year already. Woody carries his lean six-foot–five-inch frame in a manner that suggests he's spent a lot of time leaning down to be attentive to others. Chinese people are not particularly small, but he attracts incredulous stares wherever he goes. His friendly grin and wave usually transform the stares into smiles. Sandra murders the Chinese language, and they adore her. Her confidence in others' abilities and her gentle love are gifts generously given to us over and over.

The trip, changing buses twice, to their place on Sunday mornings takes about an hour, then a gasping climb past electrical wires dangling in a staircase to reach their gray apartment, clearly the "crummiest one" (Sandra's words) among the three couples' digs. It's so tiny our knees almost touch as the six of us sit together in their stamp sized room.

We alternate traveling to one another's apartments for a prayer meeting each week, after which the host couple serves lunch. The chatter and laughter erupt as we share pointers, frustrations or success in navigating the English language sea. The lunches are crowns of creative scrounging, shopping and adapting as we try to recreate American food favorites out of clearly oriental ingredients. We all look forward to this but especially Doyel "Dutch" Riley.

If Woody were a majestic sequoia tree, LuJean Riley would be a delicate bonsai. I don't believe she could stretch her eighty-five pounds to reach the four-foot ten-inch mark, but the bounce and energy of the retired preschool teacher from Reedley, California, are incredible. She and Dutch have been teaching English in the Ningbo suburb of ZhenHai for about six months. Dutch was a teacher in his former life, but his gentle talents then instructed high school students in their rural California community in pottery and photography. Dutch cringes at Chinese food and has been known to get away with refusing to sample a dish offered by a Chinese hostess simply because he's such a nice guy. We sometimes travel together and learn early on that when Dutch spots a McDonald's, we are doomed to a visit for the Chinese version of a Big Mac and fries, after which he sighs and plunges back into the world of unrecognizable foodstuffs.

It takes a full two hours by bus to get to the Riley's apartment near their campus. After negotiating several transfers, we must wander through streets and alleys to find their building (their neighborhood is not quite in the deteriorating, geriatric stages of the Wall's surroundings) and climb their stairs. We memorize bus numbers and learn to spot landmarks to find them. The courtesy and polite deference of the Chinese culture do *not* extend to crowds. Lines at a bus stop, if any, collapse as the bus door opens. People glare and shout as the gaping door jams. Scrambling bodies clutching bulging canvas bags, tugging children, and more bodies with pointed elbows. We are amused that this takes place even at the main bus station where many routes originate. The buses here are *empty* with maybe forty-five to sixty-five seats on a double-decker. Even so, the twenty or so people waiting for the door to creak open jostle to climb aboard. *Everyone* will get a seat, but something in the genes or embedded somewhere in the culture fires a need to get in *first*. We haven't been in China very long when Rob insists, "Susie, I know we're representing America here, but you've *got* to learn to shove those little old ladies aside or elbow the school kids and their lethal book bags out of the way when it's our stop!"

That is crucial because the same dynamic happens when we're jammed inside the bus and need to get *off*. The bus driver is uninterested in what goes on at the back door. It closes and the bus moves on, even though occasionally people wail and beat futilely on the firmly closed door. So I learn.

This is all to say that each Sunday two traveling pairs of Americans arrive perspiring heavily (summer) or blue with cold (winter) at the Sunday's host apartment, eager for companionship and an emotional, spiritual, intellectual battery recharge.

There can be, of course, no formal church service. The communist government officially permits worship but does not encourage it. We've seen only one building so far in our wanderings that could be described as a church, a small Catholic church in Ningbo in the process of being rebuilt over the past five years on the site of a much larger destroyed church (in the Cultural Revolution?). Since we've never seen any active construction going on there, we wonder if it will ever be completed.

One morning an early knock on our door startles us. The college president, who speaks no English, stands there with two government officials. We invite them in, hoping they're privy to the acute balancing act necessary to remain upright in our two sideways tipping easy chairs. We bring in some straight-backed kitchen chairs for the rest of us and accept the proffered bouquet of flowers— which does nothing to calm the unreasoning fear that leaps into my heart. "We're here from the government Ministry of Religion to assure you that you may have complete freedom of worship." Their lips smile, but their eyes remain wary, hooded, focused on us.

"Of course."

They tell us of a Christian group that meets in Ningbo, which we're free to join.

"Thank you." We smile too.

Apparently the officials are satisfied they've delivered their message. They all stand to leave, and for once I actually hoped our tipsy chairs might misbehave.

*"Woody" Wall, LuJean and "Dutch" Riley boarding a bus home
from our apartment one Sunday*

Sandra, "Woody" Wall, and "Dutch" Riley at dinner in our apartment

10

THE FOAM PAD

The trip every third Sunday to the Rileys is the longest of our Sunday travels. We wait just outside the college gate for the little "kamikaze bus" (our name for it) which comes wheeling by every five or ten minutes, climb aboard, hold our breath, and try to concentrate on the countryside whizzing by outside the crusty windows. We ride it all the way to the central bus depot in Ningbo, maybe forty-five minutes. Then we dodge broken cement, potholes, downed wires, mud puddles and "slickie boys," who proffer a helmet and gesture toward the back seat of their rusty motorcycles, inviting us to pay them for a ride, a *most* unlikely occurrence. We've learned to head for the number ten double-decker bus island where we wait beside the parked bus. A driver may be seated inside the bus, but passengers must wait until he or she creaks the door open. Even if there are only ten or fifteen waiting, a crush of people, often a temporary impasse, develops at the door, even though around sixty-five empty seats wait inside. We pay our fare and select a seat. Rob and I like to ride in the top section. We have to step gingerly, since spilled food, broken floor mats or spittle may slip us up, but we like the view. We can watch the cityscape and observe the interior lives we peek into from here.

We see men and women rock back in their low, bamboo chairs outside their tiny shops, nothing more than a garage with wares haphazardly displayed. Some people spread a few items on a cloth on the wide sidewalk, hoping for a buyer. Sometimes a brazier smolders outside the door. Even in cold, rainy weather, they sit outside. It occurs to me that the inside of the dull, gray blocks must not be warmer or drier than the outside. But something else strikes me as we lumber by. The neighbors chat or play Chinese chess or Mah Jongg, often laughing or arguing in ways that tell me that they have an easiness among themselves that we in our culture have lost.

We have large homes in America, with every appliance and comfort, so we cocoon ourselves in the blue light of the TV or dash from important meeting to important meeting, scarcely touching another heart. Poverty isn't cleansing or desirable, but I honor the human spirit when it rises above poverty and connects with others and with what's most important in a life well lived. I hope our American comfort and casual cynicism hasn't begun to smother it. I may be assigned to teach here in China, but that doesn't mean I can't learn, maybe much more than I can teach.

As we approach the center of town the low cement shacks give way to taller, modern business and commercial buildings. At two or three large department stores, shoppers saunter past counters of makeup, clothing and furniture, but rarely buy. Running right beside those testaments to China's entry into the 21st century are narrow alleys where the real commerce goes on. Tiny tents and shops hawk umbrellas, watches, food or plastic kitchenware as buyers scurry by, stopping to examine or chat and make their purchases.

We dismount one more time to change buses, veering off to the other side of Ningbo. The tall buildings thin as we approach the suburb of ZhenHai, the location of the high school where LuJean and Dutch teach English. It takes a little more than two hours of bumping along on buses or trudging through narrow streets to get here, and we'll repeat it for the return trip, but the warm companionship with friends is surely worth it.

We find too that the worship service—reading and discussing scriptures, heartfelt prayers for help to meet our students' needs, quiet searching for peace in a foreign world, six earnest, reedy voices joined in familiar hymns—all make the trip precious. We agree that we often attended church services at home woodenly. Now, as the off-key karaoke upstairs mingles with our own version of "Oh God, Our Help in Ages Past," the words and feelings sing back to us with a new power.

Then comes lunch. LuJean has outdone herself. She's managed to simulate an American picnic in their tiny, clean apartment with the flowered drapes which I covet. She's found hot dogs in the German-Chinese food store and something like buns, which amazingly do not have bean paste inside. Mustard is nonexistent, but ketchup is on the table. She found some beans and created a Boston baked bean dish that simmers on her cook top, sending off a mouthwatering, sugary aroma. She scalded, skinned and sliced some tomatoes, and—the jewel of the afternoon—Jell-O! with only slightly bruised bananas sliced on top. We set to. Robert compliments the cook (!) by devouring three hot dogs. In America, for dinner out I usually choose a Chinese restaurant. I smile to think of the centuries and art spent right here under our noses to create savory, succulent dishes which I do enjoy, but these hot dogs and Jell-O will nestle in my heart and mind (and Robert's) as the apogee of taste bud satisfaction.

Returning to the bus stop, as we peer into dark shops trying to decipher what each has to offer, a row of identical shops has what appears to be rolls of foam stacked from floor to ceiling. Warily Rob and I cross the busy streets lined with makeshift vendors' tables and tents. Cars and bicycles dart wherever space opens up, and we haven't learned the nonchalant pedestrian code yet. The idea strikes both of us, between leaps, that maybe we could buy some foam to ease the unyielding mattress on our bed. How much? It'll be a *big* piece of foam. The bed is comparable to a king-sized bed. Even if we could measure it (we haven't seen a tape measure here of any kind yet), how would we lug such a thing home?

Robert's ingenuity is percolating again. He prowls around our apartment when we get home and finds a piece of twine. He measures the length and width of the bed, knotting it at the appropriate spots. Three weeks later, with the string rolled up in Rob's pocket, we're ready. After our renewal at the Riley's, we saunter from foam shop to foam shop. The proprietors, startled from dozing in the darkness and amazed to see two foreigners, try to figure out what we want. We gather that the shops serve large furniture manufacturers, so our request for a piece of foam about six by seven feet is small potatoes to them. They shake their heads and don't want to cut a piece that small. Finally we find a young entrepreneur willing to sell us two end pieces that will fit on top of our mattress. Money changes hands, and we expect him to roll the two pieces so we can tote them home. He doesn't. He makes a great ceremony of wrapping plastic over the two seven by three foot flat chunks! Okay. We can either balance the unwieldy behemoths on our heads as we dodge traffic, flapping them threateningly fore and aft, or carry them like shields in front of us before we wedge ourselves and the huge slabs into the buses. We settle on a combination of both techniques, realizing that we cut a pretty ridiculous figure. Taking a more expensive taxi is out of the question since they're tiny, locally manufactured cars, barely able to take two adults into the back seat. So it'll have to be the buses.

We recall sharing space with live ducks, huge, tattered bags of household items, engine parts, items large and small we can only guess at, which are casually brought onto Chinese buses. Apparently our foreignness makes our spectacle unique. We're growing accustomed to their dropping jaws as we move through the culture here, but the vision we present now is over the top. Faces crease in smiles, even giggles, which we certainly deserve. Hands reach down to help us climb aboard the buses, and men and women scoot over to allow us to wiggle our peculiar burdens through the crowds to a space where we can breathe. The experience is unheard of, making room for *anyone* on a bus, but we're deeply grateful. We're also sure that many Chinese will arrive home breathless and say the equivalent of "Honey, you're not gonna *believe* what I saw on the bus today!"

And, for the first time since we got to China, we sink into a deliciously almost-soft bed.

11

MEETING LUCY

There was a gentle knock on the door two nights ago. We've come to expect evening visitors now that we're settled. In fact we invite our students to come to our apartment on campus to practice informal English conversation. They come in shy twos, threes and fours, some to practice speaking English, some to cock their heads silently and hope to catch maybe ten percent of what's said, which makes for some one-sided chatter on our part. The students are the very best part of our assignment at the college, which is in the midst of an identity crisis. Actually it's undergoing a name change and, with what we're recognizing now as typical Chinese optimism, a leap up soon to become a university. It has been The Zhejiang Rural Teachers' College, then Zhejiang Sunli College. Now administration hopes are pinned on adding thousands to the 1800 students currently enrolled and becoming Zhejiang Sunli University.

That particular evening, three girls stood smiling at us shyly when we opened the door at around 6:00 p.m. None was from any of our classes. They were our predecessors' students and stepped into our lives with such grace and bounce that I knew instantly we'd made an important connection. *Lu Xu Xia*—Lucy—was my immediate favorite, I'm ashamed to say. We try so hard to be evenhanded, but she stepped quietly into my heart.

All of them spoke better English than our students. They *were* a year older and had completed a year of English. They bemoaned the school policy that allowed them only one year of English study and told us that the American couple we replaced made their classes "so relaxing and fun," and "not so boring" as their standard teachers' lectures. Lucy particularly yearned to speak better and was very open about what she said is common knowledge among young Chinese, namely that English fluency is the ticket to better jobs and the possibility of a life beyond their native villages. Later I learned that Lucy was not only the first person in her family to pass the excruciating college entrance examinations but also the first in her village. Ever! The tests pretty much chart their lives, not only *if* they may go to high school, but also place them in better schools if they score high. We hear again that the days-long college entrance examinations give students anxiety, stomach difficulties, headaches, even drive them to suicide. The scores place them yes or no in college or universities and determine where and what major they must take. Higher scoring students study engineering, chemistry, or computer science. Students who score low study animal husbandry, horticulture, accounting, with *no* allowance for personal aptitude or preference. I understand that is changing slowly, but the students live and die by the test scores. It's small wonder that what we come to call "Chinese Cheating" reaches an exquisite art form when so much depends on the scores, but more about that later.

Lucy wrinkled her small nose and admitted she was majoring in "animal-raising," being groomed to return to her village to help tend the pigs and chickens. This delicate, intelligent beauty, certainly the focus of many misty eyed young men's dreams, loves her family but does *not* want to return to the pig wallows of her hometown. There was a slight chance that if she passed the English proficiency tests, she might be permitted to teach English in her village or elsewhere. As we listened to them articulate their hopes, we realized that "business" and "import/export" hold out the sweet fragrance of a prosperity they can hardly dream of. English, in their minds, is the golden key to personal affluence. And beside, Lucy tells us, proud of her command of American slang, "English is lovely and very cool."

Conversation turned to the "English Corner." We'd heard the name and were eager to hear from them exactly what it was. Every Tuesday night for the last year, the girls told us, a large classroom had been set aside for any student to come for a chance to speak informally with the American teachers. They told us that many students, unable to take an English class, look forward to the contact. What exactly would they like us to do for the English Corner? "Tell us lovely stories." "About America." "Let us play games." "American pop music."

The image of preparing and delivering two hours of lecture every Tuesday after a full week of classes quickly dissolved as I determined to set a new pattern. We may present a brief theme for the evening, but we both think we should break the crowd (the girls tell us that from sixty to a hundred students usually come to the English Corner!) into small conversation groups. That presents the challenge of how to listen in and support the groups. The idea is to encourage them to speak English, right? Lucy and her friends giggle their approval. I need to keep reminding myself that they are between nineteen and twenty-three years old. Socially, they seem much younger. Their naiveté is appealing. American twelve-year-olds whose sophistication often launches them into sex, drugs, and alcohol are leagues away from these disingenuous Chinese. The privilege of education is a huge focus here. Boy-girl stuff seems to wait until much later in life. Social activities at the college seem non-existent. Maybe that's one reason English Corner is such a draw. We're a little nervous about how we're going to monitor and help so many kids eager for a peek into a slice of American life—or maybe just a look at the two new curiosities on campus. Next Tuesday will be our coming out party!

12

THE ENGLISH CORNER

Tuesday night suppers are a hurried affair for us. Once or twice we make the mistake of postponing dinner until after English Corner. Bad idea. Usually a half dozen or so kids follow us home, wanting to extend the chance to converse in English, open to any student at the college. We'd been told to expect sixty students, so we're startled when about 130 fill the fairly large classroom the first evening. They overflow the desks and lean against the walls. They all want to listen and talk to us. Simultaneously! A reverse from our shy classroom students, some crowd around us, calling out questions. We've prepared a brief presentation about American education and a typical day for a college student in the US, since that seems to be a topic of overriding interest. The room quiets for us to speak. Wow! This must be what it feels like to be famous, with people hanging on our every word. Then we try to break them up into small buzz groups, to put together questions and speak English with one another. Circulating around to each group, we wish we could clone ourselves to spend more time chatting and laughing with each group. The sessions are supposed to run from 6:00 to 8:00 p.m. We come home exhausted.

Preparing for English Corner takes more and more time. Their questions and interests challenge us: we collect pictures and ideas to discuss air and water pollution, a big problem in China; sports in America, particularly basketball, a big interest among the males here. My cousin sends us clippings about the Jazz professional basketball team, which sparks lively discussion. Michael Jordan is well known here. One week I type up some fables—"The Lion and the Mouse," 'The Boy Who Cried Wolf," a few more—then split the students into groups. They read the fables, create costumes with bits of colored paper, string, pencils and present little playlets to their peers. We're surprised as bashful daytime students bloom on the evening stage.

One successful English Corner erupts into bedlam when we divide the kids into groups and give each group an auction sheet with fifteen sentences in English. Some sentences are correct; some aren't. They have to pretend they have $2,000 to spend for bidding, and we explain how that works. Whoever bids on the most correct sentences and has the most money left wins. After they get the hang of it, we have some very spirited bidding. At one point, a boy is close to spending all his money so he shouts, "Can I use my Visa card?" We didn't know they knew about credit cards! Ah, capitalism!

We're not sure whose idea it was originally, but both Rob and I yearn to show the kids some good American movies. After all, we reason, it's great for their listening skills, and they're constantly asking us about films. When they learned we're from California, they were convinced we had Hollywood neighbors and must be on shoulder-rubbing terms with the stars. In our travels so far, we haven't spotted a movie theater anywhere, certainly not on the campus. At our apartment we can play VHS movies on the TV, but as we poke through the dusty video shops in unlikely places in Chuga and Ningbo, we find no VHS movies, only something called DVDs. They were just on the American horizon when we left the States.

The leap-ahead technology is fascinating, much like the telephone in China. Phone service leapfrogged many land lines carrying phone signals and went directly to cell phones. Men particularly must not trust cell phones to amplify so they shout into them, making normal conversation around them impossible. I suspect that this also shows everyone what important businessmen they are. A cell phone is definitely a status symbol here. Maybe like the telephone technology, they just skipped VHS and went straight to DVDs long before they became commonplace in America.

We go out hoping to rent DVDs and find it impossible, but *buying* DVDs is much cheaper than US rental. The local joke among us expats is that there's only one real *paid for* Windows 98 program in all of China. All the rest are pirated, but computers are another story. The government is doing its best to keep the world out of China, but young people, especially in the cities, are finding ways to log on. The pirating story is true, however, in the DVD business. Shops bristle with DVDs for sale, most slash and burn Chinese movies; a very few are yanked from American films. It's a guessing game to figure out what films they are. The picture on the cover may or may not be about the movie inside, we discover. All writing is in Chinese, except occasionally the Chinese version of the English title slips through: "Robinson Grusoe." *Grusoe* makes us giggle.

We begin a campaign with Jenny to set up a once-a-month evening movie for the students. "Impossible," she says. "The only place to show such a thing is on the TVs upstairs in the teaching building. The technician who runs them rides the bus home every day at five."

"Oh? There's an audiovisual capability on campus?"

Jenny laughs because she's revealed too much. "Yes, but he must catch the bus. He does not stay here at night."

"What if we pay for a taxi once a month? He can have dinner in the school dining hall and enjoy a movie with us."

She begins to weaken, but as weeks go by and we get no word about the A/V room, we realize that to avoid a rude No, the usual polite Chinese solution is simply to ignore the problem.

Then we take the sneaky approach. Jenny is away on a trip to Europe as translator for a group of Chinese traveling there. Rob and I climb the stairs one afternoon to the forbidden audiovisual room. It's a nosebleed climb, but we corner the one man who can make our movie dreams come true. We introduce ourselves, and I use my best Chinese to explain what we hope. He agrees, much too easily, and we set up three dates for the coming three months. When Jenny returns, she graciously accepts defeat and we look forward to the first movie.

Now we have to buy a movie and have been warned that pirated movies often have faulty soundtracks, may be garbled or fuzzy. We have no way to preview a DVD since we have only VHS on our home TV, so we'll have 150 kids squirming with delight one Tuesday night and a crapshoot about what we'll be showing and the quality of the sound and/or picture. Maybe it wasn't such a good idea. But we plunge ahead, scouring the city's DVD shops and finally selecting what we *hope* is *Sleepless in Seattle*.

I climb the stairs to the aerie the afternoon of the first scheduled evening showing. Yes, our man will have everything set up. There are two rooms back to back with a standard home-sized TV facing about seventy-five hard benches in both. I give him the first DVD and smile. Jenny explained I must not give him money for a taxi ride home. "It would shame him," but she arranges for him to be driven home in the college sedan.

We're thrilled but not surprised at the crush of students who turn up for the show. The quality of the picture is fine; Chinese subtitles help the kids understand the plot, and they *love* the romance. We feel the effort's well spent. We follow up with successes like *Home Alone II*, *Mrs. Doubtfire*, *You've Got Mail*, eclectic choices, but we scrounged what we could. *Robinson Grusoe* was a bust. Lousy soundtrack.

Rob with students on campus

13

APRIL

Our students know about April Fools' Day. So much of the world outside their narrow province, even village, is so completely unknown to them, so I'm surprised when they eagerly ask for examples of jokes I have played that day when they are sure all Americans lope around wearing false whiskers and yanking chairs out from under one another. I can offer only the times in my childhood when my brother and I switched the contents of the saltshaker and sugar bowl. Then I scan my memory searching for Rob's stories of childhood pranks he and his brother pulled off. The two of them made small model airplanes and set them on fire just before sailing them out the upstairs window. That's more like it! They nod approval. It wasn't an April Fool's joke, in fact, just a boy stunt they surely got in trouble for, but I don't have much time to think of any other prank.

It is April, and winter's wet, cold-storage grip is relaxing slightly. The classrooms are still refrigerators, and while I circle around the room to keep relatively warm, the kids are doomed to shiver in their straight-backed chairs. I have an outrageous idea. "Let's go outside!" They stare at me. Even allowing for the fact that I'm a foreigner, obviously they believe I've lost my mind. "No, really! We'll stay warmer walking around, and I can point things out and tell you the English word for them." There are a few brave buds on the stark trees and bushes, and it really is warmer outside than sitting in the classroom with the wind whistling through the broken windows and the stench of the bathrooms down the hall. They look at one another. When they see I'm serious, they get up one by one to follow me. There has never been any kind of supervisor or administrator in my classroom. No one has ever suggested what we must or must not teach. In fact, the total absence of a curriculum or textbooks leave Rob and me an open trail to blaze. I know, however, that what I'm proposing is probably unheard of in Chinese teaching protocol. I've never seen students outside their very formal classrooms here and am pretty sure that the idea will be frowned upon. So I don't ask permission. I tell the students to walk quietly through the halls. Don't want teachers' heads poking out the doorways asking questions.

I quickly lead them several meters away from the classroom building windows, and a party atmosphere takes over. They explode with questions. "Do students do this in America? "How do you say this (pointing to a dead bush) in English?"

"Dead bush." No, I catch myself. My sense of humor doesn't always translate. "Bush."

A chorus of "Boosh-uh."

"No." (I begin an unsuccessful eighteen-month-long struggle to erase the trailing *uh* on the end of many Chinese students' words.)

"Bush."

"Boosh-uh."

"Sidewalk."

"Sidewalk-uh."

"Canal."

They repeat, "Canal." That one worked. I'm almost skipping, pointing out colors, buildings, trees. Their childlike enthusiasm spurs me on. Finally I suggest we all sit on a small plot of brave grass trying to turn green. I see I've gone too far. Actually sit? On the *ground*? their expressions say. They try it out. Obediently, gingerly, the girls spread their skirts and lower themselves. The boys too are obviously afraid of getting their slacks dirty. A bad idea. My vision of me—Anna in Siam—surrounded by chirping wards on a sunny lawn dissolves. It occurs to me that the kids have very few clothes which they keep scrupulously clean by hand washing in icy water and hanging them to dry, which takes days in this humidity. We've all learned a few things on this outing. We quietly return to our classroom before the bell shrieks. I'm sure they're warmer though.

Rob has made a trip on the bus into Ningbo without me, a first, and he's a bit evasive about his reasons. The hours without him near seem empty. Although we endured years of separation during the Viet Nam war and both are perhaps overproud of our independence, we've found a deep pleasure in this new experience of focusing so completely together on one job, one life. I'm distracted, though, to learn from Jenny that there are packages for us at the post office in Chuga. Our letters come through the small post office on campus. Jenny brings them to us, usually on the day they're delivered, but packages sink to the bottom of the heap at the Chuga post office. A notice comes to Jenny that they're there. Sometimes she picks them up for us, but today she has no time.

As soon as Robert shows up, I scoop up the small package notification slip, all in Chinese, and we set out for the bus to Chuga. It's a step back in time, the post office. One very grumpy man is usually the sole worker there, holding court behind his window. Stamps are not adhesive, so a small table at the center of the room offers a pot of glue. The brush has long since lost most of its bristles, or they're congealed into a cement-like, sticky mass. Glue coats the tabletop, adding its smell, something like Macbeth's witches' brew, to the ancient dirt odor of the small room. The Chinese don't queue up at the window. They shove their letters or thrust money over the shoulder of anyone unfortunate enough to be standing in front of the service window.

We've made the pilgrimage before, once to have a package for Jacques handed to us. We realized then that the postman cannot read the English letters on the packages so assumes that anything in that ridiculous scrawl must be for one of us. He can't tell us apart. I'm hoping this one is not for Jacques, since it's my birthday, and old as I am, I'm still childish enough to hope for little remembrances from our kids. Postage is hideously expensive, so we discourage friends and family from mailing items to us, but we are thrilled just the same to get care packages of comfort food, especially things like Jell-O, chicken noodle soup mix, cinnamon, Rob's favorite gum drops or anything that reminds us they miss us. Ah! Three packages for us today! One is badly torn, but the contents seem to be intact. We hurry home with our treasures.

What a bonanza of food that was once commonplace to us. There are precious photos of our family, and Bonnie baked some muffins and airmailed them, remembering that bread is a hard-to-find item here. Ovens seem to be nonexistent. She also sent some freesia bulbs, my favorite flower. I told her that I hadn't found any in the floral shops. Robin sent precious food too. I beam and bask in the love and happy birthday wishes in solid, mostly edible form, from our kids.

I met a young man the other day, an art teacher here at the college, I think. He was standing outside Jacques' apartment next door, and the two of them were talking, hand signals mostly, and paging through a book of very poor art reproductions. Jacques pointed to a painting and pronounced the name of the American or British artist. Then the young man tried to repeat the name. I introduced myself, hoping to learn if there are art classes here. My Chinese isn't yet good enough, and the artist was frustrated that he couldn't put his thoughts into English, but I learned that he is an art teacher. I think I said I would love to see his work, hoping that some day Rob and I could go wherever he works and see his paintings. As nearly as I can determine though, we agree that he will bring some things for me to see today at 10:00 a.m.

I'm delighted when there's a hesitant knock on the door. The same young man stands there with several rolls of paper under his arm. I introduce him to Robert, and he begins to unroll his paintings. Two are traditional ink paintings, very well done, then a breathtaking watercolor of the lined face of an old Chinese woman who has lived through more than her share of troubles. I can't hide my delight and appreciation of the delicacy and integrity of his work and ask if I might buy them. He's embarrassed and thrusts them all at me. "A gift," he says in Chinese, "for American friends." Now I'm in a real pickle. I try to explain that I too am an artist and understand artists too must eat. I would be honored to *buy* his paintings. He shakes his head and backs toward the door, leaving the paintings on the dining table. I see I've created a problem, so I try a different tack.

"Please tell me who your favorite American artist is."

Without a pause he answers, "Andrew Wyeth." So with many handshakes and warm thanks, I begin making plans to e-mail a friend at home, also a painter, and ask her to find the very best book of reproductions of Andrew Wyeth's work she can find. I'll reimburse her. It's my birthday, and it seems I've just stolen my own gifts. I hope the generous and talented artist will accept my gift to him.

Robert decides he'd better warn me a birthday celebration is planned for the evening. We are to go to our English Corner, as usual, and then he understands students will lead us to another room, where more students and administrators will wait with a surprise. He knows I'm not crazy about surprises and wants me to be prepared. I'm pretty at ease with my students in our classrooms but am uneasy about how I'm to behave with the spotlight on me. I gather the Chinese don't acknowledge their own birthdays, except perhaps a general celebration during the Chinese New Year. Beside, how in the world did anybody know it was my birthday anyhow? I'll try to be gracious. And surprised.

I am *truly* surprised when we're led to an upstairs Party Room I didn't know existed. We walk into a darkened room with colored lights blinking. From the ceiling hangs one of those silver balls that turn and glitter, sending shafts of colored lights dancing on the walls. A music system and dance music pushes the walls back. Best of all, I see many of my students, marvelous dancers, taking advantage of it. They all stop and beam at us as we enter, shouting, "Surprise! Happy birthday!" It's no act. I'm bowled over. They circle us like honeybees, and the look of genuine pleasure on their faces makes my eyes sting with happy tears. Yet not everyone is there. Apparently, since the room is not large, only a few kids from each of my classes were invited. That's a sad note, but they press forward and offer us crowns of tiny flowers. Then they make a great ceremony of presenting gifts, one from each class. I am hideously embarrassed when I open them and see they are not inexpensive trinkets: an oval of glass with a tiny carved wooden scene of old China, all winged roofs and arched bridges, embedded in it; an eagle delicately carved in dark, polished wood; a charming tea set; a lovely scarf. I am deeply touched but make a note to tell Jenny that I know the students have no money to spend for such things. Jenny is there too, of course, so when I whisper my concerns to her, she smiles and replies, "They all put in just a little money. It is okay."

Then comes the cake. It's gorgeous, frothy with whipped cream. It's the first cake I've seen since we left the States, and the fleeting thought that I may well be throwing health cautions to the winds dissipates with the first moist, creamy bite. But I'm jumping ahead. Before I sink my teeth into that light, vanilla confection, I cut and serve pieces to all the guests. The students make a ceremony of taking their piece and wishing me a very happy birthday, with a grin.

Robert startles me too with a large, peculiar-shaped brown box with a bow stuck on it. (He never was one for fancy giftwrapping.) He's bought a guitar in town! So *that* was the goal of his clandestine trip! The kids crowd around, begging me to play for them. They don't know I haven't played a guitar in several years and wasn't very good at it then. Rob just knows that I miss my music. He secretly wrote to our daughter, who sent a guitar songbook for my birthday. He produces it, and everyone quiets expectantly. Now I'm really in a bind. Rob sees my dilemma, and suggests they restart the music. They have a better idea. They turn on the karaoke machine. Karaoke may have originated in Japan, but the Chinese have wrapped themselves around it as their own. Our upstairs neighbor broke us in to the craze in this country with his microphone cranked up to full volume and his just-a-little-flat renditions that go on well into the night.

Now the kids take turns at the mike. No false modesty here. They choose a song from the menu on the TV screen, and the professional backup music begins as the words scroll beneath romantic pictures. The dancing starts again too, often girls with girls. We recognize many songs from our own culture and some purely Chinese love songs. They really love to waltz or foxtrot, steps American kids never learn. They applaud when Rob and I step onto the dance floor. I'm a little ashamed that I'm really enjoying the attention, and we show off a little, dipping and jitterbugging.

The happy euphoria stretches into the evening. Finally I agree to try my new guitar. The resulting rendition is warmly received, but I tell myself I'll never again sneer at my upstairs neighbor, and I vow to practice. Quietly. At home.

14

CHINESE LESSONS

I'm sure of one thing: I want to learn to speak Chinese. Languages have been fairly easy for me to absorb, maybe because I spent several growing up years in Germany when my father was appointed military governor of Würtemburg-Baden right after World War II. I studied French in college, so I'm pretty confident I can at least make myself understood in Chinese. I learned in Germany and on visits to France that even stuttering attempts at the language earn deeper friendships.

Jenny is dubious when I ask her to recommend someone to teach us Chinese. Robert has decided that he wants to be in on it, determined he can make a go of it. Although he's a very smart man, his ear for languages is tone deaf. I tell Jenny the deal is to be strictly business. We want to pay a language teacher. "Yes" she nods, but she's smiling her "maybe."

A few days later, Jenny brings a petite, smartly dressed woman with owl glasses, about Jenny's age, and introduces her. Chen Ying Chun. She speaks precious little English, has never taught anyone Chinese, but yearns to better her English. The deal: we will teach each other our native languages, hour for hour in our apartment, two afternoons a week. I see I've lost the round where I insist on a cash deal. Ying Chun giggles and ducks her head in embarrassment often. Although she has never taught Chinese (she's a social studies teacher at the college), she is insistent we learn the calligraphy, not the Pinyin or phonetic spelling. We agree since we're ignorant of the thousands of characters to be learned. In the brief language training we had in America we learned about the four phonemic tones that convey meaning. The word *Ma* said with four different inflections can mean four entirely different things from *horse* to *mother*. We settle on a time, and Jenny and Ying Chun leave chattering happily.

Ying Chun writes simple characters at our kitchen table, repeats them, and we try to figure out what they mean in English. She scowls when we try to replicate her tone and makes us repeat over and over until she's satisfied. We learn the words for *spring, summer, hot, cold,* and *water*.

Our drinking water comes from five-gallon bottles in a holder in the kitchen. Jenny coached us to telephone the small shop on campus that sells candy, school supplies and water. We're assured the proprietors will deliver the requested bottles to our apartment. The couple running the shop speak no English, of course, so we repeat the single word *schway* with a swoop in our voice like our question mark at the end of the word. After a stunned silence the man or woman on the other end of the line figures it must be those foreigners wanting water since that's the only thing they require from the shop. The man jumps on his motorcycle (really!) and roars to our door with a five-gallon bottle of water on the back.

Our request is not always successful. Sometimes we wait until it's clear they haven't decoded our word. Sometimes we hear disgusted chatter on their end of the line as the disconnect tells us that our one-word message simply didn't translate. Both Rob and I try our one-word mantra into the phone, and he finally shakes his head and grumbles that, even though to his ear my *schway* sounds identical to his *schway*, I seem to have a better batting average. I learn over time that making a more complete sentence for them gives them more time to figure out what in the world I'm saying. So perfecting certain words and phrases becomes crucial.

Our Chinese lessons continue. I have the teaching materials and some experience now to help Ying Chun with her English. Like so many here, she can read fairly well, but speaking and understanding are tough for her. She brings one slim paperback book for us to study Chinese. (Almost all books in China are paperback, printed on cheap paper. There are no color pictures, so our colorful magazine photographs enchant our students.) Her lesson book harkens back at least to the 1940s, with drab little paragraphs of very improbable conversations and storyettes and a few vocabulary words beside them with the Chinese character alongside its English and Japanese counterparts. Ying Chun knows no other way to teach except the way she was taught, the way all Chinese students have been taught—by rote. She reads the paragraph to us, quizzes us to see if we grasp the meaning. We generally don't. Then she tries to explain, often with comical results.

We quickly break through her serious demeanor, and she clowns with us but is very determined that we replicate her sounds. Robert loves to tease her. At first she stares at him, unsure of his meaning, then giggles and even pretends to scold him playfully. He works hard for a few sessions but then decides it's not worth the effort, that progress comes at a cost that he's unwilling to pay. After all, he reasons, he's here to teach English. He shouldn't have to lapse into Chinese to instruct them. Beside, it's too darn much work. Ying

Chun and I hit upon using a tape recorder. After an hour or so of working together on a paragraph, she records it so I can listen and try to duplicate her sounds the next session.

Maybe the best part of our time together is when I ask Ying Chun a bit about her life. I learn she has a son, about five years old. (Getting the age of children right here is a real puzzle for a Westerner. The Chinese say everyone turns a year older at the Chinese New Year in February, and that can be a little tricky for people with a more precise date in mind.) She loves her son, but like most children here, he is in school much of the time. Her husband (she screws up her little face) is not much of a factor in her life, but she yearns for a daughter. The Chinese adore their children, and the little girls I've seen are petted and loved almost as much as the Little Emperors, the sons.

It's interesting to look down the road to what the one child per family policy will mean in the future. Of course, the country has hordes of people to feed, and the rule may seem draconian, but the leadership figured they had to do something. I ask Yinig Chun what would happen if she had another child. "Oh, I would be punished. No more money!" She shakes her head sadly, signaling the end of the conversation. For years people here have been controlled by their *danwei*, or work group. They cannot simply move to a new job or city or even buy food without the proper *danwei* papers. I understand that life is not quite so harsh now and people are gaining more mobility, but wages and monetary support are still closely controlled. Either Chen Ying Chun and her husband would get less money from the government if they had a second child, or they would be fined. When we see a rare Chinese family with more than one child, we say to ourselves, "They must be very rich." And what will happen to extended families? No more true aunts and uncles, no cousins. One couple will have to support four grandparents. I'm grasping that when our students say *my brother* or *my sister*, they very likely don't mean biological siblings. Maybe a cousin or a family friend.

I yearn to speak, even haltingly, but Ying Chun holds me resolutely to the written page. She helps me when I ask for specific phrases for the market or downtown but seems baffled when I try to explain that I want to *speak* fluently.

My debut comes on the rickety bus coming home from Chuga. Rob and I are clutching our backpacks and packages bulging with snow peas, potatoes and onions. The bundles are common here, but backpacks are a novelty. Furthermore, we're the only foreigners for miles around (except for Jacques, our French colleague, who rarely ventures into the village). The bus is crowded as usual, and the smell of human bodies, cigarette smoke, live chickens and gasoline stir into an aromatic stew that will always be China for me. A gaggle of men look us over and comment on our strangeness, nothing really offensive, just curiosity. They discuss us as if we were ducks or pigeons being evaluated for food value, assuming as most Chinese do, that we are too ignorant to understand them. As we get up to leave the bus, I give them my sweetest smile and say in Chinese, "Please be careful what you say. I can understand you."

Their jaws drop and I read the look in their eyes: "The duck speaks!"

Rob with our Chinese teacher/friend

15

TEMPLES AND
DONGQIAN LAKE

What a glorious day! After two weeks of rain and mud, it's magnificently sunny and warm enough to eliminate the long underwear that has been our accustomed garb since we landed in China. We had a tourist day with Jenny. She arranged for a car and driver, and we left the college at eight-thirty this morning for a drive through the countryside, winding up the hills, past men ploughing fields with lumbering water buffalo, snaking through villages, gazing up to see hillside graveyards with families carrying large, brightly colored, round paper fans to decorate the graves. Our goal was a Buddhist temple built in 300 A.D. Because the day was so gorgeous and a Saturday, many Chinese families and others had the same idea we did, so we shared a festival atmosphere. As we left the car and circled on foot around the pool at the entrance to the temple, incense and the dark smell from sputtering altar candles tingled our senses. We joined the chattering clouds of excited school children and equally holiday-spirited adults. Gold, red and saffron banners fluttered about the entrance, and I felt completely and wholly deep in the heart of mainland China.

There are 999 rooms in the temple, Jenny told us, one of the oldest and most revered in China, especially by the Japanese who believe the ancestor of their nation sprang from here. Many Japanese make pilgrimages to come here. We wandered from room to room, inspecting even the enormous wok which the gentle monks use to cook their food. I admired the many golden Buddhas, some clothed in elaborate fabrics, some with offerings of food (even Pepsi bottles!) placed at their feet. As we wandered through the rooms, a drum boomed deeply, calling the monks to prayer. I felt the vibrations before I heard them, the sound so soft, yet insistent. About fifty men, heads shaved, in robes of brown, orange or saffron floating around their bare or sandaled feet, hurried past us toward the temple's main chamber. It didn't seem irreverent to follow them, along with all the Chinese tourists. There we saw what few Westerners have. The metallic bass gong washed over us as its heartbeat gathered the faithful monks. Jenny explained that the color of their robes denotes rank or the level of their progress and training. They sang and chanted their prayers, nodding and bowing, completely oblivious to the crowds around them.

The day didn't end there. We went on to Dongqian (*Dong Chien*) Lake. Robert and I had been there on our own already. We took some students' advice one Saturday and tried to hike there, since they assured us it wasn't far. After an hour on foot along the busy road with no sidewalk, the gnat-like three-wheeled trucks, busses, and lumbering trucks narrowly missing us, we flagged down a pedicab and finished the trip behind his bicycle. But today Jenny told us the history of the lake. It is manmade, quite large, with bits of hopeful grass indicating one spot where the eye can rest on something beside concrete. We wander through a peculiar temple that falls into the US

Highway 66 roadside attraction category. Within the crumbling walls are strange, gaudy, life-sized figures, obviously depicting some story from history, lost on us. A museum displaying hundreds of pictures of animals, all done in butterfly wings, is beautifully grotesque: peacocks, tigers and dragons (one five feet long!), all sketched with millions of butterfly wings. The butterfly population must've set off a triple alarm when they saw the artist coming with his net. Or maybe they didn't. Now that I think about it, I haven't seen a butterfly or heard a bird since we've been here.

We went to the hotel by the lake for lunch. Jenny ordered for us. I'm sure one of the dishes was snails. Jenny encouraged me to try them. I pulled one out of its little shell. Okay. I ate two of them to be polite. I loved the soup, which had an unidentifiable green vegetable in it. I tried to get from Jenny just what it was, but she couldn't find the English word. Maybe I'm happier that way.

Lazy sampans bobbed on the lake, but after lunch Jenny led us into a very fast speedboat to career across the lake to an island and another temple. By then we were more interested in the school groups, organized into circles doing elaborate *tai qi* or seated on the sparse grass. We still attract curious looks from most, but they were so content with what they were doing that we were free to wander at will.

We picked up a brochure at the hotel as we were leaving and are chuckling now at home to read in the multicolor, expensive brochure:

> *Wanjin Hotel, gifted with eleven scences of Dongqian Lake is lacated in Dongqian Lake, the largest presh water in Zhejiang province. It is the first choice to spend holiday amuse in Zhejiang province. It is a best place for you to amuse, spend holiday, and discuss business. The Hotel consists of standard guest rooms, deluse suites,*

compound amusement suites with central air-conditioning and tele-
phone. In the amusement center. There are sauna equipment
into-duced from finland. Japanese automatic shuffling machine,
beauty center, healthy hall, billiard ball, children's paradise, etc.
Especially American system with quick bottle arrangement and ball
return is imported in bowling hall. It is the most advanced equipment
in the world! Wanjin Hotel, everyone goes, everyone says well.

I find the amusing, childlike English gloriously displayed in neon signs or captured in glossy programs endearing. But it does underscore two things: one, the Chinese long to leap into the larger world of economics, tourism and business in English; and two, either there are mighty few native English speakers around to help with accurate translation, or the locals are loath to ask for assistance.

A case in point comes soon after that day trip. Occasionally Jenny or someone from another department comes to us with something they've put into English, wanting us to correct or polish it. We're very happy to oblige and hope to avoid the kind of head-scratching Chinglish the Wanjin Hotel put out, but it often leads to a careful dance with the translator.

"Let's see, what is it exactly that you'd like to say here?" That's Robert or me. We try to question our colleagues without letting them know we haven't the foggiest idea what they are trying to say. I say this, shuddering at the thought of trying to put an intelligent thought into proper Chinese. I admire their efforts, but trying to unscramble the convoluted, ultra-polite Chinese manner of writing and speaking into intelligible English is often a challenge. If we know that someone needs to write something in English, we try to catch them before they translate. Trying to untangle their written English is much harder than sitting face-to-face and having them explain in their own spoken English what they want to convey. We were too late with the lovely first-of-its-kind brochure Zhejiang Sunli University put out.

We've heard a little about the supercharged woman who is the power behind the Sunli education group. Apparently our school is to be the Chinese test case for setting up a private, tuition-based university. We've glimpsed the forty-something lady who feels completely at home among the dark-suited men on her board of directors and Communist Party administrators. She's the mighty engine turning this sleepy three-year teachers college into a proper four-year university at dizzying speed. Jenny brings the multi-paged, color brochure, meant to attract foreign teachers and students and asks us to look it over for mistakes. Well, it's already printed. We see photos of ourselves on the pages glorifying the university's magnificent English department. The pictures were taken without our knowledge while we had our classes outside, pointing out the glories around us. In English, one presumes. The brochure praised the college English department, surprising since the college doesn't yet *have* an English department, but the Chinese are given to hyperbole. Rob and I looked it over, while Jenny beamed at us and came to the final page, the ultimate push for foreign investment and participants, praising the "*intercourse*" to be enjoyed here. It's too late to correct that. So we hand the brochure back to Jenny, smiling. "It's wonderful, Jenny."

16

MAY 6, 1999
MOTHER'S DAY

This Sunday is different. The phone's shriek wakes us at around 6:00 a.m. A tense Shen Wei Qi (Sam) from the college administration is on the line. "Please stay in your apartment today. NATO has bombed the Chinese Embassy in Yugoslavia. Chinese citizens have been killed, and many people in China are very angry. It may not be safe for you to be on the streets now."

We whisper, "All right," and hang up. Why in the world would NATO or America bomb the Chinese Embassy? We know that as we left America in February of 1999, the news warned of the ethnic cleansing and hatred boiling between the Serbs and Bosnians. News here has alluded to American and world "intervention in local affairs" in that part of the world with no mention of "rape hotels" or whole-sale slaughtering among the "local affairs" of the inflamed neighbors.

We deeply feel the disconnect with world news here. Chinese media, the one daily half-hour English evening TV news, and the English newspaper hammer out praise for the benevolent Chinese premier's successes in encouraging world peace and the astounding growth of China's economy. World news, if mentioned at all, is through the rosy film of China's glowing world stature or "the West's grasping, bullying tactics" in world affairs.

As daylight grays lift, the eerie quiet on the campus is palpable. Sunday is a workday here, but no hammers or cement mixers cut through the heavy fabric of silence. Our college doesn't have classes on Sunday. Most Chinese colleges do not, but many schools do. Businesses are open as usual on Sunday. Still the sound of traffic is strangely muted. We turn on the TV, hoping for a glimmer of current news. Blank. Nothing. All channels are dark.

I call Sandra and Woody, which is a challenge in itself since I have to *speak* the numbers in Chinese to their college switchboard operator, always an opportunity for misunderstanding. But I get through immediately and hear the worry in Sandra's voice. "Do you know anything more?" I ask.

"No, only that we think several busloads of students were taken away, probably for a spontaneous demonstration. It's happened before," she tells me. LuJean and Dutch are also worried and isolated on their deathly quiet campus. We won't be getting together today.

Our old computer creaks to life. Before coming to China our idea was to use it to e-mail home since an Internet hookup is questionable here. We told ourselves we would invest in a new computer after returning home and get serious about plunging into the Internet world. No reason to take a new computer to China where its use would be severely restricted. Our dilemma is that now we have no access to international news. Jacques, the Canadian, next door! He has a fully functional computer and the wit and skill to use it. Maybe *he* can find out what is stirring the turbulent world in Yugoslavia.

Jacques is already crouched in front of his screen and has a bit more information. American bombers in fact unloaded on the

Chinese Embassy in Yugoslavia. At least three people were killed. American authorities claim confusion about the location of the embassy, saying their maps don't show a Chinese Embassy at that spot. They believed they were bombing an arms depot. Then Jacques starts having trouble with Internet reception. A coincidence? We've heard our letters and e-mail could be censored, although we've never spotted any tampering. Sandra told us that several months ago her sister sent her a letter with some photos. It arrived without the photos, but a week later a letter from another friend arrived—with the photos.

Jacques tries e-mailing some friends in Quebec. We realize it's still Saturday night in Canada and the US. Most people there have turned off their computers and gone to bed. "Keep trying, Jacques, and we'll do the same on our dinosaur of a computer. Come over later and we'll have dinner together and swap information."

So begins our longest day. It's Mother's Day in America, but the flowers and family hugs are a lifetime away. While our friends and family in America sleep, we check and recheck our e-mail, sending SOS for *any* news. Meanwhile the silence crouches outside our door. Waiting. Rob suggests we pack our backpacks with passports, emergency foodbars, water and a change of clothes. If we *have* to leave quickly, where would we go? To the Chinese we are so clearly American that there would be no slipping through a crowd unnoticed.

Let's try the TV again. It leaps to life, filling the room with hate-contorted faces, mobs burning the American flag, a man (the father of a dead Chinese journalist?) sobbing as he hugs a bloody blanket. It's a steady loop of high decibel rage and grief. The narration is in Chinese, but the message is clear. *Now* where could we go? Our very American faces and hair give us away. We are a very long way from an airport.

I feel the walls beginning to close in. Breathing takes careful effort. All the fears I pooh-poohed before coming to China leap back at me. Strangely, my sense of smell seems painfully sharp. The odor of bleach sears my nostrils. The smell of years of dirt embedded in the worn carpet almost strangles me as it mingles with the smell of crushed garlic and ginger. Even the muted noises outside bring icy heat prickles to my skin. What am I listening for? I invent reasons to stay close to Rob, who stares at the computer screen like a submarine sonar expert, *willing* the ancient computer to life.

There's an incoming e-mail! A friend in Washington state glanced at his e-mail before going to bed and saw our plea. He gives us a concise summary of what he's read and heard about the bombing and mentions student protests in China. After that one message Sunday morning, our sources of information go blank for the next twelve hours. We close and lock the iron security door and glance at the barred windows. We laughed uncomfortably at them when we first came, feeling hemmed in. What might they have to keep out now? We don't turn on any lights, trying to keep a very low profile. We spend the dreary day trying to prepare for tomorrow's classes. That keeps my mind from dwelling on my thumping heart. While the US sleeps, the gloomy day here at Zhejiang Teachers' College mirrors our turmoil. We have no idea what is happening in the world or even in our immediate surroundings. We both acknowledge it is certainly the time for prayer.

Our Canadian friend arrives for dinner and tells us he has been out on campus and had some threatening gestures from the normally friendly construction workers. He is clearly shaken since until now his youth and "foreign expert" title have attracted students' friendship, even adulation. The young Chinese teachers he was close to turned away from him when he approached them today, so Jacques says he plans to leave China as soon as possible. He thinks we're sitting on a powder keg and he doesn't care that he signed a contract with six months to run. We're aware that we're the only three non-Chinese faces for miles!

At about ten o'clock Sunday night (10:00 a.m. on the US east coast) our family and friends finally turn on their computers and, realizing our information vacuum, start shooting messages to us. For the next three hours it's newsroom central in our apartment. We receive a message, reply with a few comments or questions, and find two more messages in the in-box. I'm not sure whether we feel better or worse as the story clarifies. President Clinton is apologizing for the huge mistake, telling the public that the military used apparently outdated maps, that they had no idea the Chinese Embassy was in the building, that the intelligence indicated firearms were being stored there. My brother Dick in Virginia sends whole news clippings and tries to answer our questions and catch us up on news that never appeared in China. We know nothing of the disappearance of thousands of Kosovo Albanians or ethnic cleansing. Man's inhumanity to man has been truncated in the Chinese media as simply another example of the rich American bullies interfering in the private internal affairs of another small, weak country.

Our little laptop doesn't jam once, which is incredible! In the past if we got a particularly long message, the inbox ground to a halt so that we could receive neither that message nor any e-mails that followed. The only way to clear it was and is still to phone the one computer guru in Ningbo. When we have the problem she deletes all the inbound messages on the computer, which often takes days. We never know whose messages we lose, so we *beg* people to keep their notes short and *not* to send photos.

The miracle *this* night is that there are no glitches in the flow of messages back and forth. Our hookup works smoothly, and if there are any censors wanting to keep information out of China, they're occupied elsewhere. We finally sign off at about 1:00 a.m. Monday, drained and desperate for sleep. We're determined to teach tomorrow unless instructed otherwise.

The first class Monday morning is one we team teach. We set out for our classroom with a plan. Outside, the students seem more reserved, not the usual eye contact and chirping *hellos* and giggles as we walk across the campus. The TV images and hoarse voices of impotent rage and hate are burned in our hearts and memories, so we're unsure of our reception in the classroom. Will anyone *be* there? If the students are there, will they register the shock and rage all of China must be feeling now? Will there be glowering government officials? We may not be personally responsible for the bombing, but we're Americans and we're *here*!

The usual kids *are* in their seats, holding their breath, their eyes trying to read us as we enter. I quietly ask Yu Li Ping to come up front and stand beside me, and I explain what we want her to do. "While you speak English rather well," I tell the class, "we want to be *sure* you all understand us, so I'm going to speak a bit in English and ask Yu Li Ping to translate." Deep breath. "Mr. McKee and I want to apologize to you for NATO's bombing of your embassy in Yugoslavia. There is no way to tell you how sad it makes us. The American president has publicly apologized for the mistake. No one ever intended to target Chinese citizens. It was believed that ammunition to be used against innocent people was stored in that building. The NATO maps were old and did not show the Chinese Embassy there."

Yu Li Ping flushes and puts my words into Mandarin after each sentence. Is there a collective exhale of relief? A buzz erupts among the students, then quiets. Li Ping turns to us, her eyes brimming, and says, "Mr. McKee, Mrs. McKee, you do not need to apologize to us. We know that you love us, and we love you." Our eyes and hearts overflow. Each class after that gives us similar reactions.

Chinese citizens, old or young, never hear of President's Clinton's apology. State controlled TV and print media smirk at the preposterous suggestion that wealthy, swaggering America could actually bumble and drop bombs on an unintended target. They cannot explain why the Chinese Embassy was singled out for punishment but are sure it was intentional.

We still haven't unpacked our quick-flight bags but think we can resume our quiet lives here. We're praying for cool, wise hearts and minds, particularly for world leaders who could learn a great deal from these trusting young people.

ROB'S BIRTHDAY AND
EVENING CLASSES

I t still feels a little ragged here after the explosive outpouring following the US bombing of the Chinese Embassy in Kosovo. Our own raw, mental images remain of the sudden violent TV pictures—an inconsolable father hugging a blood-soaked blanket and the masses in Beijing flogging an Uncle Sam dummy, while American flags smolder in the background. I'm sure they're not erased in the minds of our students and the staff either, although they are all courteous. We hear rumors that thousands of students in cities throughout China, including Ningbo, were bussed to rallies and "spontaneous" anti-American demonstrations. We don't know if any of our students were taken to town that day. A curtain of secrecy we can't penetrate slides silently across certain areas of life here.

It's been a week since the bombing, and we need to venture off campus to restock our empty pantry. Jenny and Sam nervously agree that we may go to Chuga to shop, but Jenny will accompany us—in the college staff car—no bus. Rob and I loathe the picture of us pulling up in front of the marketplace in the black car that emanates privilege and rank, but we have no choice.

Is it our imagination, or are the vendors quieter today? People scurry past the writhing tubs of fish as usual and the long row of stalls displaying an incredible assortment of eggs, the women vendors vying for attention. One points in disgust at our usual egg lady's eggs. By now I understand that she's not yelling insults at us. She's saying we always buy from that other woman. "Her eggs are old. Rotten! They stink! Come buy my eggs today." After that outburst everyone enjoys a good laugh, including our usual egg lady. We smile, shake our heads, and buy from our stand-by.

That seems to clear the air, and we move up and down the aisles, past the stench of fish too long in the market, past clouds of flies that rise in annoyance from slabs of pork. No purchases here! We continue, choosing among the pungent smells of vegetables, green and purple, until our backpacks and string bag are full. We make our usual stop in the tiny grocery store for rice, wander past the outdoor stalls shopping for apples, bananas, perhaps some tiny sweet oranges.

On the way home, Jenny announces that the staff wants to honor Robert on his May 16th birthday.

"No, Jenny! The best birthday gift you can give us is for you to stay home one night with your family after your trip translating for the Canadian delegation. Beside, we are embarrassed and unhappy about the embassy bombing. Nerves are raw, and we wonder if it's wise to celebrate right now."

She smiles and nods, but we know that we're beaten. Why can't we win an argument with Jenny?

Six members of the staff pick us up Monday night for dinner downtown, including Jenny and the college's new academic vice president. He's excruciatingly polite. His English is extremely good, but we can't read behind his eyes. He studied for a year and a half in the American Midwest. His field of study? European history. We tease him that perhaps America wasn't the best choice for his chosen field, but he only smiles. We're taken to a private dining room in a big hotel and have a sumptuous meal. They give Rob a large bouquet of flowers, a magnificent fabric scroll, a wall hanging of a crane and a pine bough—symbols of longevity, they explain—and some audiotapes of traditional Chinese music.

Afterward our hosts take us to an entertainment complex. Apparently, Rob mentioned some time in the past that he likes to bowl. The neon sign above the building flashes two words in English script: Bow Ling. The bowling lanes look quite new and modern, all computerized. Everyone is very friendly and typically curious when we enter. Evidently the sport is quite new in China, because around us we watch the lousiest bowlers I've ever seen. As dropped balls thunder on the polished alley floor I expect to see gaping dents. We're not particularly good bowlers either, but Rob enjoys it, and our hosts seem pleased with the evening.

We decide to make our first solo venture into Ningbo after the bombing. It's time to go high tech and buy an overhead projector. So far we're limited to very dusty chalkboards for visual aids. We check our classrooms for a functioning plug, and all but one have one. That one has loose wires sticking out where a plug should be. We ask to have it repaired, and in a few days it is. Our negotiations downtown for the projector are lengthy and amusing. I'm sure we will be the source of conversation for the store clerks and the bus patrons since we haul it home, a monstrous box looking a lot like a wounded stork with one leg folded on top. It's worth it though. Our students have never seen one before, and we can project pictures or cartoon sequences that I prepare. Everyone can see them, and the students get a kick out of creating stories to go along with what they see.

Spontaneous discussion is what we're after.

Robert has one class, all mechanical engineers, who need a lot of remedial help. There is *no* discussion. After the students respond to his, "What is your name, please?" it's all uphill. He's tried everything to get some comprehension and participation. Finally he discussed giving them some extra help with the administration. Later the administration let him know they'd arranged for the entire class to come one extra evening a week. Traditionally here evening classes simply don't happen. Imagine telling a college class in the States they should show up for an extra class one evening because they're doing so poorly! But the Chinese students *come*. They're all smiles, even applaud when Rob introduces me to help him for the evening. The class is mostly young men with three or four girls scattered in the class. I suspect that this major, in spite of its fancy name, has to do with perfecting the Chinese miracle of using discarded wire, rags or mud to repair virtually anything. We tell them there will be no quizzes, no homework for the evening lessons, just as much help and fun as we can manage—speaking English.

I draw a quick cartoon on the chalkboard of a lion and a mouse. We invite two students to come to the front and read a simplified version of the fable. We go over unfamiliar words (a lot of them), and then they reread it. They get quite a lot of fun out of that. Their childhoods are filled with fables and myths, so these appeal to them.

After class several kids cluster around the desk as we gather our things. One very shy girl, who Rob says hasn't uttered a syllable all term, thrusts the back of one of her theme papers at me and asks me something I can't understand. One of her classmates volunteers that she wants me to draw the mouse for her. As I scribble a mouse, she actually caresses it and tells me she plans to send it to her mother.

Hong Li walks at my elbow all the way home, and I learn that she loves to draw. After this, she materializes at my side at odd times during the day.

The evening classes continue. Tonight we brought a stack of magazine ads. Each student selects one and studies it for a few minutes, then one at a time they tell a story or describe what they see in the pictures. The colored photos and the happy foreign-looking people beaming out at them enchant them.

One boy pores over his picture until his turn comes. His nose almost touching the shiny page, his eyes have a faraway look. Rob whispers that he hasn't opened his mouth in class yet. The classroom stills as the boy gathers for one momentous effort. Finally, holding up a Volvo ad, "If I would have this car, I would be *wild* with joy!" His classmates gasp, and we all applaud.

18

CHINESE CHEATING

As the weeks pass, both Rob and I feel more at ease in the dusty classrooms. We try out the various English workbooks we brought and the shelved ones left for us in our apartment and find that the kids can't cope with the more difficult ones. Their spoken English is still basic, and their comprehension of the spoken word even fuzzier, even though they're able to read fairly difficult texts out loud. Comprehension? That's another story.

Then too, we discover a huge lack of understanding in the folks who write the textbooks. Chatty written paragraphs about amusing little anecdotes that happened while on an airliner are so far removed from our students' lives that they have no context for them. They have probably ridden a rusty bicycle in their short lives but may never ride in an automobile. They almost certainly will never own one. Their chance of being on an airplane is about on a par with being struck by lightning. The books' chummy references to American movie stars or grinning sports figures make no sense to them at all.

Almost by accident we see that they love stories and pictures of daily American life, especially of kids their own age. We write and e-mail friends and family and ask them to take color pages from magazines and send them to us. They are enchanting jumping off spots for questions and discussion.

We settle into our own teaching styles, coaxing our students to relax and laugh at their mistakes. Both of us use an occasional Chinese word in class. Even when we massacre their names, the inevitable laughter is always a case in point. Learning another language may be serious business, but mistakes happen. If we're afraid to try something new, we never make progress. That becomes our mantra. My guitar, the cartoons, the hammy acting we both do, the stand-up games, even Simon Says, are techniques that simply don't appear in a typical Chinese classroom. Laughter and smiles are the oils that grease the tense students' efforts to open up and try. Grades, however, seem to flip a switch to terror again.

As we get to know them better, we learn that they live and die by examinations and grades. King Lake, Lucy, Stone, Richard, all of them tell us the same story, reinforcing what we've learned. In their villages, exams determine which students will go on to junior high school; then more tests and, if they pass, high school. Until fairly recently most villages had no school at all. Now a child who fails to measure up at test time is yanked from further schooling and sent to work in the fields or factories, often a dank, dark room where they count ball bearings day after endless day. High school is generally the end of the road for most students, but those who pass the tests with high marks go to trade schools (like this three-year teachers college) or to various levels of colleges and universities. Then day-long tests determine not only what college or university they attend (in their home province) but also what their field of study will be. Our hearts sink when we hear their stories of yearning to study science or computers but their test scores place them in animal raising (pigs and chickens) or accounting. So much depends on the test scores that they have perfected *helping one's comrade* or as Rob and I refer to it with awe, Chinese Cheating.

We're required to turn in grades for our students, although we wonder if grades assigned by foreign teachers count. We rather doubt it. How could English be weighed as heavily in their grade point average as such important classes as *Thoughts of Deng Xiao Peng* or social studies (more of the same) or computer science? By the way, we listen to the kids list their classes and see there's no such thing as core subjects or trying to broaden a student's education. They take only the subjects related most narrowly to their assigned field, with the exception of political speeches by the latest revered leader (Mao Tse Tung is out; Deng is in). Yet we give occasional quizzes and tell them we grade classroom discussion participation. Our folders with the photos and names beside them leave room for notations about who tries to speak up. We stress that we ask them only to try, not to be perfect. We try to design tests to reinforce what we talk about. We've seen examples of their state-mandated English exams, which seem designed to trick the test-taker with unimportant, technical grammar questions that would throw a native English speaker. No wonder they're gun-shy. Since we try to encourage natural conversation, I give at least one essay question on each quiz. Okay. I'm a glutton for punishment, but reading almost incomprehensible handwriting and figuring out the writer's intent is becoming my specialty.

The college also requires a final examination. That's the only way they know how to educate. Test. Test. Test. We argue that a final written test for oral English doesn't make sense. Linda, the English Department chair, smiles and shrugs. Her English is probably better than most Chinese English teachers', but she's extremely nervous and unsure of herself. She doesn't know what to do with us. The same smile greets our repeated requests for a desk or two in the English teachers' office. Then nothing. There's no such thing as a teachers' lounge, so between classes teachers come into the office and put their heads down on their desks and nap. We learn to open the office door quietly. Our hope is to hold office hours for the kids who are too shy to come to our apartment for help. So far no desks, but back to Chinese Cheating.

Robert notices it first: the almost silent hum, like a distant generator, in the classroom during a written test. We saunter up and down the aisles between the double desks. There it is again! If you lean down you can hear a whisper, but no lips are moving! If you actually perceive a student speaking to a neighbor, he laughs and says he didn't realize he was speaking. They are *good*! So good that we try an old tactic, handing out two different tests so two students sitting side by side have the questions in different order. At first we got an "X test" with all "Y" answers from time to time. We also spread the test-takers out with an empty desk between them. They just don't look at cheating the way we do. We ask the Walls and Rileys and learn they have the identical problem. A lifetime of pressure means students help one another against The World Out There. China is a nation of the community, not individuals. We point out that using another's knowledge on a test won't help them when they're on the job in the world. They smile and nod. And cheat.

Once when Rob was giving a final written exam in a large auditorium, two more Chinese English teachers came to help proctor the exam. He arranged for his classes to be there at the appointed time. The kids produced a photo I.D. and displayed it on their desks. Rob asked one teacher why they did that. "Oh, they must do that during examinations to prove they are the correct student taking the test. Otherwise they may send in a friend, a better student, to take the test for them." Of course, by now we know all students by sight, if not by name, so we'd be tough to fool, but that is not the case for other teachers.

On that occasion, about a half hour into the silent test, three self-important men in dark suits typical of the Chinese strode into the tense room. Rob had never seen them before, so he went to shoo them out. They stuttered protests in Chinese as they backed out of the room. He noticed the kids watching in amazement and heard some snickers. His two proctors rushed to the front of the room and tried to intercept him. "Those are important officials, here to be sure there is no cheating," they sputtered.

"I don't care *who* they are. This is my class, and I can monitor it myself," he insisted, adding when he saw their faces, "with your help, of course."

So we feel our way each day, teaching in ways we hope reach the students, using structure, no structure, laughter, music, movement, textbooks, no textbooks, sometimes even tests, using all our senses to try to see that each student produces his or her own work.

Chris, whom we inherited from our American teaching couple predecessors, gives us a heartbreaking insight into the impact of tests on Chinese students' lives. She must've told us her Chinese name the first time she came, but I don't remember it. Chris is the English name she got from a junior high (Chinese) English teacher. She's in only the eighth grade, she tells us, but her quiet drive to better her English brought her on her bike on Saturdays to visit with Renee and

Ed, our predecessors, long before we arrived. She figures we will continue the arrangement since we're their replacements. We do. She's very shy about speaking, which makes us wonder why she's so determined to learn to speak English. She tells us she lives with her mother "who must work very hard every day so is not at home very much" and her father "who brings home many men with ugly faces. I do not like them. They sleep in my room. I must sleep on the floor by my grandmother." She adores her grandmother, who is her real caregiver. In fact, she begins to bring us delicacies her granny makes. Fortunately she doesn't insist we enjoy them while she watches to see our reactions to very sticky rice wrapped in grape leaves or moon-cakes or some homemade jelly-like substance that looks and smells like glue.

What thrill us—well, me at least—are Chris' own artistic creations. At first she shyly brings us origami birds, exquisitely folded, tiny colored paper birds, then other fantastic shapes. One day she arrives bearing something large hidden under a scarf. Beneath the scarf is a mobile of exquisite twisted paper shapes and tiny sequins about two and half feet across and just as tall. She admits it's hung in her room this year. She made it, she tells us ducking her head, "in my spare time," and she wants us to have it. Her hands twisted and folded for hundreds of hours to give birth to the paper masterpiece. Now she wants to give it away. To us. She studies our faces to see if we accept her treasure. There is so little of beauty and comfort in her young life that I yearn to urge her to keep it for herself, but her generosity awes me.

She always stays overlong, especially since the conversation is rather one-sided with me, the magpie, doing all the talking. Robert tends to wander out of the room after greeting her. She generally answers only in monosyllables, so I scour my brain for simple topics she can grasp. She smiles and nods or answers a simple *yes* when I ask a question. Sometimes she brings a schoolmate, Jack, with her, taller than she, but that isn't the reason she seems to shrink in his presence. His brash self-confidence is almost a slap at her gentle manner, and I find I dislike him a little. His English is much better than hers, but I wish she wouldn't let him answer every question or assert his opinion. His sharp, beaklike features contrast with her soft, round look. He leans back in the chair, and his eyes sweep our room. He clearly wants us to know of his superior grades in school and his plans to be a successful businessman.

To help Chris, I begin sending her home with English books and sometimes accompanying audiotapes we find at the Ningbo bookstore. I use them for our students who are ready for a little more meat beyond the milk of our class studies. She gobbles up the slim paperback love stories, shortened versions of English or American novels, and adventure stories, bringing them back each week with questions and a hunger for more. Jack insists he also wants to borrow the books. I cherish the times Chris comes alone. She may not speak much, but the tenderness and the simple pleasure she communicates at being in our home warm me.

One Saturday Rob and I decide to strike out on our own and take a long distance bus to Xi Kou, the birthplace of Xiang Kai Sheck, the ousted leader of China, driven to Taiwan in 1949 by Mao Tse Tung's troops along with the Chinese Nationalist army. The town, only about two hours' distant, is supposed to be a lovely mountain village surrounded by tea fields, and we're curious to see how the communist Chinese handle this bit of their history. We manage to get the right bus and are amazed to find a TV blaring a Chinese movie of screaming gangsters and bloody battles at full volume from the front of the otherwise comfortable bus during the whole trip. A white-gloved stewardess also serves no useful purpose on the "deluxe" bus, as we speed on the first real highway we've seen in China, pretty much deserted except for our bus and a few government sedans. We attract curious glances from fellow passengers. We look out the windows at neat rows of tea bushes all up the mountainsides.

Xi Kou is indeed a charming town, with a river with grass and parks alongside it. We find Xiang's family home and see that the former general and opponent of the communists gets a nod in Chinese history. At least the propaganda doesn't vilify him.

We return home in a heavy rain just before dark, triumphant and tired. We see a shadow near our front door as we approach. It's Chris! Standing ankle deep in the lake that accumulates at our door with each rain now, she and her bike are awash. "How long have you waited?!"

"Oh, not too long. I thought perhaps you would come home soon."

I'm almost in tears at the picture of Chris standing waiting, hopeful, maybe for hours. Rob says, "Chris, please telephone us before you come to be sure we're home. Sometimes on Saturdays we may be gone for the whole day."

She hangs her head, and we realize she doesn't have a phone. "It's OK I can come. If you're not here, I will wait."

The school year is almost over. Chris appears less and less often. Finally she tells us she has no time for my books and tapes. She must study all the time for her examination. She has frequent headaches and complains of stomach aches. If she doesn't pass the upcoming test, she will not go on to high school. She hopes Jack will help her study. He's supremely confident not only that he will go on to high school but also that he will be accepted for the top high school in Ningbo. She wishes she were such a good student.

After an absence, she tells me her grandmother took her to the hospital since her stomach "hurt me so much." The doctors found no serious problem, but we all knew she was tied in knots, worrying about the exams. She tells me she can't eat anything. I have a precious box of Ritz crackers I've hoarded and offer her one, thinking maybe it will sit well on her nervous stomach. She likes it, so I send her home with a sleeve of crackers. The days drag until the exam. We don't see her for several weeks. When she finally comes, we ask how she thinks she did. She shakes her head. "I don't know." Her childish roundness seems to have evaporated, and she's a worried young woman now.

"When will you find out if you passed?"

"Soon I think."

Several days go by. Then both Jack and Chris ride their bikes to our door. Jack strides in and selects a chair, taking charge of the room. Chris follows.

"Well, please tell us. How did you do?" Jack is eager to confirm that he will be going to the academically superior high school in Ningbo. "And you, Chris?"

Almost inaudibly, "I passed the test but not so well as Jack. I will go to the high school in Chuga."

"Congratulations, Chris, Jack! Well done, both of you!" I don't dare hug Chris. In China nobody hugs in public, but I ache to wrap my arms around her and assure her she's done wonderfully well.

And I don't believe she cheated.

FACE LUMP

I've been trying to ignore a hard nodule just to the left of my nose. It feels the way it did before I had a root canal done in the States several months ago. The swelling is painful to the touch, and I refuse to believe the problem has returned after that dental surgery. But it has. I can't bear the thought of going to a dentist here. The level of cleanliness I've seen, even in hospitals, reminds me of stories I've read about our Civil War battlefield tent hospitals. Surely there are well-trained, competent dentists here, but I have no idea how to find one.

I e-mail our dentist friend who did the root canal: "Help! Can it be that the infection has returned?! What can I do?"

He and a doctor friend reply that "it's possible that a tiny root was missed and has become inflamed, but if you take an antibiotic, it should quiet down until you can have the tooth looked at. There should be no long term damage to your health."

Oh, fine. Just how do I get the antibiotic? I mention it to Jenny, the lady-who-accomplishes-anything. She listens patiently then tells me to walk over to the college infirmary and ask the doctor there to have a look in my mouth.

I step into the infirmary, which at first seems deserted, suddenly stir-ring up the dust. A white-coated lady steps out from behind a filing case and asks what I need. I try to explain in a combination of English and Chinese. She scurries into an adjoining office and returns with a simi-larly white-coated man who is all smiles. He speaks absolutely no English, but he's the doctor and my ticket to the antibiotics, so I try to describe my problem. He reaches over and presses the swelling on my face gently, then gestures for me to open my mouth. When I do, he takes a tongue depressor, which looks none too new, from a cup on his desk and, placing it in my mouth, peers in. His grunts and nods tell me more than his comments that he sees the problem. He smiles to reas-sure me, nods and puts the tongue depressor *back into the cup*. My mind wrenches through images of other mouths explored with that tool. The lady interrupts my thoughts and hands me a packet of *Amoxicillin Capsules*, the words in English hidden among the many Chinese char-acters on the packet. It's exactly what my doctor and dentist friends prescribed, though this is half the dosage, but I know how to take two. I flee back to the apartment.

Jenny appears later with more of the same antibiotic that she picked up at a drugstore. In China, apparently, one can just go into a drugstore and obtain such a thing without a doctor's prescription.

I realize late one afternoon that the pain has subsided and the hard knot is gone from beside my nose. The lump has gotten softer, and there is a slight bloody taste in my mouth. Maybe the antibi-otics are working and the mysterious crud will not resurface, at least until I'm back in the United States. My doctor friend assures me I'm not doing serious damage to myself by putting salve, so to speak, on my symptoms.

20

KING LAKE

King Lake! That should be the name of a body of water, not a sleepy-eyed boy slightly shorter than his peers. But King Lake is the English name he chose for himself. He was Rob's student before he decided to befriend us both. The first time I met him was when he came to our door one afternoon shortly after we began teaching and invited us to "come and play with us." I was tired that afternoon and really wanted to do some preparation for the next day's classes, but I fastened a smile onto my face as Rob and I stepped out into a brisk wind. I remember thinking we really should clue the kids into the fact that grown college students probably should not use the word *play* to describe their leisure time activities, which are pretty scarce. But I tried to be a good sport as we trudged along, wondering where we were going. King Lake bounded in front of us, and I thought maybe "play" still applies to this man/boy who giggles with delight at the surprise he has for us. The light dusting of a mustache on his lip is most unusual here, and I think he is rather proud of it. But he seemed very childlike.

The tidy sidewalk of the main campus quickly gave way to debris and chunks of cement as we rounded the corner of the boy's dormitory. The odor of wet concrete is always in the air here, of dirt and rotting green things. Building and destruction are the two sides of the modern Chinese coin. All around the college and all over China, old buildings are crumbling or being demolished to make way for new ones. I stumbled a few times over the rubble because our eyes were fixed on the two kites soaring over the heads of about half a dozen students. They grinned at us as we approached. The kids' genuine pleasure that we came replaced the odors, the irritation at disrupting my plans, and our scramble over debris to get there.

"Would you like to hold one?" a shy girl asked me.

What else could I say? "Thank you." The kite's tug, the feeling of being on the wings of the wind, yes, I was playing again, maybe for the first time in many years!

They were not the fantastic creature kites we buy in America labeled "Made in China." When one spun out of control and nose-dived onto a chunk of broken concrete, I saw it was a homemade affair of sticks and paper. Again I recalled that the students come from villages where money is so scarce that toys are a luxury, but ingenuity and resourcefulness fill in the blanks.

That's the first time I remember meeting King Lake. Maybe we'd chatted earlier. He was one of the monitors for Rob's class and thus a self-appointed "sherpa" (our name) who appeared smiling at our apartment door before class to help carry the stacks of books we hauled from room to room. The monitors also carried the books back home at the end of class or to the next classroom. They seemed to enjoy the special privilege of coming into our apartment and having a look around. I'm trying to recall King Lake specifically among the four or so sherpas per class who swarmed over our apartment every day, touching photographs on the wall, even tapping on our decrepit computer, opening desk drawers. The invasion of privacy appalled us at first, but we tried to tell them gently that we preferred they ask before they opened something. We figured there is little privacy in their lives, and they're so curious about us and our things, so they think it's natural to explore.

I am more relaxed now, less fearful of what our adventure holds for us. King Lake is probably one of the reasons. He is unfailingly smiling and friendly, and I've recently noticed that he lets himself walk beside a girl on campus. That may not sound unusual, but in China, boy-girl dating at this age, even flirting, is discouraged to the point of driving it underground or out of sight. No boy-girl intrigue on a campus? Impossible! I'm sure there are surreptitious romances, but by and large girls sit with girls and boys with boys. If I try to seat a girl beside a guy, junior high school giggles erupt. King Lake defies the unwritten edict, however. And he's chosen well.

He brings Barbara (her more common English name) to our apartment the first time. She's very self-conscious about her English and smiles constantly, hoping we and King Lake will bear the burden of conversation. He nudges her from time to time, urging her to try to speak, but she rolls her eyes and ducks her head. His tenderness is touching. He asks us to take their picture and actually holds her hand! She's only slightly shorter than he is, with cropped hair, glasses and a dynamite smile. He's smitten, and I think she is too. They're classmates, he tells us, both in ornamental horticulture. At the end of our first get-together, he brightens at the idea of the two of them cooking a Chinese meal for us in our apartment. I'm ashamed to say my first reaction was to recoil. My regime of scrubbing, soaking in bleach-water, boiling and generally decimating any lurking evil germs on what we put into our mouths is threatened, but they're so earnest. I immediately worry that they can't possibly afford the ingredients, but I don't want to offend them by handing them money. Yet that's the only alternative I see, and there! They are delighted to accept a few bills and assure us there will be some change. They bound out of the apartment after we've settled on the appointed time for the feast.

Is it possible to dread and look forward to an event at the same time? King Lake and Barbara arrive laden with plastic bags bulging with mysterious long green bean things, a protruding fish tail (oh, no!), packages with labels incomprehensible to me, a chunk of pork that looks to be at least fifty per cent fat, and other items buried in the depths of the bags. All that, and King Lake hands me much more change than I expected. I lead them into the kitchen and stand back. They rinse off the pork slab, running our non-potable water over it, rubbing off the flyspecks (or did I just imagine those?) and dried blood. Then the chopping begins. King Lake handles my large cleaver with an expertise I envy. They ask for my cooking oil and the wok. Our American predecessors left a large plastic bottle of oil out of which I've used a small fraction. Barbara pours what looks to me like a lot of oil into the wok and turns one of the two cooktop burners on high. I can *feel* the oil seep into my pores and permeate the walls I so recently scrubbed, but the sizzle and aroma of crackling onions and pork, fat and all, chase my misgivings away. I'm invited into the chopping fraternity and told how to cut green and white vegetables which are completely foreign to me. I give up worrying about cleanliness as I watch Barbara rinsing the dishes I've scalded with pots of boiling water before I put them into the cabinets. She takes plates from the cupboard and runs them under the tap before she puts the meats and vegetables on them. The clank and clatter of the dishes, cleaver, pots and chopsticks, mingle with our happy mostly Chinglish conversation, reminding me that a kitchen is a magical place for forgetting trouble and making friends.

Odors I cannot identify assault my nose. Garlic, of course, is comforting and permeates other subtler scents. King Lake chops ginger to a fare-thee-well and adds it to dark powders that whisper of long ago emperors and quiet silks. I see that, instead of tasting dishes as they go, King Lake and Barbara press their noses close to the steaming wok and inhale the aroma, adjusting the spices accordingly. That amazes me, but why not? I come from the taste-as-you-go school, but isn't the sense of smell even more reliable? No one here seems to consult a recipe, and they seem confused when I ask if they're following one. "How did you learn to make this?" I ask.

"We watched our mothers and fathers" they respond, wondering, I guess, how else one might learn to cook.

After almost two solid hours of cooking Robert and I scurry to set the table. Some dishes they proudly place on the table confuse us. One is a plate of corn, kernels from the cob, and peas, vegetables cold but presented as delicacies. Both Rob and I come from areas where you happily gnaw on an ear of fresh, tender corn, dripping with butter and salt. But we try to be politely pleased with the offering. Then the hot dishes come. The pork has been transformed with garlic and ginger and tossed with bok choy and onions. Delicious! By now we're salivating, and even the whole fish, presented head, tail and all, seems edible. We have eggs they've bought from one of the many street vendors. These brown eggs are boiled a long time in tea. We often pass women near our bus stops with vats of bronzed eggs, wondering what exactly they are. They're surprisingly tasty and tender.

Naturally, no one has a dinner plate. We eat Chinese style with chopsticks, dipping into the many plates of food in the center of the table. To drink we offer the omnipresent Pepsi or 7-Up. We still giggle at all the Chinese writing on the Pepsi bottles. (Coke is big too, but Pepsi seems to be the favorite here.) Somehow the drinks don't seem very glamorous, but King Lake and Barbara don't want water. Eating is a very social affair here, and conversation flows or waits on the appetite. Comfortable silences are honored, and I'm relieved I don't hear the belching and spitting I'd read were once common, even expected, at Chinese tables. We praise the food extravagantly as King Lake and Barbara insist, with Chinese courtesy, that they are very bad cooks. They worked very hard to produce the meal for us, and we are deeply grateful. We know they have a lot of homework to complete, and though they want to help clean up and do the dishes, I insist I can take care of the kitchen. They are persuaded and leave with a handful of Hershey's candy kisses, my Big Find at the German-Chinese joint venture supermarket. The Chinese apparently don't go in much for dessert, but I've discovered a chink in their armor—chocolate.

Barbara and King Lake come often to visit. Barbara is shy but enjoys our company. She gazes up into King Lake's eyes and giggles at his jokes. He apologizes for his English, as most students do, but we see he's taking advantage of our invitation to all of our students to come practice their English with us.

Once he comes alone, something on his mind he wants to talk about. We first have a little something to eat. All our students are very curious about what Americans eat! Then he inhales and begins,

"I wanted to ask you and Mr. McKee what I should do. You can see that I like Barbara very much, but I'm not sure if it is fair to be her boyfriend. We are so young, and her family is much richer than mine. What do you think I should do?"

Advice to the lovelorn was *not* in the volunteer's training manual! He looks earnestly from Robert to me for an answer. I hedge a little. "Why don't you ask *her*, King Lake? Maybe your wallet is not what she finds attractive." That doesn't satisfy him. He fears he won't be able to provide for her in the near future and that it's unfair for him to mislead her. The Chinese don't generally marry until they're in their late twenties or thirties. King Lake and Barbara are probably in their early twenties but seem much younger. Their tender love, however, seems precious and unique among their peers, but he thinks he's not good enough for her. Interestingly, both men and women expect to work all their adult lives. It's never the case that the man is the sole provider, as nearly as I can determine. A man often lives and works in a city far from his spouse, so his protective attitude confuses me a little.

We were warned before we left America that our classrooms, even our apartment, might be bugged for comments, religious recruiting or any conversation deemed inappropriate by communist authorities. We could be sent home summarily, but our real fear is that we might jeopardize students—like this earnest young man who has to live here. What do we say? We speak of the many unknowns in the future and in the strength of love between two people to face and embrace whatever comes. Ultimately our "you must make your own decision" answers must be unsatisfactory to him, but we are honored that he trusts us with his questions.

Tonight is very peculiar. King Lake arrives after dinner wearing for the first time a jacket like the letterman jackets popular in American high schools, only his jacket has a huge American flag emblazoned on the back. He's very elusive about where he got it, something about his sister, so we don't pursue the matter. He has a packet of papers in his hands, so we assume he has homework to do and offer our dining room table. He readily accepts the offer. We expect he wants help with some English translation or reading. He looks up and grins and thanks us but says he probably won't need our help.

Okay. We sit at our desks too, working on tomorrow's lesson plans. We know that lights out in the dorms is a no-nonsense ten o'clock when the doors are locked, so we're surprised when he doesn't show any sign of leaving. The night noises settle down outside. We can hear the boys' dorm clearly. The noisy horseplay goes up after homework, just before "uncle" switches the lights out, one floor at a time. King Lake is absorbed in his writing and clearly has no intention of leaving.

Rob asks, "Hadn't you better hurry back to your dorm?"

"No, the doors are locked. I must finish this paper tonight and can't work in the dark there. May I stay here for the night and work?"

It's a good old American all-nighter, but the twist is that the paper he's laboring over is, now he tells us, his application to be accepted as a member of the Communist Party. Oh fine! Two American service volunteers harboring an earnest young student applying for member-ship in the Chinese Communist Party. In our home. Wearing an American flag on his back.

We give him some blankets and a pillow and go to bed.

Barbara and King Lake prepare a meal for us in our kitchen

21

LIBRARY COPYING

O ther than the boys' and girls' dormitories only four buildings on campus really count. The four-story teaching building offers the only classrooms for 1800 students. The library, the administration building, and the dining hall complete the four. We want to explore the library resources. It's newer than the classroom building, smaller and three stories tall. A large, stark room downstairs with tables and chairs is obviously for studying, although there are no reading lamps, just dim, overhead bulbs. Then we climb upstairs to the stacks. We try not to look too flabbergasted when we first step into the main portion of the library. We're amazed to see the holders magazine shops use to display their magazines, all facing front. That's how most of the dogeared paperbacks are housed, all spread out so the shelves look full. Most elementary school libraries in the United States would be ashamed of the collection. We wander and find some hardbacks shelved normally, and after a lengthy search locate some English language books, maybe fifty or so, mostly out-of-date textbooks, technical books, few that invite reading. About what a couple of American neighbors might put out for a weekend yard sale.

An important building looms at one end of campus, the administration building, where Jenny's office is, along with the college president, vice president, and all the other functionaries. We have little reason to spend much time there, though Jenny insists we're welcome to climb the stairs to her office whenever we like. Stairs are a way of life here. Elevators are unheard of except in city department stores (none in Chuga!) or fancy hotels. The college leaders have window heating units too, unknown in the students' living and learning areas.

Since English language teaching materials are at such a premium, we ask Jenny how to make copies of pages to use in the classroom. She takes us back to the library and introduces us to The Copy Lady. We discover one grinding, ancient copier and a white-gloved lady presiding over it. The notion we might run the copy machine ourselves is not to be entertained. The Copy Lady must be approached and the number of copies requested formally. Her hours of operation are limited and strictly observed. We think the Chinese teachers probably make their requests in writing, but since we're linguistically challenged, we can be forgiven that step. I need to polish up my numbers and add new phrases to my Chinese vocabulary: two-sided, two to a page, one-sided. The Copy Lady smiles sparingly, impressed with her own importance. The cartoons I occasionally draw to illustrate a point or spark a conversation in class do not amuse her.

An exploratory walk around the campus takes us past several one-story, one-room concrete boxes linked together. The tantalizing smell of spiced meat cooking draws us. Round bamboo steamers rest on the outdoor brazier at the door of what looks to be a tiny snack shop for the students. The charcoal Americans use isn't used here. Instead large bricks of a foul-smelling substance are standard, so the come-hither smell of the *jauza*, steamed pork-filled dumplings, mixes with the acrid odor of the smoldering bricks. Side-by-side in the crumbling cement compound is one more shop, sparsely furnished with bottles of Pepsi, or *Bazi* as our students pronounce it, with its familiar logo, the label emblazoned with slashing Chinese characters. A few displays of what we assume to be candy and other mysterious items attractive to the kids line the shelves. An ice cream freezer chest reveals disappointing contents. The Chinese do not drink milk, and ice cream simply isn't available. We've tried peculiar wannabes that leave us yearning for the real thing. The other doors must lead to the store proprietors' and possibly some teachers' living quarters. The ubiquitous clotheslines are strung outside the doors, and the ever-present mud and weeds line the walk.

Speaking of mud and muck, the only place set aside for recreation is the soccer field, smaller than regulation but generally crowded with boys any time classes are not in session. Any lines once marked on the field have long since disappeared. The broken goal markers lean, but that doesn't dampen the competition and fun that erupts from the sloshy games. They have uniforms too. Each major field of study in the college—computer science, animal husbandry, so on— has its own colors, and classmates come out to cheer the teams on. Girls stand around the field watching, and I wonder what they let them do for recreation. They tell me that there's a Friday night disco dance on campus, but that looks like the only real socializing that goes on here.

I haven't mentioned the dining hall. There are two, three if you count the small upstairs room where teachers eat in some privacy. My introduction to student and teacher dining, before we even realized what the buildings housed, was a walk past the side of one long, low building where three or four workers were rinsing out bowls, trays and pots under water spigots outside. No soap. No scrubbing. No hot water. We saw rows of red and blue thermos bottles lined up there, which we later learned is the only hot water the students ever get. They replenish their supply at one spigot outside the dining hall every day.

Typical student complaints about institutional food, with shy admission of bouts of diarrhea, help us decide to eat in our apartment. Most teachers don't have that option, since they ride the college-provided bus from and to Ningbo, where tiny apartments are also college-provided. That is typical here. Their *danwei*, factory—in this case, the college—provides housing.

The loudspeaker. I'd read about the omnipresent drone of slogans barked out through amplification crashing through closed windows and bombarding the eardrums everywhere in China. During class hours, however, the loudspeakers are quiet. At other daylight hours, encouraging pep talks and martial music are the norm. It's amazing how quickly I learn to tune the noise out. I figured the students didn't hear it until we met Richard.

Richard is a self-confident freshman international business major, the epitome of Chinese hopes and dreams. Actually, Rob met him first on the track at the soccer field early one morning. Robert jogs before classes to stay in good shape. A few Chinese boys were running there when the Chinese national anthem blared out on the loudspeaker, and the large crimson flag with one large gold star and four smaller ones curving around it slid up a pole at one end of the field. Rob stopped and stood at respectful attention. The boys did too, after which one fairly tall student jogged up to Robert and said,

"Thank you for honoring our flag."

"Of course. I like to think we all honor one another's countries and flags."

Richard then opened a conversation in good English and eventually bragged that he'd been chosen to host a program on the campus "radio" (loudspeaker). Would Rob help him select some American music for it? We sensed the beginning of an interesting friendship.

Richard drifts into our lives, cheerful and somehow incongruous among his peers. He loves to tell us that he's good at tennis. It's easy to picture him in tennis whites, although there's certainly no sign of a tennis court on campus. In fact, I have a hard time conjuring up a mental image of a tennis court in all of China. But he assures us that he has access to courts in his hometown of Hangzhou. He would fit into the country club set, if such a thing exists here, with his glib charm and gift of gab. He seems to come from a fairly well-to-do family. We bump into evidence of a definite class system here. Certainly the communist officials enjoy luxurious homes and are driven in the few black sedans on the road. Hoards of little taxis shuttle the fairly wealthy, while swarms of bicycles and buses take care of the rest.

Richard becomes a stalwart of our English Corner. He's a great help in the weekly dog-and-pony shows we're expected to put on. He's one of the few Chinese students confident enough of his own ability to speak English. We count on him to help the small buzz groups that chat on a particular subject, and his tail feathers spread as he perceives his status.

22

CHINESE LAUNDRY

I promised to tell more about our clothes washing machine. We understand the appliance crouching in our bathroom (aka The Swamp) is a luxury most Chinese don't even dream of. I'm pleased to be able to get our clothes clean without resorting to what most people do—plunge their swollen, red hands into icy water and scrub their knuckles raw trying to remove the grit. I see both women and men bending over the murky waters of the canal outside our apartment doing just that. Our students think they've joined the modern world since they have sinks in their dorms, albeit cold water only, to wash their bodies and their clothes. Dryers have not even made an appearance in this corner of the world, so clothes sag from every window and on lines strung across dark alleys.

I try to appreciate the gift of the washer, but it's become personal. The Machine and I are not on civil speaking terms. Most days are gray with heavy overcast. Thin sunshine occasionally peeps through the damp clouds and lifts my spirits. Perhaps today I can do a load of wash and actually get it dry outside! The washer must be rolled to the center of the bathroom. Remember the floor drain in the center? There's no pump in the washer, so when it's finished with a tub of cold water (all there is), it burps through a hose in the bottom. Gravity is working for it, so out goes the water through the drain, the cement-filled peanut butter lid set to one side. Before it does that, however, it fills with icy water to which I add hot water with the hand-held shower nozzle from the tub. Clever, eh? There is no agitator; the tub just humps up and down, *annoying* the clothes in its bowels. Then it spins. I give it high marks for spinning much of the water out of the clothes. Then it refills with cold water and again chugs, no swishing, sometimes humping a two-step across The Swamp floor.

The washer has a complicated dial for settings, none of which I understand, probably *long wash, spin, rinse, etc.*, but it has an audible language as well—belches, grinds, hums, chortles. Two coughs signal a change in gears. I keep my ear cocked to its mood to catch it when the clothes are spun to the least-soggy mode. Time is of the essence to get them out on the line to take advantage of the failing sunshine. No mater where I set the dial, thinking at last I've found the shorter cycle, The Machine calculates when I'm busiest and fills the tub with icy water before I can pull the plug. I stand beside it listening when I think it's about run its course, but somehow it outsmarts me and refills the tub over and over, leaving me with a mass of dripping clothes, zero sunlight, and sunken spirits. I asked Jenny to decipher the Chinese characters on the dial. They don't make any sense to her either, and we're embarrassed to realize that she's likely never used an automatic washing machine.

I'm left either to do as the Chinese do, hang the clothes outside for days on end in the rain or, Rob's suggestion, string a line inside our apartment. The apartment is not large, and we live in *all* of it, yet we zigzag a line through the living room, sticks supporting it here and there, with the heater and the fan pretending to be the sun and the breeze. An ordinary load of underwear and lightweight clothes takes roughly two to three days to dry in that fashion. Heavier things take longer.

Meanwhile we have an open invitation for students to come to our apartment to chat. We learn to unstring the laden line quickly to let people move around inside or admire Chinese inscrutability as they simply look beyond the inconvenience while we all pretend our apartment doesn't feel like something out of the *Grapes of Wrath*.

After one particularly bruising session between me and The Machine I was on the mat. I'd missed the telltale two-cough signal that the clothes had finished spinning, so might (if I were fast enough) be ready to hang before another cascade of cold water drenched the soggy load. Rob led me away from the dripping scene and volunteered to take over the laundry chores. That from a man who for thirty-five years honestly believed that his underwear, socks and shirts arrived magically clean, folded or pressed in his dresser drawers, slacks neatly hung in his closet. His generous offer probably saved our marriage, salvaged my sanity and cleaned our clothes.

We live close to one of the boys' dorms and daily see their shirts, slacks and bedding on the line strung behind their building or dangling from the windows. The baffling bit is, the boys don't use clothespins, so the laundry ends up in the mud and weeds below, sometimes for days. Presumably they must be collected and rewashed. I found and bought clothespins here and wonder why the students don't catch onto them. Well, kids are kids wherever they live.

Rain, drizzle or torrent isolates us from the rest of the campus. Early one morning we woke up to giggles and gasps outside the back door where the stairs from the upstairs apartments touch down. We peered out the kitchen window and saw the women teachers who live upstairs slipping off their high heels, the gentlemen rolling up their pants legs, and stepping into the unavoidable lake accumulated from the storm the night before. One man dragged a piece of scrap wood to make a bridge over the huge mud puddle. It sagged into the muck, but everyone accepted that as just another of life's hardships to be endured. Umbrellas bloomed everywhere, but these teachers went to class with soggy feet.

Both Rob and I had classes later that morning. We checked the front door and saw we were marooned. Rob scooped up a few loose bricks near the door and splashed them into the puddle there. When it was time for classes we were on our own: no sherpas braved the slosh; we had no boots so shoved our hiking boots into heavy plastic bags and tied them at the ankles. We loaded our books into backpacks, put on all the raingear we owned and hopscotched onto the bricks that at least kept us up two or three inches higher in the lake than we would have been without them. No jokes about walking on water, but our sides ached from laughter, still do, at the hilarious sight we must have been.

Just when I think I've conquered my fears of being deep in communist China, we were jolted awake at six in the morning by a crash from inside or very close to our apartment! Rob keeps a sheathed Army Ranger dagger near his bed, something he's done since he returned from Viet Nam. He's on his feet, unsheathed dagger in hand, before I even sit up in bed. He crouches at our bedroom door and peers into the living room. We hear voices just beyond the living room wall. Our wall is intact, but then we hear the voices counting in unison, Ee, Ar-r, SAN! (One, two, three!), then another crash and a cheer. The wall shudders. Rob throws open the front door.

We are face to face with a team of grinning workmen who have just shoved down the brick wall separating our apartment building from the village just beyond the campus. It fell against our wall, leaving about fifty meters wobbly but standing. My shoulders sag with relief, and Rob slides his knife out of sight. The men set to work on the remaining wall, pleased to have an audience. The wall is bricks and mortar, no rebar. Hands and shoulders bring down the next section. We gather this means that at the end of the semester, this building will come down.

23

THE HAIRCUT

Rob and I are looking pretty shaggy. We need haircuts. Chinese men and women have extraordinarily handsome hair and are well shorn. Where do they get their hair cut? On our walks through Chuga, as we shake our heads *no* at fruit-sellers offering an apple or heavily bruised bananas for inspection, we've seen ancient barber chairs in the narrow alleys and no shortage of customers as the wiry barbers wield straight-edged razors on men who seem quite comfortable in those torn, filthy chairs. We shudder to think we might be at those barbers' mercy for the next year and a half, as bicycle pedicabs dodge around them and disinterested shoppers kick tufts of fallen hair out of their way.

We leave the streets that are our customary haunt one day, having bought enough vegetables and fruit for a day or so. We don't need to stop at the dry cleaners, an open stall on the street that amazes us by returning clean, pressed clothes from a dingy, shallow storefront. We inspect endless rows of shops displaying nuts, bolts, rusty and new mechanical components, as well as fabric shops where I've never seen anyone buy anything. There follow endless displays of kitchen plastics, buckets, spoons, crockery, always in the same pink floral pattern.

We take some turns and find a quieter street which brings us nose to nose with a large glass window and the fragrance of shampoo. In the window, photos of glamorous Chinese men and women with spikey hairdos affirm that it's a beauty shop. Cautiously we open the door. No customers, but it looks relatively clean. Three young women giggle and gesture for us to take seats at one of the lounge chairs. A haughty young man, slim as a pencil, in a flamboyant silk shirt tries to act nonchalant at the other end of the shop.

I nudge Robert. "You go first."

"No hair wash," he hisses. "We have no idea how clean this place is, and they probably don't have hot water."

We indicate that he wants only a cut, as our eyes search for a price chart. Nothing. Rob sits on the edge of the slim young man's chair, and the barber makes a ceremony of opening a large leather case displaying varying sizes and shapes of scissors and combs. I notice he's wearing a pair of scissors in a holster, something American cowboys would never have thought of. He sets to work on Robert's hair, snipping and crouching, studying the head from all angles. I watch in fascination. The barber obviously enjoys an audience. More flourishes, but he's giving Rob a very fine haircut. After more than forty-five minutes, Rob is squirming. How much time can it take to style a man's thinning, silver hair?

Okay, I'm convinced. I say I want a haircut too, and decide to take a deep breath and go for the whole deal. A young woman leads me to her chair and swathes my neck in a clean towel. She offers several bottles of shampoo to determine my preference. I smile and point to one, wondering when we're going to get up and walk to a sink. She squirts from one bottle—water—then shampoo (smells vaguely flowery) and begins working up a lather. I'm a trifle confused since I'm used to dunking my head under a running faucet or streaming water over my head in the shower. Where are we going from here? She doesn't lose a drop of water or shampoo from my bubbly head and massages the suds into my happy scalp. Just when I think she can't go on, she taps my shoulder and beckons me to follow through a curtain into a room with several sinks and chairs. I sit at one, facing the sink, relieved to have a real source of water and comforted as the warm water rinses the shampoo off my head. We complete the exercise, and I expect to be escorted to the young fancy shirt for my haircut.

No, she leads me back to her chair. She tells me to lean forward over a towel folded on the counter facing the chair and begins massaging my neck, head, arms and back. She kneads, pummels, squeezes, stabs, uses her hands and fingers in ways I can't even picture, thrumming up and down my spine, pressing my temples until I want to yell. After what seems like an hour, she sends me to The Scissors.

He circles me, evaluating my short, straight, mostly white hair, remnants of dishwater blond at the back. Obviously today is the first time he's touching hair that is not black. After taking careful stock of my coiffure, he starts, snipping miniscule bits here, combing and gauging with his eyes what to shear there. I enjoy the experience and don't much care what it looks like in the end.

Then I see it! A curling iron, carelessly tossed on the floor. To say my fine hair is limp is an understatement. Phyllis Diller once called her own fine locks *lint*. That's about what mine is, so I use a curling iron to lift it and give it a bit of body. The one I brought from America won't run on Chinese electrical current, so I figured the limp look might be permanent while I'm here. I point to the curling iron and indicate we should use it on my hair.

"No," he grunts in disgust, "can't use such an old-fashioned tool," as he rolls the cord around it and kicks it out of reach. I consider grabbing it and running but instead put together enough Chinese to ask him where I can buy one. "In Ningbo," he sneers. Not true. I've dragged Robert through every department store and shop which might have one.

After the lengthy dance he does around me, snipping and examining my head, I have to admit it's probably the best haircut I ever had. He uses a hair dryer like a magic wand. I can tell he wants to ask me something. He speaks over my head to the girls in the shop, and I understand he wonders how old I am. I answer in Chinese, "Sixty." They are truly flabbergasted. I would be flattered except that I've seen a lot of wizened women here, who are probably younger than I, bent almost double, deep creases in their faces, caring for their children's babies. Their eyes speak volumes of agony and heartbreak survived with patience. They wear their age with dignity.

When we ask the price of our afternoon, much discussion among the workers ensues. A price is agreed upon, about $8.00. For both of us. I'm sure Jenny will scold us for not bargaining, saying we were overcharged, but we believe we got the bargain of the century. We'll be back.

On the way back to the bus stop, we notice a man in dark clothes sitting cross-legged on the broken sidewalk. Something writhes at his feet, and a few shoppers are quibbling about price. He reaches into a net bag on the ground and pulls out a small, wiggling frog and hacks the legs off the living creature with a bloody cleaver, then dispatches several more the same way. The stench and sight sicken me, and we hurry across the street to flag down our bus.

24

YO MEI YO

Yo mei yo isn't a name. It's a shrug of the shoulders, a flip of the hand meaning your request isn't worth bothering about. It also means a salesclerk won't search the stock to see if he in fact *has* what I'm asking for. Literally it translates something like *have, not have*. A comprehensive translation would be, "I don't think I have what you want, and it's too much trouble to check." There's no profit motive here, no commission on sales, and Chinese sales clerks have mastered the art of bored condescension. They are also, however, fiercely protective of the goods they are masters of, and customers may *not* touch an onion for inspection, a bolt to assure a proper fit, or, as I learned, a piano keyboard.

I miss the keyboard. I thought I could do without music for a year and a half, but my fingers and my heart fidget for my piano. Rob urges me to shop for one, and I rationalize that a portable keyboard would be helpful in my classes and our English Corner. The Chinese love music and count on us for news of American pop songs, but they have to settle for our folk songs and simple singalong tunes. Still my pleasure is a factor, and I reason I'm entitled to my own "weapon" when our neighbors crank up their karaoke mikes and wail off tune long into the night. Our students, especially the girls, adore hearing and singing the theme from the movie *Titanic*, old news in America maybe but a very hot item here. It's the *only* movie many of our students have ever seen, because Chairman Jiang Zhemin casually commented once that it was a good film. Now that I think about it, I've never seen a movie theater in China. The song's haunting melody and tribute to undying love are two unbeatable draws for young people, so we make an odyssey through the three department stores downtown, searching for the musical instrument department. I have to admit, the *uhu*, a one-stringed violin-like instrument held vertically on the knee and played with a bow, intrigues me, but I try to stay focused on the piano keyboard. I know I want one with the full eighty-eight keys. The few we find are encased in plastic wrap, and there's no way to plug one in to hear its sound and feel the action of the keys. The clerks scowl and scurry over when we approach a keyboard. Gestures and language collide as they insist I may not touch them. We seem to be at a dead end.

I mention our frustration to Jenny, saying I must try one out to know how it sounds and feels before I know if I want to buy. Are there any real music stores in town? She consults her colleagues and comes up with two addresses. When she asks the price in the department stores, she's aghast! That cinches the deal. *She* will come with us and show how the Chinese bargain, she says. They are taking advantage of our American-ness.

When she has some free time and we have an afternoon with no classes, we take off on the bus to locate the music shops. In the first, Jenny tells me that, yes, I may play the keyboard, but the salesman can *assure* me it is the highest quality. He also says if I take the plastic wrap off and play it, I must buy it.

We go to the second store. There the clerks actually let me play their pianos. None has a sustain pedal, so I feel a little like Mozart (minus his genius) at his clavichord. I just can't hear my jazz renditions of "Slow Boat to China" or even a gentle version of the *Titanic* theme without a mellowing sustain pedal. One of the *eight* clerks "helping" us (typical, too many clerks who know too little) assures us that no, *mei yo* sustain pedal. Doesn't have one, not possible. While I prowl through the shop, Rob takes the owner's manual out of the pristine plastic wrapper (causing an incredulous gasp from the clerk), finds the English section and finds—*Shazam!* mention of an optional sustain pedal which can be ordered. We find the corresponding Chinese version of the manual and indicate that *this* is what we want. A young clerk calls to order it. We *think* he will call us when it comes in. Then follows a serious price bargaining session between Jenny and seven of the clerks. One remains aloof. Jenny grumbles at the outrageous cost they finally agree on, but is placated when the store offers us four tickets to a piano/violin concert in Ningbo that very night. A bribe? A bit of face-saving? Who knows? We accept. Happily.

Outside I ask Jenny what all the discussion was about. She says she told them the department store price for the same model, "But I don't tell him the *real* price." She smiles triumphantly.

We've paid what we think is a fair price for the keyboard and lug it home, all boxed up, in a taxi. Rob and I grab some dinner, get cleaned up and jump back onto the bus for an evening out, our first in Ningbo. We barely arrive at the fairly large, little-used concert hall, find Jenny and her young son Ya Ya, who's five, and get settled in our seats.

It's a marvelous concert by a young Chinese man who studied and won many awards in France. A young woman, who probably plays on an instrument from "our store," accompanies him. We notice that easily half the audience is made up of children under ten. You can imagine what a tough audience wiggly but interested youngsters would be. Jenny explains, "When I was young, I didn't have the chance to hear this music [mostly western classical pieces]. That's why many parents now also bring their young children to expose them to it." We bask in the music too and try to imagine hearing it through their ears and hearts.

A sidebar: when Robert tries to assemble the stand for the keyboard, there are no screws. The instructions are quite emphatic that only the screws provided may be used or the keyboard may be damaged. Jenny is busy with a visiting delegation, so we ask a student to phone the music store and explain the problem. He does, and they apologize for the error. We make another two hour round trip bus trip to pick up the missing screws. That is simply the way business happens here. Patience, even resignation, and a healthy sense of humor are very handy.

Three weeks after we order it, the sustain pedal comes in. I now have a complete keyboard and am awash in pleasure and music. My fingers haven't forgotten how to dance.

25

LUCY AND THE KEYBOARD

I'd like to think that buying the keyboard was an inspiration. Mostly, though, I just yearned for my piano. But something magical happens! This evening after dinner, we hear the expected tap on our door. It's Lucy, all alone tonight, apologizing that her friends have "other things they must do." I notice her eyes straying to the keyboard and ask her if she'd like to play.

"Oh, *yes!*"

"Do you know how to play, Lucy?"

"No, never in my life have I dreamed I could touch such a thing."

"Well, come on. I'll teach you."

Our Chinese friends, especially the young, are eager to perform if they think they can please you. "Would you like me to sing?" or "I can dance for you, if you like," are quite common. They're not showing off. They genuinely want to please. There's no false modesty here, just a desire to share what they can to make you happy.

Lucy and I sit side by side, and I search my brain for what to do to help her begin. Here's a simple duet every child in America has tried. Lucy absorbs my demonstration like a thirsty sponge. I even draw a cartoon of a sponge for her when she doesn't understand the word.

We giggle when she grasps my meaning. Suddenly it's 10:00 p.m., and she's embarrassed that she's stayed so long, but the precious moments have taken me back to joyous times with my own children at the piano. Lucy has lost track of time too. A precious picture that will stay in my heart is the memory of Lucy's eyes turned to mine at the piano. Her smile, a toothpaste ad, she says, "Oh, Mrs. McKee, I am so happy." A laugh of deep pleasure, a joke I can't share with her, bubbles up as I realize that I've been teaching *her* to play "Chopsticks." I hug her, and she accepts it without the usual Chinese reserve. The culture, eager in friendship and courtesy, nevertheless rarely allows public hugging. Holding hands as they walk is not unusual, even boys with boys, but a public hug is rare.

I scour the shelves of the one bookstore we know has music. The beginning piano books are either for very young children and quite poor, or they're too difficult for a new student. I buy one or two and then I capture the prize, good old *John Thompson, Book One*, in Chinese. They have only one dusty copy on the shelf, and word has traveled among our young friends. Several girls are anxious to learn to play my keyboard. Okay, I have access to the school copy machine. I *am* using it for English language comprehension, and I hope the copyright gods will forgive me.

Lucy comes almost every night, sometimes while we're eating dinner. Completely at home, she amuses herself while we finish or offers to help in the kitchen. I catch myself humming and smiling as I remember times with my own children doing homework or practicing the piano in the evenings. Lucy's enchanted to watch how and what we eat and sometimes eats with us. Mostly though she loves to sit at the keyboard and practice her latest lesson. When I'm free, we two sit at the piano, and I strain to stay ahead of her. She is so in love with the music and learns so quickly that I can see she'll be beyond my simple book very quickly. Music, obviously, is embedded in her soul, and I ache to think that when I go, she will no longer be able to caress the keys and enjoy the sounds they make. I make rather pathetic paper keyboards for her and for the other girls who come for lessons so they can practice in their dorm rooms.

One night she wants to teach *me* a melody from a famous Chinese myth comparable to our *Romeo and Juliet*, the star-crossed lovers. In the Chinese version, the lovers are turned into delicate butterflies. Later I found and bought a tape of a young Chinese woman playing the song on the violin, but the tender beauty of the melody can't match Lucy's clear voice. We pick it out on the piano, and she tries to form my American lips to the Chinese words.

Other girls come and touch the keys reverently. We *all* play "Chopsticks" together! Several are enchanted by making music, but none quite so thrilled as Lucy.

"Oh, Mrs. McKee, I am so happy!"

26

MOVING FROM THE APARTMENT

When we packed up all our furniture for storage in the US and rented our home to a family while we are gone, I sorted through the items I thought I might bring to China. At first I set some watercolor supplies aside to take but then reasoned that, one, the trip was not a vacation or an opportunity to paint exotic scenes; two, space was limited to two suitcases, so summer and winter clothes, everything had to be culled; and three, if I weakened and found time to paint in China, surely I could buy art supplies there where painting and calligraphy began.

Now I'm wistful when I pass a shop and see colored pencil boxes or tins of watercolors for school children, but my time really is packed with lesson preparation, teaching and the unbelievably time-consuming chores like shopping or feeding ourselves or riding the buses to pay bills in person downtown. This, by the way, is the only way to take care of them. I have, however, been working on two chefs d'oeuvre that will help our students understand English definite and indefinite articles. They can't get the hang of it, since Chinese has no articles (no *a* or *the*), nor can their Chinese English teachers. The eight or ten local teachers, all trained in China, are polite but distant.

Rob and I wonder why they don't want to deal with us but finally guess they're self-conscious about their own English, especially since they're teaching it. Some speak very poorly.

So I hit upon the simple—I thought—idea of buying a large piece of paper and making a chart outlining examples of correct usage of English articles. I assumed I'd find such a chart in one of our grammar books. No chart. It's one of those things so pervasive and simple for a native speaker, so *mysterious* for non-natives, that the texts just don't cover it. Think about it: A banana is yellow, Bananas are yellow, Fruit is delicious, The fruit is good. Subtle meaning shifts. Then we come to plurals (which Chinese does not indicate) and must explain count and no-count nouns. I thought a chart might help. Robert calls my charts (two of them) my Master's thesis. I make colorful cartoons to boil down the rules, but I find that our language, a mongrel made up from so many languages, often defies its own rules. Yes, I bought some colored pencils and markers. Even if I don't help our students, I'm learning what a challenge learning English as a second language is. And I'm having fun.

By the way, we have eaten "hundred-year-old eggs." I *don't* need to do it again. When we dine in a Chinese home, any home, we eat what's offered, especially since they treat us like honored guests, and we sense their sacrifice of work and scarce money. We're very conscious of our obligation to be gracious. We encountered the hundred-year-old egg at the home of a sixty-seven-year-old man and his wife. We met him through a lawyer in his seventies, whose English is excellent yet wants a weekly language polishing at our apartment. He usually produces a list of questions he hopes we can answer, digging into the finer points of English grammar.

I remember the final question one rainy afternoon. He adjusted his glasses and read: "At the conclusion of the lovely evening, the gentleman took the lady home." He removed his glasses, looked from Robert to me and asked, "Whose home?" He is always very formal, and Robert usually defers to me to answer the technical questions, since I majored in English and literature a lifetime ago. But the question shattered our polite demeanor.

"I guess you can decide for yourself," was the best I could do, going on to explain that it was unclear without any possessive pronoun, "but fun to think about, don't you agree?"

He stared at me for an instant, then threw his head back and permitted himself the first real guffaw since we met him. Maybe that's why we were invited to his friend's home for dinner.

His friend, very proud of his new set of teeth, said he'd heard that in America one spends great sums of money for dentists and false teeth, but "here in China, it is all free." He didn't say how he came to lose all his teeth at sixty-seven. Whether it's the new teeth or his thrill at being able to "swim in the English sea" (his words), his smile was expansive and generous. His congenial wife and a neighbor had slaved, I figured, for days to produce dish after dish, which they brought to a table that took up all their living space. Woody and Sandra Wall, who introduced us to the two men, joined us at the feast. Dishes paraded proudly from the miniscule kitchen I could see through the door. The neighbor bustled across the hall to her apartment and scurried back, laden with more delicacies to impress the foreigners. We dipped our chopsticks into the dishes, hoping the inoculations we had before we left home would stand up to unfamiliar parasites and viruses.

The hundred-year-old eggs gave me pause. They were black. I know they're not actually a hundred years old, at least I desperately hoped they weren't. Our hostess smiled and placed the dish within my reach and nodded for me to try one. She spoke no English, and my Chinese *Xie xie* (thank you) sounded a bit hollow. I don't think I actually bit into it. I pretty much swallowed it whole. Sandra explained the technique to me some time ago, and I winked a thank you to her.

Jenny was obviously nervous the other day when she came to our apartment. We know our apartment building will be demolished at the end of the semester. The workmen are swarming over an area where, we're told, the *Foreign Experts' Villa* will be built, but it's only mud, a huge pile-driving machine and the omnipresent concrete mixers right now. Jenny tells us that we must pack all our belongings for storage for the summer since our "villa" won't be ready until the fall, and this building will be taken down soon. Questions pop from our mouths: "Where will we live during the summer months, Jenny?" "Where will our things be stored?" "We'll be happy to pack things up, but does that include all the dishes and things provided for us here?" "Can you find some boxes for us?" "When do you think our new home will be ready?"

She backs up physically under the bombardment. "Yes, I will find boxes for you. Yes, please do pack the kitchen things. Our technicians will take care of the furniture, and we will find a place at our college to store all of these things." Then the most important answer, "We don't know where you will stay for the summer. I think you said that perhaps you will return to America for your son's wedding. Why not remain there until your apartment is ready?"

We'd decided to make a two-week trek to California. We're thrilled that Wes and Bettina are marrying. Our organization leadership here in China has no objection to our return to America. Our classes will be finished soon, the campus echoing with the sounds of massive construction. No students. No classes. We have no job when there are no students, but our commitment is a complete dedication to serve in China. We hope to be a positive influence here, even during the summer months, and we think staying in the US for two months would be weaseling out on our service responsibility. Jenny hints we will end up in a hotel in Ningbo for two months. Gloomy prospect.

With our summer whereabouts still uncertain, we pack up yet again into the cardboard boxes Jenny continues to bring, a few at a time. Boxes are stacked all around the apartment when she asks shyly if we could come with her to her son's school one afternoon after classes. We've met little Yang Yang (pronounced *Ya ya*, like the Chinese word for duck). He's more like a five-year-old lion, full of untamed energy, a rascal, a charming one. Of course, we'd love to. "Will you also bring your guitar to sing for the children?" I've been practicing and can do a creditable job of strumming along, accompanying myself and my students in simple songs. "You Are My Sunshine" is a favorite; they love cowboy songs; the theme from the movie *Titanic* they adore, and thank you John Denver for "Country Roads"! Try to picture thirty black-haired kids who've never been outside their own province wailing, "Take me ho-o-me, country roads, to the place I belo-o-o-ong. West Virginia, mountain mama, take me home, country ro-o-oads." But what can I sing for the little ones? "Jingle Bells" is a favorite. We hear children singing incomprehensible English to the tune year round. Those seem to be the only English words they know beside a *Hello* followed by a giggle hidden behind a hand. I'll go with that and maybe nursery rhymes.

The cold's grip has suddenly relented. It's early June, and tiny shoots of green struggle to be seen among the weeds and discarded colored plastic bags along the streets. Robert, Jenny and I lock up the apartment with its packed boxes stacked near the door and catch the double-decker bus into Ningbo. Just as we reach the city center, the heavens open, and torrents drench the city. I've been in exciting rainstorms in California, but the downpour's sudden ferocity is impressive. Jenny grimaces and reminds us that the monsoon season is beginning.

For the first time, we're out without coats, not even the ever-present umbrellas. I see the worry on Rob's face too, and I know he's thinking of our clothing and storage things near the front door. During far less ferocious storms in the past, water poured in under both doors, floating the worn carpeting at the entrances. He decides to jump off the bus at the next stop and catch a taxi home to salvage whatever the water damages. I see Jenny's disappointment, so I agree to go on with her.

When we get off the bus, we are instantly drenched. We step into deep puddles at the bus stop, the water above our ankles, and splash through unavoidable rivers in the streets and sidewalks, trying to protect my guitar in its cheap cardboard case.

It's not a long walk to the school, but no matter because once we're wet, we can't get any wetter. The school, tucked into a residential neighborhood, tall apartment buildings on all sides, surprises me. We pass a small, inviting courtyard and go in the front door. We're expected. We try to keep from dripping too much on the clean tile floors as a smiling teacher leads us to the principal's office. The principal, a woman, greets us, politely overlooking our drips, and offers us some fruit, lichees, I think. I'm anxious to meet the children, but she's a gracious hostess, and the fruit enchants me, something I've never seen or tasted before. It tastes vaguely melony but looks like grapes on steroids.

At last we come to a large room where about seventy-five preschool children sit quietly on the floor. I can't help wondering how long they've been sitting there waiting. They applaud as we enter the room, and I ask Jenny if she knows if any of them speak English. "I don't think so," she smiles, so my face, my cretin Chinese and body language will have to do.

I launch into "Twinkle, Twinkle, Little Star" and roll through my repertoire for wee ones. They seem enchanted. A small young man, the English teacher for the entire school, translates and helps me go through a rendition of "Itsy Bitsy Spider." It works in any culture. Then he suggests, "Please tell them a story."

"In Chinese?"

"No," he says, "I will put it into Chinese as you tell it."

All I can think of is *The Three Bears*. Well, maybe they could be pandas. Papa Bear's voice gets gruffer, and my gestures get wider as the story progresses. It really sounds better in Chinese. When Goldilocks dashes out of the house and into the woods, the wide-eyed children listen, breathless, for the Chinese conclusion, which sounds much longer than my version. I believe the English teacher gave it a Chinese twist with a stern moral. At any rate, it must have been successful because the children were led away reluctantly and replaced by another crowd of slightly older children for the second show.

After all that, Jenny and I get a tour of the facility. Such a contrast to the college's stark classrooms. The walls are painted bright colors. We step aside to let an obedient queue of children pass us on the winding stairs. They all hold bowls and are obviously headed for a dining area. We peek through a door window at a busy art class, the little dark heads bent over all sorts of inviting paints and paper. We come to a room with neat rows of tiny beds, all made with a pink cover tightly tucked in. The room is not just for naps, since most of the children, I learn, stay here all week since both parents work, often some distance away. They go home Saturdays and come back to school Sundays. The school buzzes with childish energy and kind teachers, but I wonder how the Chinese manage to maintain a strong family bond with so much time away from each other.

Finally it's time to go. We wave goodbye and thank the principal and friendly guides and head back to the bus. The rain has stopped and the instant lakes just as quickly almost dried. I reach the apartment just before dark and find that Rob had moved the boxes out of the flood's way. I'm sorry he wasn't able to soak in (a pun?) the sweet charm of those precious babies.

27

SUMMER TRAVELS

We're getting excited about the prospect of doing some real sightseeing in China, as well as flying back to California to see all our kids and attend our son's wedding. We'll soon complete our teaching responsibilities for the semester, and I'm sure the administration here will be glad to be rid of us. Our sponsors see no reason for us to remain in China with no students to teach, and we're paying for our own round trip tickets. Our apartment will be demolished to make way for a new girls' dorm, and our new digs won't be ready for months. Construction all over campus continues at a furious rate. The weather has suddenly turned hot and muggy. Ningbo is famous for it's blistering heat, made even more unbearable by the humidity. Our energy is sapped, and I buy my first straw hat to shield me from the scorching heat. The kids, in fact all Chinese, solve the weather problem, summer and winter, with umbrellas. Men and women carry them. At first we were a little surprised to see even boys on campus with floral umbrellas, but the wisdom of having one on hand for rain or sun becomes clear.

Rob's been studying guidebooks and has mapped a route for a three week trip before we fly home. Dutch and LuJean are going to accompany us around China. Great! They're wonderful company, not the travel warhorses we are but happy to trot along on our sweep through must-see China. We promise our students we'll take lots of videos to show them Beijing ("You're not a real man until you have visited the Great Wall" a Chinese saying goes), Datong, and Xian, where the thousands of terra cotta warriors were unearthed. They beam as they describe the lakes and treasures to be seen in various cities of China, but when we ask if they've actually been there, the answer is always, "Oh, no." We hope to give them a tourist's eye view of their own country. Several students have invited us to come to their homes in their villages. We feel honored to be invited and hope we can do it. They give us snapshots of themselves. We'll miss them this summer.

Suddenly, exams are over, the kids vanish, and we and the Rileys take the Chinese airline to Xian, an adventure in itself. Seats on the plane are assigned, just like at home, but getting off the plane is a replay of the bus exit strategies, only in a tighter place. Americans sit obediently, strapped in their seats, until the plane comes to a halt. The Chinese leap to their feet, reach over one another, pull down their bulky parcels, umbrellas, suitcases, even before the wheels touch down. They cram into the aisles and shove toward the door while the meticulously dressed, doll-like stewardesses shrug their shoulders. LuJean, Dutch, Robert and I feel like we've survived a rugby match as we stagger off the plane in Xian.

Our four American friends who trained with us in America greet us with smiles at the airport. We tried the patience of our Mandarin Chinese teacher then. We shared long study sessions, ESL training, meals, and six weeks of shared struggles cemented our friendship quickly.

Thrilled to see them, we introduce LuJean and Dutch. We're eager to hear about their experiences living and teaching at a small, private elementary school in Xian. They adore the little ones, and when they speak of their students who call them *Nie Nie* and *Zu Fu* (Grandmother and Grandfather) and crawl into their laps for hugs, I recall the pleasant experience at Yang Yang's preschool. Their living arrangement is a little different from ours. They live in small apartments with no cooking facility and take all their meals at the common dining hall like most Chinese teachers.

Their movements are far more restricted than ours. Karin tells us that at first an "interpreter" always accompanied them, even on browsing excursions downtown, "for protection." When our visit loomed, she put her small foot down with the principal. "We are adults. Our friends are coming, and we *will* stay out past eight o'clock at night *alone*, if you please!" He agreed, she tells us, but pled with them to be cautious, since if anything bad happened to them, he would be held accountable. She could see that would be very severe for him. Their school sedan whizzes us and our luggage to the school for a delicious lunch in their dining hall.

In the dizzying week that follows all eight of us visit every temple (Rob cries, "Enough temples already!"), pagoda, museum, drum and bell tower, walking atop Xian's beautiful old wall which encloses the city, about thirty-six feet high and thirty-six to forty feet across, wide enough to drive a chariot along. Xian governed China for over 1,000 years. We're awed by the over 6,000 life-sized terra-cotta warriors, some on horseback, an amazing tribute to a brutal emperor 2,000 years ago.

We barely escape with our skins when we run the gauntlet of trinket sellers, many of them children, who surround us like army ants as we leave. It feels like Hitchcock's *The Birds*! Dutch makes the mistake of making eye contact with one young boy holding up small warrior replicas, but then our friend wants to buy one! We look back over our shoulders as Dutch disappears, surrounded by a hoard of eager salesmen. Too bad. We're not going back in there for him! He eventually emerges, not too battered, with a sheepish grin and a small clay warrior.

Our experience with museums in China so far has been disappointing. With so many glorious years of art and history, most museums are dingy, the display cases grimy and poorly lit. The word *seedy* comes to mind. Caretakers sleep beside dusty displays. It's sad to watch as irreplaceable art and antiquities crumble, but in Xian we enjoy some excellent displays. One exception to Xian's well-protected and displayed past is an archaeological museum we dart into one rainy afternoon. We can't read the few signs, and the roof over the archaeological dig leaks badly. Someone has tossed plastic sheets under the leaks, but they have tumbled askew, leaving ancient shards and pots exposed and dissolving.

We also eat real ice cream. You'd think we were children at a county fair instead of eight grandparents as Karin and Jerry proudly lead us to their favorite ice cream place on the streets of downtown Xian. They've found *Magnums*, which actually do taste like the real stuff: creamy vanilla ice cream coated with rich dark chocolate on a stick. Our American taste buds do a jig! Rob and I had noticed we'd shed a few pounds since we came to China, ten or fifteen pounds of good ol' American padding we could well afford to lose. We've been eating well. Maybe it's the lack of ice cream in our diet?

At night Xian lights up like a holiday, tiny white lights lining the crenelated walls and people smiling and enjoying the downtown streets and parks. The northern and western desert winds blow sand and grit across the city, making breathing difficult, but we mingle with the happy crowds, smelling spicy kabobs in the

Muslim quarter, stuffing ourselves with juicy steamed dumplings, and savoring our Magnums.

As new foreign guests to the city, we're invited to be on an evening radio talk show designed for people who want to better their English skills. It's a live call-in show! There is a downpour the evening we're to go to the studio, but the radio station sends a car to pick us up. LuJean, Dutch, Rob and I are sweating by the end of the show. We think we presented a fair and good picture of Western/American education and life. We hope so. The driver who takes us back to the hotel evidently wants to avoid the huge puddles backing traffic up in the streets, so he drives blithely up onto the sidewalk and careens along, passing startled (a little) pedestrians. Now we're *really* sweating! We've learned that this is typically Chinese. You make up your own traffic rules and don't slow down while you're doing it.

The next leg of the adventure is an overnight train to Datong. We share a "soft sleeper," a compartment, really quite comfortable, with two bunk beds. China has four classes of train travel: "hard seat," inexpensive, packed wall to stained wall with Chinese peasants with their chickens and possessions, zero comfort; "soft seat," a little more expensive for additional comfort but not found on most trains; "hard sleeper," six people in an open compartment with six hard bunks, all open to the corridor, the lights and speaker system blaring all night. "Soft sleeper" cars are hard to come by, but they're air-conditioned (if it works), four to a room, with a closable door. We're lucky to snag one.

Before dark we glide through fascinating countryside that probably few tourists see. We're off the beaten track, passing crumbling villages, fields of corn and unidentifiable (for us) crops, donkey carts, goats, vast expanses of land that even the Chinese can't live on. We travel through mountains, long tunnels, newly built towns and finally arrive in coal-dusty Datong.

After a night on the train, my kidneys are bursting, and I invite LuJean to go with me to the end of the car to visit the loo.

She shakes her head. "I can wait."

I can't but am driven back momentarily by the stench as I near the bathroom. It's incredibly filthy, a hole out onto the tracks, and a tiny sink with dribbling water. Trash is not a problem on the trains since the conductor walks through now and then, heaving beer bottles, food remains, discarded paper and refuse out the windows.

The attractions of Datong are two, though one is *not* the coal-choked city. Outside town are Buddhist grottoes carved into the side of a sandstone cliff dating back to 500 AD, over 50,000 statues of all sizes, from a foot tall—massed in niches that honeycomb the grotto's walls—to unbelievably huge. I pose tiny LuJean for a picture by one forty foot behemoth Buddha looming over her.

Then we bounce in a rickety bus for more than an hour, but it's worth the prize, a hanging monastery clinging to a cliffside over a once-raging river that often flooded, taking many peasants' lives centuries ago. Building the engineering marvel was, the peasants thought, their only hope of appeasing the gods. Now for tourists, it's an incredible sight all alone in a gorge far from any village.

After two days, we board the train again for a seven hour day trip to Beijing, a city of 12.6 million people! There we walk through Tiananmen Square, feeling quite different, I'm sure, from the many Chinese families relaxing in the sparse shade trees along the sides of the vast square, large enough to accommodate a million people. They seem quite unaware of the events that happened here eleven years ago. Any signs of the gruesome iron fist their government showed students who grew too outspoken in their cry for more freedom have been obliterated. Surely some who saw the tanks and the blood spilled that dark day remain. Horrified foreign TV crews filmed the tragedy, but the Chinese government pretends it never happened, and most people here accept that—or simply don't know.

Chairman Mao's face and little red book have almost disappeared in China, but his image still looms at the gate to the Forbidden City at Tiananmen. In fact, we saw a fairly large line of people waiting patiently at the center of the square. First, seeing Chinese in an orderly line whips our heads around in disbelief. We ask and learn that Chairman Mao is buried here—frozen, actually. At certain hours his body is raised in a glass case, and citizens pass by to see their former leader. The frozen body remains on view only briefly, for obvious reasons in the heat. We opt to skip the sight, instead spend the day loping from palace to palace, peering at the lavish architecture and through smudged windows at what's left of the obscene wealth once part of the emperor's prerogative. We take the buses, metro, occasional taxis, mostly walking in heavy, humid heat, but we see it *all*. Robert's months of homework with his guidebooks produced a well-planned campaign. We climb uncountable stairs from building to building in the Summer Palace and gardens, evidence of the opulence of the 18th century emperors, visit museums, temples, bell displays. Somewhere LuJean, who's only about four feet ten inches but with the heart of a lioness, finally admits that her ankle is sore and thinks she'd better stay in the hotel room a day or so to recuperate. Dutch grins and seems eager to join her. She threatens to write a book entitled *Following Robert Through China*.

Drinking water looms large in our travels, in all our life in China. Bottled is the only safe source of water, and the summer sun brings out the vendors with ice chests filled with cold water. It's the hottest item for sale (!). Everywhere we go, in the summer especially, we make sure we have one or two bottles in our backpacks or hands. Rob insists on bargaining for water, never pays more than two yuan (a quarter), maybe three yuan in remote areas. It becomes a matter of principle. We always wonder exactly where the bottles are filled. The caps are "sealed," but never question Chinese ingenuity. We just have to trust them.

LuJean limps gamely along the day we hire a cab to take us on the three hour trip outside of Beijing to the Great Wall at a location yet quite undiscovered by the hordes of tourists who vie at spots nearer the city center to buy gilt Buddhas with belly clocks or chartreuse T-shirts emblazoned "I Climbed The Great Wall." The vendors here are few and lethargic. After we pay our fee and ride the lift up the mountain all by ourselves, we walk along the top of the wide wall snaking its way along the ridgeline as far as the eye can see. We stand quietly, soaking in the timeless, grinding human toll it took to build the unending but futile barrier, begun in the sixth century BC. Of course, the costumed Mongolian warrior who leaps out at us from behind a parapet, slashing his rubber saber, threatening to dismember us—for a photo-op fee— dashed the reverence of the moment. Not many tourists here, but the locals have plans for those who do come.

We take our time to examine the impressive walls: about twenty-one feet thick and about as high. With firing ports and overlooking guardhouses every 3,000 feet or so, it was impenetrable to the techniques of warfare of centuries ago. Most guidebooks suggest that the guards could be bribed or plied with alcohol, so the wall never proved foolproof. Coming down the mountainside later, we can't believe the Disneyland slide, but we climb gamely aboard and swoosh down to the waiting taxis.

After about a week in Beijing, we have seen everything there is to see, thanks to Rob. LuJean and Dutch fly back to Ningbo, and we catch the plane to America. Home. And our son's wedding.

LuJean Riley, Sue and Rob on the Great Wall outside Beijing

28

THE WEDDING

The flight to America is agonizingly long, more than the seventeen scheduled hours because an unfortunate bird was sucked into the engine intake, forcing a return to the airport. Finally we're standing in the immigration line at LAX. Another wait. Robert mutters, "I hope Wes and Bettina appreciate this." I believe they do. First we sag into the arms of our waiting niece Debbie, her husband Andy and their bright little girl Jamie. They look hot and tired but have a cooler in the car packed with sandwiches, root beer, gumdrops, everything they can imagine that we would hunger for after six months of Chinese groceries. The drive to their home in Glendale isn't long, and our chatter fills the time. As it happens, it's the Fourth of July. I see tears in Rob's eyes, but not too clearly, since I weep too when we pass American flags dancing from many homes and businesses. We've been away from our country many times in the Army, but never quite so far away as in China. This return, especially because it's so brief, is poignant. That flag stands for joys and freedoms and sacrifice our new friends in China can only dream of.

Andy grills steaks for dinner. We haven't *smelled* beef for six months! We both think we'll eat until we founder but find that a few bites are enough. Suddenly we're woefully tired, so we shuffle gratefully to the master bedroom Debbie and Andy have ceded to us.

We spend a few precious days in our children's homes, where they continue the wonderful treatment our niece and family in Los Angeles started. Overfed and petted, we lap it up! Mostly we bask in the love and happiness in their homes. Bonnie and Rod, in our hometown of San Luis Obispo, are busily preparing for five weeks of bicycling through Europe, leaving a couple of days after the wedding, so we enjoy seeing their bikes with saddlebags all packed to go.

"How can you travel with only one change of clothes?" as we drag our giant suitcases upstairs.

"We have camping gear, all we'll need," Bonnie explains. "We just wash our clothes and let them dry in the wind as we ride along."

Wally the Cat, who lives with Bonnie and Rod, decides we're not assassins just as it's time to leave and drive up to Robin and Bob's in Monterey. Their life too is rich and full: Bob is busy with his mortgage business and excited about beginning the remodel of their charming Victorian home; Robin is directing *The Merry Wives of Windsor* for the Colorado Shakespeare Festival in Boulder and commuting for rehearsals. She'll return to Colorado right after her brother's wedding. Meanwhile, she is busy at the office preparing for the Carmel Performing Arts Festival she brings to Carmel and Monterey each October. Our heads spin as we watch all the activity, but we also have time to walk along the beach with them, relax in their beautiful garden, and fix some delicious meals together.

As soon as we reach Fresno a few days before the wedding our assignment is to take over the care of Jordan, our only granddaughter, Wes' child by a former marriage. It's almost her ninth birthday, and we have lots of missed hugs to gather and plenty to store up for the coming year. We enjoy scooping up her new cousin-to-be, Bettina's niece, who's Jordan's age. The two girls love to play together, and it's fun to watch them "porpoise-ing" in the hotel swimming pool. We also help prepare Wes' home for the backyard barbecue planned for Thursday, as friends and family gather from out of town. A high point for me comes when my brother Dick and Miriam fly in from Virginia. Dick's kidney removal was successful, and we savor his good health. We squeeze a lot of catching up and love into the precious hours. There is talk among Wes' chums of a pre-nuptial golf game, their favorite way to hang out. My courageous brother, another golfer, joins the young lions the next morning and acquits himself quite well, according to all reports.

Fresno shows off with a perfect summer evening Friday for the rehearsal dinner. There's a balmy breeze at Bettina's sister's backyard. Floating candles and flowers adorn the pool, and a band serenades us during a catered Mexican dinner. It's a storybook evening, and we all have a magnificent time. We are the hosts, but we have the easy part: pay the bill. The new in-laws and Bettina and Wes did all the planning and hard work.

Saturday arrives. The wedding is touching and memorable, the dinner party that follows, marvelous fun. The young cousins sing a song they composed to honor the new couple. We dance and laugh and discover that Bettina's family really does love to party. The groomsmen don't want the party to end either, so they pay the band to stay through the wee hours. We finally kiss the bride and groom good night and goodbye, since we leave the next morning to head back to China.

29

INTERIM APARTMENT

The problem of where to put us, now that we're back in China, is solved. Sort of. Jenny meets us with a car and driver and takes us on a very long ride to a part of Ningbo beyond any of the three rivers that join at its center. Most of our boxes are already here on the new campus owned by the Sunli Education Group, which Jenny explains now owns our college as well. (Is capitalism raising its head?) In fact, wheels are turning to make our small teachers' college into a four year university. Soon. We follow her, lugging our suitcases up four steep flights of stairs to our interim apartment. The British term *walk-up* applies to every apartment in China, and almost all Chinese live in apartments. *Struggle-up* might be more appropriate. Elevators don't exist in the multistoried buildings.

The apartment is quite new and the whole campus deserted since this brand new school is a boarding school for kindergarten through high school students and it's midsummer. We thank Jenny and the driver, find the bed and fall into it. (Our foam pads didn't follow us, but we're too tired to care.)

In the morning we realize we don't have drinking water, so we must begin our quest, like little summering animals scurrying around in search of what we need to sustain ourselves. We put on the lightest clothes we own and set out. As soon as we step outside, even though it's early morning, sweat drizzles into our eyes. We need to learn to move slowly in this heat! Our apartment has a balcony that looks out over a gorgeous green playing field, one of the few manicured lawns we've seen in China. We hike around it toward the gate we recall driving through the night before. The whole fenced campus is surrounded by rice paddies, canals, fields of rubble and winding paths disappearing into more fields. The smoldering smell of burned off, harvested crop fields pervades the air. We ask the friendly gate guard how we to get into town to buy food and water. He explains that if we wait, a pedicab will come to take us to the end of the bus line where we can catch a bus into Ningbo, about a forty-five minute ride. Is that a blessed breeze? The moving heat only stirs the stale, fetid air, swollen with unshed rain. No relief.

The pedicab comes, and the driver seems pleased to have a fare. We sit in the buggy portion of the bicycle, supported by the two back wheels, and watch him climb onto the business end of the vehicle, his small but muscular calves pumping us along. A tarp, ragged and dirty, drapes over our part of the pedicab. We're mesmerized looking at the cyclist's lean back bent over the rusty handlebars, his slim waist supporting a baggy pair of trousers. After about a fifteen minute ride, which I spend feeling guilty about the cyclist's exertion in the humid heat, he pulls up to a small shack. We dismount, and Rob pays him the paltry amount they negotiated before the ride. (We learned that the hard way. We'd climbed aboard our first pedicab in Ningbo without agreeing on a fee beforehand. The cabby overcharged us and waved his arms and shouted until a crowd gathered when Rob protested. We paid the fee, our red-faced driver suddenly beamed at his good fortune, and we knew we'd paid for a lesson.) The bored lady in the shack looks up from her reading. She's surrounded by trinkets, a few drinking water bottles (aha!) and some packaged items we don't recognize. We buy water and look around. Behind her shack is a row of equally shabby-looking, low buildings, the last tentacles of the city before it becomes farmland. A few people stand around, apparently waiting for the bus that soon arrives.

We mount the bus. No shoving today. It's too hot and only four or five others to get on with us. We learn to sit on the side of the bus away from the brutal sun. There's no such thing as air-conditioning on most Chinese buses, so the first ones on can ride on the shady side. The stench of bus fumes, trapped in the dense air, mingles with the smell of factory gases, decaying cement and human excrement. We strain our eyes to look out the streaked window, trying to spot something that looks like a market or food store. Where do all of these people shop for food?

Eventually, buildings other than factories, housing or hardware shops begin to appear, and Rob and I think we see a likely choice. We get off the bus and start walking, knowing just how a shaggy bear emerging from hibernation feels. We walk past paint stores, factories with great slabs of concrete pipes, then, yes! A door opens into a small grocery store—not the open stalls of Chuga I've grumbled about. No smiling egg lady, no moist, fresh-looking bok choy, no grinning meat sellers with their hunks of unappetizing pork. Am I wishing I could inhale the aroma of rotting fish again? We at least find some things we can put together to eat. We make our purchases, then repeat the transportation saga in reverse, finally dragging up the stairs to our apartment with a few eggs, a bag of rice, what I hope are soup mixes, and water. Our search for food and water took us only five hours.

I need to pause at each landing of the stairway to lean against the dank wall to steady my breathing, using every ounce of my resolve to slow my heartbeat. Am I on the second or third level? Sweat runs between my shoulder blades where the backpack sags under the weight of the groceries. If I take my straw hat off and fan my puffy, red face, maybe that will quiet the blood pounding through my heart.

A window air conditioner in the apartment churns importantly but ineffectually day and night. When we first step into the room from the airless hallway, our skin and lungs feel some relief. It's not cool, but our bodies recognize a perceptible loosening of the fist of heat and humidity and begin to relax. Soon we again think the only hope for survival is to flop onto the bed, glazed eyes on the ceiling, arms and legs splayed. That we do until we fall into a lethargic argument about who can gather the strength to stand up and fix us something simple to eat.

It doesn't occur to us at first that we're both ill. Some nameless grip has squeezed our core; no cocky juices remain, only grit and hope that our energy and bounce will bob back like Halloween apples in a bucket of water. I sink into worry mode. Could it be more than exhaustion and heat? Is some parasite or disease manifesting itself? I try to shake the idea, remembering the countless shots we had. Slowly, after many days of lethargy, we begin to stir.

I put a call in to Jenny and ask if we could have our refrigerator, about a third the size of standard American ones, stored at the college. The miniscule model here simply won't do because I'm determined to make a run in a taxi to The Metro, the large German-Chinese joint venture store overflowing with produce and food. We intend to stock up so we won't find ourselves marooned again. I also ask for the washing machine. I miss it glaring at me from the bathroom, and I don't relish the idea of washing everything we wear by hand for the remainder of the summer.

The next day, a slim, sinewy man, at least sixty, maybe five feet two, arrives at our door and mumbles that he will bring up our refrigerator and washing machine. I hover at the head of the stairs to hold the door open, expecting at least two men to haul the two beasts up. No. The lean worker from the college appears at the bottom of the stairwell with our refrigerator on his *back*, his dark, calloused hands clasping it low, behind his knees. He leans forward slightly and steadily bounces up all four levels without pausing. He sets the refrigerator down in the tiny kitchen, turns, not even breathing heavily, and returns with the washer. He gestures that he will hook the washing machine up now. Amazing!

Even in the finest Chinese hotels, only a curtain separates showers from bathrooms, and no lip on the floor contains the water. Instead, a drain somewhere on the bathroom floor (remember The Swamp?) leaves the whole bathroom floor awash during and after every shower. This apartment is no different. The technician sees only one hot and one cold outlet in the room, so he hooks the cold water up to the washer and leaves. We thank him but know this means the only hot water we have comes out of the nonremovable showerhead. That would be okay, except that the one small appliance we find dependable is the on-demand hot water heater. It doesn't heat a whole tank of water as most US hot water heaters do. It lights and heats the water as it comes through the coils to the spigot, providing piping hot water instantaneously. Even a quick Navy shower—

turning the water off while you soap up, rinsing quickly—doesn't work here. Scalded like lobsters, we stand soapy, red and miserable. I know. I try it. Rob puts his brain and skills to use and works out a system whereby we disconnect one appliance or the other and control the water temperature for both systems. We think we can get through the quarantine period.

We rarely see anyone on campus. When we feel stronger we wander through the buildings, peering into empty classrooms, marveling at the sparkling rooms with overhead fans, whiteboards, even some with large screens and overhead TVs. I discover a music room with a number of keyboards that makes me envious. On one of our prowls we find some little ones in the kindergarten play area. Children's voices at play are the same the world over. I smile as I watch them, wishing I might be in there with them, but their watchful teachers hustle them inside and make it clear they are a self-contained unit. When we mention to Jenny what a well-heeled school this appears to be, she sniffs and says it is for people who have "too much money." And we thought everyone was equal in China!

One day I see a cloud of white birds descending on the rice paddy just outside the wall beyond our apartment building. They're cranes! I've grown almost accustomed to seeing water buffalo plodding at their own pace through the paddies, but the flock of birds is unique. Suddenly, all the Pearl S. Buck stories I loved as a girl flood back to me. Cranes! Such a symbol of China. Then I hear the growl of distant thunder rolling almost continuously across the fields. The cluster of birds, maybe two dozen of them, reorganizes, rises and disappears into the roiling clouds.

After an earlier venture outside, we put our umbrellas out on the balcony to dry. This morning they're gone! No one climbed up four stories to steal two cheap umbrellas. The wind must have picked them up and deposited them up-ended neatly in the harvested rice paddy where the cranes touched down the night before. I would've liked to see that happen! Like something out of *Mary Poppins*.

Robert and I peer over the balcony railing, and beyond the twelve-foot high wall we spot our umbrellas, tumbling about in weeds and rice stubble and muddy water. I vote we buy two new umbrellas on our next trip to town. Robert prowls around the apartment, then disappears. He reappears wandering around outside. The skeleton of another faculty apartment building, almost finished, is behind ours, but there are no workmen there today. He comes back upstairs, and I realize I'm doomed when he mutters, "It's the principle! I can do it." We watch the umbrellas rock in the wind and occasional spatters of rain. Rob pulls on his jeans and goes downstairs again to the rescue. I lean over the balcony, assuring him in my sweetest, wifely tones that if he breaks his neck I'll be *really* mad at him!

All I can do is watch as he finds a ladder at the construction site behind us and leans it against the wall. He tests it, climbs up, straddles the wall and peers down the twelve-foot drop into the weeds and muck on the other side. He returns to the construction site and finds yet another ladder, pulls it to the top of the wall, and lowers it on the opposite side. He climbs down and collects the dripping umbrellas and returns to our side. The runaway umbrellas are scrubbed and back in our possession, the ladders returned, and Robert carves another notch in his holster.

KUNMING

W e've worked out a sort of armed truce with our living conditions here "on the edge." Just gathering food and keeping ourselves clean consume a lot of time. We make stabs at getting ready for next year's teaching but are still unsure of exactly who our students will be. We had been assured we could keep the various classes we started last February to complete one full year with the students, but we also hear that since there will be an entirely new English Department in the fall, we might have new freshmen. Robert the prior-planner cannot believe that a "university" does so much by the seat of its pants. My personality is more of the proverbial squiggle, so I'm content to have a general plan but let the day-to-day events dictate the lesson plans.

The cloud that hangs over us, though, is that we're lonely and feel useless. I refuse to say it was a mistake to fly home for the wedding and bask in the love and joy of our family, but the contrast is stark now. Our kids have all dashed off to plunge into their own lives, so staying home would've had us foot-shuffling and wondering just what to do with ourselves. We've been back in China only a few weeks, but the time until school reopens at the end of August, possibly the middle of September, stretches on without end. Imagine a college or university that can't tell you exactly when its classes begin in the fall? This is the end of July!

The phone jangles the oppressive quiet in our apartment. It's James/Zeng Jia Men, from the Foreign Affairs Office in Ningbo. Who would've fingered James, the slim, quick-speaking official who recruits and oversees foreigners in business and education in the Ningbo area, to offer an escape from our isolation? He invites us to join the Walls, Rileys and several from his office for an eight day trip to southwest China, Yunan Province. We like James, who prides himself on his rapid-fire English. His staccato style, almost like a Las Vegas gangster, is his own creation, I think. His English is not always accurate; sometimes his words and/or pronunciation need to be sorted or rearranged, but his meaning generally comes across.

Rob and I view our service here as primarily a good will, people-to-people cultural exchange. Of course, our main assignment is to teach English, but we hope we can learn from one another. As our Chinese students absorb English from us, we hope they also view us as human beings who care about them.

Relationships of respect and trust go both ways. We also need to open our eyes and learn from their strengths and culture. But our view of China is restricted to the Ningbo area, so here is a chance to broaden our experience. James is excited to show us that part of his country (and hope we'll take a good impression back to America). We'll travel to Kunming, Dali and Lijiang, all cities southeast of Tibet. The reason for going now is a horticultural fair in Kunming, with floral and gardening setups from countries all over the world on display. His office will make all the hotel and travel arrangements. We need to be packed and ready to go in a few days.

Ten of us fly out of Ningbo on a Thursday afternoon. I'm grateful that Jenny is with us, especially because, as we're screened to get onto the plane (and this is pre-9/11), the guard rummages through my carry-on bag, pulls out my curling iron and shoots a horrified glance at me as he holds it up in triumph. My curling iron! Jenny knows what it is and quickly explains. He's doubtful, certain he's uncovered a clever plot to overcome the pilot with a foreign ray gun. A blistering argument that I can't follow ensues, but in the end he returns the curling iron to my bag and lets us pass.

We land in Kunming, "Spring City," which lives up to its name for balmy weather. Since we'll be back here at the end of our circuit, we spend only one full day in the city, mostly wandering through the Stone Forest, a large area of rocks exposed thousands of years ago when the sea receded. The Chinese love giving descriptive names, such as Turtle, Dragon, or Fighting Dog to the rock formations left behind. My imagination has to stretch to find some of them, but hordes of Chinese tourists cluster around each and enjoy themselves immensely. We wait our turn at ponds and clusters of rocks to scramble up for a better view and the inevitable photo op.

That evening we attend a stage performance highlighting the various ethnic groups living in and around the city, including dances from the Bai, Mongols, Naxi, Tibetans and more than twenty other ethnic minority groups. The show seems to honor a true melting pot of cultures, all intended for tourists and visitors. Discussing Tibet or any non-Han groups (Han are the ethnic majority in China) is off-limits for us. We have no visa to cross the border to Tibet, and the issue is delicate to our Chinese hosts, so we don't press it.

We're struck by how clean the city is. After the swirling litter in Ningbo (the worst), Beijing and Xian, the contrast is clear. James tells us that anyone throwing litter on the streets is fined, since they're very tourist conscious. That surely would be an incentive, but we suspect it must be cultural too, since so many people here spring from other cultures. I have always thought the Chinese were culturally monolithic, but in fact their beauty and diversity are marvelous! Rob notices many unique facial features. Such fine-looking people! The hair color may be the same, but the faces are strong and very individual.

After the show we dash to the station to catch the night train to Dali, a gorgeous city surrounded by mountains. Again the cleanliness impresses us, as well as the tremendous amount of agriculture in the valley. We can identify some crops: rice, tomatoes and cabbage. We eat in the restaurants our Chinese hosts select in the towns here, tasting unusual and mostly delicious food. Sometimes we're seated upstairs and can look down on a courtyard where the food is cooked. We see young women washing and chopping, the discarded bits dropping to the ground. Plastic tubs, red and blue, filled with bok choy, snow peas, long green beans and eggplant cover the courtyard tables. It is a chaotic symphony of movement.

Plates of steaming food arrive, and we plunge in with our chopsticks, tasting and nodding, conversation rarely flagging. James carries on a happy monologue, which makes up for Carr, who works with him and insists he doesn't speak a word of English. A young boy, maybe twelve or thirteen, the son of the "boss" of the Foreign Affairs office, comes along. If he speaks English, he doesn't try it with us, but he seems quite comfortable with James and Carr and Jenny. James makes a point of telling us that during his recruiting travels in Canada and the United States, his stomach always gives him trouble. "The food in those countries is simply not edible," he tells us.

Since most Chinese in China believe American food consists of Kentucky Fried Chicken or McDonald's (the only food chains we see outside a few others in Beijing, Shanghai or Hong Kong), we ask James, "What kinds of restaurants do you go to in America or Canada?"

"Oh, always Chinese restaurants!" he tells us. We tease him and suggest other possibilities. There's *good* American cooking, French cuisine, Italian food. He just shakes his head and repeats, "When I leave an American restaurant, I am always hungry, and my stomach hurts."

He can't possibly be hungry after sitting down with us in his own country. For a man who weighs not more than a hundred and twenty pounds, he puts away a huge quantity of food. When we all lean back in our chairs, gazing over the empty dishes, James asks for another bowl of rice. He grins and tells us he has a little corner that needs filling. I can't imagine where he stores it. His belt would whip around his waist twice with no problem. One of James' favorite responses is *No problem*. That's a handy attitude for the fellow who arranges our trip.

I spend one wonderful afternoon watching local women doing tie-dyeing. It's a cottage industry here, and we're invited into a courtyard where huge sheets of cobalt and pale blue fabric flap on a line criss-crossing above huge wooden vats. A woman sits on the step of her home, and a little girl peeps out the door at us as her mother darts a needle in and out of the yards of fabric heaped on her lap and spilling onto the stoop. She sews intricate patterns and pulls the thread taut so when the material is dipped in a waxy solution, then in the deep Delft-looking blue dye, the protected parts remain light. The blue fabric treasures waving in the clean breeze remind me of Pennsylvania Dutch handmade quilts—also proudly displayed on clotheslines outside the orderly farms, hoping for tourist dollars. Here, I think, the fabrics will be cut and sewn into tablecloths, clothing or bags to be displayed for hard currency return.

Rivaling tie-dyeing as my favorite part of the visit is the boat trip. We bobbed across a huge lake, where sampans fish as they've done for centuries, to an island and a small fishing village. We wander through twisting lanes past enclosed compounds where we peek inside the occasional open gate. We see the residents, many in colorful costumes though not necessarily intended to please tourists. Food is often cooked in the courtyards, and women bend over short brooms to keep the grounds tidy. The compound walls sport painted dragons guarding the gates. We stumble onto a fish market where we peer at sea creatures or, I suppose, lake creatures I could only guess at. Dried fish hang on twine, and various home articles made from shells are also for sale. I'm most enchanted by the mothers with babies slung on their backs, papoose fashion. The scarlet slings are brilliantly embroidered with outrageous color combinations. The babies are completely oblivious to the folk art on those slings. They know only the love that embraces them.

We watch dragon boats races on the lake. Oarsmen skim boats decorated with fanciful painted dragon heads across the lake as their supporters on the bank yell encouragement.

One morning we board a small bus for the three-hour drive to Lijiang, north of Dali near Tibet. Traveling on the small buses is an adventure in itself since the Chinese love to be entertained and failing all else, entertain themselves. There is a microphone on the bus, so we're encouraged to join in on some sing-alongs. Since Chinese songs are not our forte, we take turns coming up with American folk songs. Dutch, LuJean, Sandra, Woody, Robert and I do our best with "Home on the Range," "She'll Be Coming Round the Mountain" and "Where Have All The Flowers Gone?" When we're all out of ideas, to our amazement, James, Jenny and Carr erupt in a rousing song (in Chinese, but they translate) about how "father, Chairman Mao, our great leader, is always watchful, always leading for our benefit." We try not to look too amazed or disrespectful but wonder how educated people who have been outside China can still sing about a leader responsible for the death of millions of their people. The cult of Mao Tse Tung is no longer alive, so surely they know about his ruthlessness and weaknesses.

A tour of the old city of Lijiang has been arranged, so we dutifully admire the city wall, the butterfly museum (now I know why there are no butterflies in all of China) and the old town with its craftsmen making and selling their wares. Our plans for the next day include Tiger Gorge and Jade Dragon Snow Mountain, which rises about 18,000 feet and sports an impressive glacier. During the night, however, grinding stomach cramps hit five of the six Americans hard. Only Robert is up and chirping in the morning. I spent a sleepless night on or near the bathroom floor. Phone calls between hotel rooms tell us Dutch is especially hard hit too. LuJean won't be touring today, either. Sandra and the usually solid Woody are weak and unlikely to leave their room. Jenny offers to take us to the hotel doctor. Does it mean something that three and four star hotels keep a doctor on staff? I hope a day in bed without eating may clear out the violent food poisoning. The others vacillate whether to go for Chinese medication or not. I'm not entirely sure what they do for the next two days because I spend the time alternating between a haze of twilight sleep and nibbling bananas and sipping water, the only two things I can think of that might not start the spasms and agonies again. I remember James sticking his head into our room, a very concerned look on his face, then disappearing.

I urge Rob to go ahead with our Chinese friends. He can scoop me up in a body bag and throw me over his shoulder on his return. Why he isn't part of the fellowship of food poisoning I'll never know. Maybe his years in Viet Nam taught his insides to handle all sorts of invading germs, but he agrees to go and leave me to my private misery.

Rob rides the gondola up Jade Dragon Mountain to about 15,000 feet, then climbs another 1,000 feet to a viewing platform. To hear him tell it, the day was extraordinary. He is grateful for the heavy parkas provided for tourists, but mostly for the oxygen tanks all tourists are given. The day was a strenuous one, he tells me, exhausting, exhilarating, amazing as they looked out over the glacial undulations, breathing from the oxygen tube from time to time. What he doesn't realize, and discovers later, is that even the Chinese start suffering that day, one with altitude sickness and two others with coughs and colds. He sits blissfully unaware at dinnertime that night, the party considerably shrunken, and cleans up several untouched plates. That's my boy!

What started out as a jolly group of ten is a sad-looking troupe when we board the plane bound for Kunming again. I grit my teeth and struggle to keep my head up for the trip, and the other four don't look so well either. Dutch, especially, is sagging, not the robust, grinning man we're used to. The main purpose of returning to Kunming is the 1999 Horticultural Exposition. Before the flight, we food poisoning victims submitted to pills, capsules, and even a trip downstairs to the hotel doctor for a shot. (My syringe.) My hotel room is the only spot I want to see in Kunming, and the Rileys feel the same way. Woody and Sandra gamely agree to accompany the small group to the exposition.

Again I have to pass along Rob's description of the day. He says the Chinese portion of the Expo was beautiful, a garden representing each of the thirty-two (more or less) provinces of China as the centerpiece. Other countries presented displays in keeping with the horticulture theme: Japan, Thailand, Egypt, Indonesia, Russia, the United Kingdom and Chile. Others, such as Pakistan, ignored the *horti* and concentrated on *culture* to sell their country's arts and crafts—and sell they did. The USA exhibit was a great disappointment and embarrassment. He says a sign blazed *Texas House of the USA* over a single story, non-descript 1500 square foot building that was nothing more than a sales outlet for T-shirts and vitamins, of all things. Nothing to do with horticulture. Outside the non-display was a patio with dirty, worn benches and chairs and a couple of vending machines. Of course, we have no way of knowing who in the US was invited to present a display. Perhaps no one. Some roaming Texan may have heard about the Expo and posed as a proper representative. I can't help wondering if some Chinese bureaucrat didn't smirk at the slap at the American image here.

We stumble aboard the plane for Ningbo, the walking wounded heading home to lick their wounds. Dutch has to be hospitalized and requires IV fluids as soon as he gets back. I just want to curl up on my bed and wait for the world to spin around a few times before I re-enter life. My clothes hang a lot looser on my frame now. As soon as I can tolerate thinking about food we'll scour Ningbo in search of those ice-cream-on-a-stick Magnums. But not yet.

Rob and I dressed in ancient costume for a tourist photo op

3 1

BACK ON CAMPUS

Rob makes a solo trip from our isolation ward to the campus. For the first time in six months we'll be apart for several hours. We always functioned independently in America, but the past few months of working so closely together on a common goal has strengthened and matured our love. My fears about being too closely monitored by this guy, so self-disciplined, such a planner, were groundless. We've found a team pattern that's comfortable, even fun. I feel pretty glum when he leaves. We've been moving like automatons around the sweltering rooms, trying to cajole each other to make the effort to put together something to eat. Then we flop back down on the bed. A bug has hit us, and we can't shake the lethargy. He insists he's up to the all-day effort to find out about the progress on our new apartment, *when* we might be able to move back to campus, *when* classes will begin. I just don't have the stamina yet for the bus routine, so I wave him goodbye.

It's almost dark when he stumbles up the stairs. I'm glad to see him and eager for news. "Well," he begins as we sit to a light supper, "classes are supposed to start on August 28th, but if the new English Department gives us only freshmen, classes with them could start later."

"Why?"

"Freshmen have five weeks of military training before their classes begin."

"When will we know?"

"Don't know."

"What do you *think*?" He shrugs and rolls his eyes. This man carefully plots every *day's* activities. He can hardly conceive of a college, no, a university staff, that doesn't plan and print schedules far in advance. He's spent a bewildering day trying to squeeze answers from unyielding Chinese school bureaucrats.

"When do you guess we'll be able to move back?" I have little hope of a definitive answer.

"They tell me the apartment will be ready in about a week, August 28th."

A date! Something I can pin our hopes and plans on! But do we dare? "Were you able to see the place?"

"Yes!" He brightens. "I actually walked through it. Susie, it's . . ." He can't find the right words. "It *is* a villa!" We squirm when Jenny and other Chinese officials refer to the Foreign Experts' *Villa*. The Chinese can't resist hyperbole, but Rob's glowing description of the fabled apartment-to-be seems way over the top. He tries to transform my picture of the littered construction site I last saw into the gleaming new fourplex that is to be our new home. "There are two bedrooms. We can use one as a study and a guest room, if we need it. There's a living room, a dining room. The kitchen's smaller than the old place but much cleaner, and, Susie, the *pièce de résistance*, the *bathroom*! Two real sinks with a marble counter *and* a big mirror with decent lighting. We won't have to comb our hair in Braille anymore! There's a new Western toilet and a bathtub! The floor is white tile, and it's *dry*! In fact, all 850 square feet have gorgeous hardwood floors that shine like a flooring ad."

I squint, trying to imagine this palace. "Any furniture?"

"Yes, it's all in place. The dining room table and chairs from our old place, but the living room has built-in lighted shelves all along one wall. The side-tipping chairs have vanished. Instead we'll have typical Chinese wooden chairs and a loveseat."

"What about the beds?"

"Yup, our old bed is in one bedroom, and a new double bed is in the other." Before I can frame the next question, he adds, "Yes, our foam pads are there."

Wow! Now I'm really eager to settle in and get to work. All the extravagant window drapes I've seen in shops (never any customers, however) come to mind. "What's on the windows?"

Robert grins and shuffles his feet. "Uh, try to imagine a really nice, uh, pizza parlor. Y'know, Chianti bottles on the tables with candles stuck in them and wax melted all down the sides."

I think out loud, "Red and white checkered tablecloths?" That's all that comes to mind.

"Yes! That's it!"

"What? Hardwood floors, marble countertops and red and white checks draped on the windows?"

"Yup, not only on ours, but they must've gotten a deal on 'em. All four apartments in our building and the six apartments in the companion building have them. I walked through 'em all."

Where, oh, where are the tender silks and brocades that whisper *China*? Oh, well.

32

THE FOREIGN
EXPERTS' VILLA

Mercifully, the new Foreign Experts' Villa is completed on schedule, and we reverse the moving exercise. Our summer aerie was isolated, lonesome, and we chafed and prowled with no teaching responsibilities, though we appreciated the roof over our heads. The *new* roof and everything else in our new apartment is marvelous! I smile at the red and white checkered drapes on the windows. I love it all, but ah! The bathroom! Clad in palatial white tile, there's even a ceiling vent fan. Clean and dry never looked so good!

Our teaching schedule is still a mystery, so we busy ourselves adding finishing decorating touches. We buy new sheets and comforters in the linen department of a Ningbo store, the only paying customers and the source of much curiosity. I decide that instead of trying to match the pizza parlor drapes, I'll just ignore them. Color choices are limited, so I opt for blue. The jaunty American red, white and blue is my private joke.

Several bus trips to find pads for the unrelenting wooden living room chairs finally yield thin, purple flowered cushions that will fit. That's okay. The windowless room is permanently gloomy, though swags of the ubiquitous red and white adorn the French doors. All the rooms have windows except the living room, which has only the door that opens out into the patio overlooking the canal and the village. It's a fine source of light and air on pleasant days, but gloom takes over when it's too hot (despite the cherished air-conditioner!), too cold or too miserable to open the door. Whoever planned the glitzy indirect lighting over the shelving must've fancied the red glow for reasons of his own. I think it looks like a flashing *Beer On Tap* sign in my living room. Since there is no other lighting in the room, we need to buy lamps. The door leads to a very nice balcony we'd call a deck in California. With the door open on good days, we get light— and clouds of flies from the sluggish canal five steps beyond. Screened doors or windows are unknown. When winter sets in, we'll have to close the door, but for now Rob bends his mind to creating a screen door.

The door opens outward, so hingeing one, even inside, is out of the question, he decides. Lots of head scratching. He uses twine again to knot the measurements, and we pace through Chuga in search of screening material. We duck into a tiny, dark shop one afternoon to find a young mother watching her little girl playing on the floor. I've scoured my English-Chinese dictionary and pieced together phrases gleaned from Ying Chun, my Chinese teacher, to explain our needs. The young mother bobs her head and disappears into the living quarters. Her husband joins us and nods that he understands and says he will build the framed rectangle we require. Two days later we pick the door up, pay him, and haul our precious screen door home on the bus.

It fits! Perfectly. It's a bit cumbersome to open the wooden door, then fix the screen over the opening with bungee straps every morning, but the light and occasional almost-cool breezes some days are worth it. We're especially glad to be rid of the hordes of flies, and I wash the bloody little carcasses of past kills off the new white walls.

Our apartment building has four units. We're on the ground floor. The school vice president lives across from us. He's from Hangzhou, where his wife and daughter live, 130 miles west of Ningbo. He spends most of his time at the college, and we've never seen his family here. That is pretty typical for a Chinese family. Living and working apart is the norm. The apartment above him is for the university president. His wife lives with him, but we rarely see either. The unit above us is reserved for temporary visitors, so it's generally empty. Another brand new apartment building next to ours has six units designed for department heads and future foreign teachers.

The balcony doors open onto the canal, and across the canal, like a sudden step back in time, is a typical Chinese village. Our gleaming, white, pseudo-Mediterranean building and their mildewed, mud-spattered concrete cubicles contrast sharply. The people living there find us just as fascinating as we find them. We can see their simple, rectangular houses, and, through a clearing, the town square where a water buffalo sometimes hangs out and people shuffle or ride rusty bikes on their way across the village. Chickens and ducks waddle through the square, pecking at weeds growing up through the cement, sometimes darting through an open door.

One day I was on my hands and knees scrubbing the tile floor on the patio when three ladies across the canal waved. I smiled and waved and called out what I hoped was a pleasant hello. Maybe they took that as an invitation because they pulled their low, bamboo chairs up for a front row seat of my solo performance. Their animated conversation accompanied my efforts for quite some time, and they were *really* interested later when Rob put up a makeshift clothesline on the patio. The hope that we can improve on our indoor drying protocol from the old apartment springs eternal in our breasts.

It's fascinating to watch the water activity. No home across the canal has running water. (Anyone who tells you everyone is equal in communist China has never been here.)

Day and night, villagers come with plastic bowls full of laundry to scrub in the canal. They brush their teeth, roll up pants legs to bathe themselves, and urinate in the same water they wash their vegetables in. Mop buckets scoop up water for indoor chores, and lots of visiting goes on at the canal's edge just beyond our patio.

The water flows in two directions, since the larger canal that feeds the side canal often stagnates a few feet beyond the corner of our building. Sometimes it ebbs and flows. Floating garbage, plastic bags, Styrofoam chunks, food remnants, floating greens growing in the water, all move to the right for a while, then back to the left. People lean over the water and stir a spot to move the flotsam aside and clear a "clean" entry for their needs.

One evening recently I heard such a squeal of agony that I leaped to the window expecting to see a child in trouble. The shrieking did not stop as I tried to locate the source in the fading light, finally gurgled and faded to a halt as I spotted a man holding a bleeding pig over the water by its hind leg. He'd slit its throat and was draining it. Patiently.

Apparently we will be teaching mostly new freshmen English majors. We're disappointed we won't stay with our former students for two reasons: we like them and were looking forward to continuing with them; and it seems unfair to promise them a full year of

English, then drop them to take care of the influx of "rich kids." Since we're the only foreign teachers, a source of prestige and status to the university, we may have a class or two of International Business students from the old guard, but apparently we will be the honey around which the English majors cluster.

We *are* excited about having an English Department and hear that the incoming freshmen, particularly the majors, will have a better command of English. We'll see. Our open house invitation stands for both our former students and the new ones. The only difficulty now is that we have trouble working dinner in. Finally Robert insists they telephone us first to set a time to come over. They nod, then just show up.

Our students visit often. Lucy comes almost every evening to play the piano and chat. We finally feel comfortable enough just to prepare our meal, sit down and invite them to join us, which they rarely do. Others arrive as the evening wears on, and suddenly it's nine thirty or ten. Some nights we have six or eight kids here, which confuses us a little since they tell us they're very busy and have "much to do," yet never seem in any hurry to leave. Even when we say we haven't had our dinner yet or have something else to do, they don't take the hint. Sandra, who's been in China longer than we have, tells us we must be assertive: "It's very nice that you could come over. Now you must go." That seems a little harsh, but she tells us she had the same problem at first and found she had to be blunt and tell their students to *go home*.

Our new apartment on campus

View out our back windows from the new apartment

33

THE OPENING
CEREMONY

Classes have started for our former students. The new freshmen, though, drill in the brutal sun out on the basketball courts every day. Their classes start after their military training, in about five weeks. They wear military fatigues and sneakers, marching with uniformed army and navy leaders, executing right and left turns, occasionally resting in what shade they can find. Rob says it's not unlike college ROTC in the States, where students train for a semester or more. From a distance it looks much the same, except for all the black hair here.

Excitement is in the air, now that we *think* we're officially a university. The name on the brass sign on the school gate changed before the end of last term, in both English and Chinese, even though it wasn't yet a fact. A lot of accreditation remains to be done. Even now we get the feeling the administrators *hope* the school will be granted university status, but like so much of life here, brave fronts and hopes often mask uncertainty and doubt. They go to *lots* of pain to welcome the new freshmen, since they're a different variety of student from the current students here.

To attend the new university students pay a hefty fee, particularly
for China, where the lucky and the gifted once studied virtually for
free. These youngsters' families pay 20,000 yuan as a one-time
investment, plus 10,000 yuan per year for three years. (They offer
only three years this year, like the teachers' college, but with full
accreditation they'll bloom into a four-year institution. Even so, the
incoming freshmen will pay 50,000 yuan (about $6,000) for their
education, which won't really include a university degree. Balance
that against a top-notch teacher here earning about 24,000 yuan
(about $3,000) a year. Most teachers average only about 10,000 a
year. The staff's attitude toward the students is interesting. They're
anxious to please them and to offer the advantages of a well-estab-
lished university. Concern to polish up the school's image swallows
up last year's ho-hum attitude.

Our front door looks out onto the boys' dorm and beyond them
to new basketball courts that materialized during the summer. The
lightning speed of demolition and construction constantly amazes
us. One fairly decrepit building was whisked away during the latter
part of the school year, and we watched in awe as a new soccer field
with a track around it came to life day by day. The much-praised
new classroom building, five stories with two open courtyards,
crept higher and higher every day behind the flimsy netting
surrounding it. Swarms of workers plinked away, sleeping near the
site in red, white and blue canvas tents, cooking and warming
themselves and their families last winter. Suddenly now it's ready
for students and teachers

The clean, inviting classrooms thrill us. No more choking chalk
dust and grime. Whiteboards. Overhead fans to move the air.
Screens on the windows. We soon learn, however, that our

students don't understand the concept of screens. They dislike the flies and insects but insist on sliding the screens aside, saying they keep air from coming into the room. Keeping the fans on is a running battle. The kids tell us they can't hear when they're on, although they are silent. We guess the changes are major for the students, so we go slowly.

Audiovisual networks in two of the larger classrooms include overhead projectors controlled by a computer. Our own giant leap forward! Of course, the rooms are tightly locked. We learn from Sandra and Woody that they once arranged for a huge shipment of books to be shipped to their school from the States. A church had donated books and paid for a full sea van to be brought from America to Ningbo College. The Chinese made an enormous fuss over the gift of badly needed reference material, effusive thanks, and then all the books were carefully locked up. Woody and Sandra pled and argued for students to use them and met a polite but stone wall. The reasoning was that if students actually used the beautiful books, they might damage or even lose them. The bureaucrats' solution was to lock them up where they remain untouched to this day. We see signs of the same mentality circling the wagons around the fine, new audiovisual equipment, so we begin lobbying right away for keys to the rooms.

Our request elicits polite smiles, sucking sounds between clenched teeth, dubious headshaking, but we at least get desks in one of the two offices for English teachers, part of the new loosely organized English Department. We're pleased to meet some newly hired teachers; some even speak English fairly well. Sunny, whose smile matches her English name, is probably in her mid to late 30s, as are most of the new teachers. There's Ruth, eager to please as a puppy;

May, at the college last year, whose dark, good looks and intelligent eyes make her popular with her students. Another May is an older woman, very well educated. The three older men who teach English, all married, are more aloof. Then there's Charlie, a slender boy/man petted and teased by the women teachers in the department. I mustn't forget Lily! The class clown! What English she doesn't know she makes up. Her laughter fills a room, so I can't picture her as a typical Chinese lecturer. Linda is designated department head. She's probably in her forties, also well schooled. Her English is jerky but competent. She seems in over her head as department chair but tries to keep things on course.

Rob and I have desks across from Sunny, and Anna, whom we met last year. She had run to catch up to us as we were walking on campus and introduced herself breathlessly. We were surprised to learn she had lived several months in Australia, which explains her good English pronunciation and syntax. Travel and study outside of China are extremely rare, so we were struck when Anna confided she's been struggling for more than eight years to get a visa to work for a master's degree in America. She still corresponds with an American English teacher from Ohio, who taught at her high school, who's working on arranging a teaching assistantship for Anna in Akron. How much education means to some shows in the fact that Anna will have to leave her young daughter and husband behind, possibly for years, if she realizes her dream.

I'm instantly drawn to Anna. There's a deep sadness behind her eyes, but she's eager and intent on learning all she can about America. We learn early in our friendship of her un-Chinese weakness: she adores butter! She acquired a taste for it in Australia, so when I casually mention at the office that we're going to shop for food at The

Metro and offer to pick up anything anyone wants, she shyly asks, "Oh, butter, please. I will, of course, pay you for it." Her office mates screw their faces up in mock disgust. I start slipping butter to Anna clandestinely after each shopping run. I can't give her too much at a time, since she doesn't have a refrigerator (too expensive and too costly to run). The unmarried teachers live three or four to an apartment, very sparsely furnished. Rob and I have eaten in some of their apartments, and we usually bring our own chairs.

Have I mentioned the incredible new landscaping done on campus over the summer? It's mind-boggling! The place is transformed! We joke about "technicians" who can't repair a leak, who use string and rags to jerry-rig a repair, but that's hard to reconcile with the army of gardeners who transplant mature trees, create hills and rock gardens, and lay grass where yesterday there was only filth and rubble.

We discover that though the transformation is for the overall beauty of the campus, it's particularly aimed at the ceremonial opening of the newest capitalist-style university in China. Ling Ya Fen, the lady powerhouse who drives the transformation, is opening a pay-as-you-go Western style university in a country where capital flows into the hands of anyone who recognizes that education and business are closely allied. Chinese periodicals describe her as an "excellent young entrepreneur" and "fine Communist member," having "endured great hardships for pioneering," and—most Chinese of all—"First Rose in East Wind."

Tremendous balloons and roof-to-ground red and gold banners proclaim the "glorious success" and "march into an honorable future" for Sunli University. Even Jenny's calm is a mite ruffled when she asks one day to use my iron to press her uniform skirt for the formal ceremony where all the dignitaries will deliver endless congratulatory speeches. Uniform? We haven't seen any uniforms yet, except for the freshmen's fatigues. "Yes," she tells us, "all the teachers and leaders have uniforms. Do you and Robert want one? We wear them only for special occasions."

I examine the tailored navy blue skirt and jacket with the accompanying white shirt and tie. "No, thank you. If it's okay, we'll just wear our own best clothes for the day."

The day arrives, and hundreds of flower pots are carefully placed to best advantage, trash swept away, red carpets laid to the dignitaries' stand. Balloons sway in the breeze that's a bit stiffer than hoped for on this day. Rob and I get cleaned up. I choose a soft green dress and high heels, and Robert decides that this is one of the rare days on which a suit is appropriate. We walk over to the new soccer field at the appointed time. The freshmen are already on their benches on the grass, their splotched camouflage uniforms matching the muted and overcast sky. The older students file in, and *they're* in uniform too: white shirts and dark skirts or slacks. Finally the teachers all march in to canned music on the omnipresent loudspeaker, wearing dark suits and ties. We are escorted to our seats and are amused to find various levels on the stand, appropriate to the status of the guests. Our chairs are to the right and below the main stand where the mayor of Ningbo will sit. Madam Ling Ya Fen and the board of directors, the university president and four vice presidents all will be on the highest level too. Black limousines with flags spill important people who are escorted to the stand with much handshaking. Just as the proceedings are about to begin, a rain starts, not a hard rain, just a soaking sprinkle. Miraculously, little green packets pass from hand to hand down the rows of teachers and students, and lightweight plastic hooded raincoats bloom over three thousand people! In an institution that still can't tell us exactly what day classes will begin and whom we will teach, somebody did some astute planning to have those raincoats ready.

The dignitaries don't get raincoats, but people materialize with umbrellas behind everyone seated on the dais. Obviously the show must go on. The Chinese national anthem comes over the loud-speaker, and everybody stands facing the flagpole while the red flag with its gold stars climbs slowly up the pole. The strong winds pick the flag up and flaps it open, and a collective gasp rushes through the crowd. The flag is *upside down!* The white-gloved man at the base of the flagpole hesitates, and everyone senses his horror. An upside down flag is an international distress signal, may be a dishonor to the flag, and the man whose job it is to raise the flag before a crowd of Important People is living a nightmare. People murmur and gape at the flag and one another helplessly. Rob leans over and whispers, "They've *got* to do something!" After an excruciating pause, the flag is lowered and raised again, right side up. We could feel and hear sighs of relief ripple through the crowd. The first speaker comes to the podium, his umbrella-holder trying to be invisible behind him. The speeches drone on for only about an hour. All the while I'm sorry for the flag man, wondering what will become of him.

*Faculty and students in the drizzle at the opening ceremony of
our new university*

34

MOONCAKES AND
ENGLISH MAJORS

Mooncakes have always evoked taste bud-tingling dreams of dainty treats in exotic far-away lands for me. We're in a faraway land all right, and here in China it's Mid-Autumn Festival when mooncakes are a centerpiece of the celebration. Our former students parade to our door like army ants, laden with boxes of mooncakes. We learn they are a kind of puffy cookie with various fillings from fruit (not too bad) to black bean paste (ghastly!) to meat (ugh!). Must be an acquired taste, but I don't think we'll be here long enough to acquire it. Fortunately our young friends usually don't expect us to consume their gifts before their eyes. We receive their heartfelt gifts graciously and put open boxes out on the table for other guests to enjoy later.

We are invited to a party in the evening put on by and for the "new and young teachers." Since we are neither, we feel honored to be included. Fruit and the inevitable mooncakes cover the tables. They ask us to participate in a talent show. I came prepared with my guitar and the words to "You Are My Sunshine" for everyone. I wow the crowd! The Chinese *love* karaoke and do it at top decibel level in specially designed rooms in restaurants, complete with TVs programmed with menus of lyrics and backup music. There is no fear of the microphone here. They love to belt out a song, and "You Are My Sunshine" fits their natural inclinations just right. The high point of the evening, however, is being invited to play musical chairs and to *last five rounds* with a crowd of native Chinese. To appreciate this properly, go back and reread the description of boarding a Chinese bus!

Starting tomorrow, though, the fun and games end and the teaching begins. We had magnificent summer trips and experiences but are more than ready to meet our new English majors and plunge into the real reason we're here.

The university has enrolled 144 freshman English majors, and we each have two classes of International Business majors as well. Our initial contacts in the first classes are encouraging. They seem to have a better grasp of the language, and their eagerness to learn is even (hard to believe!) stronger than last year's students. It's a good thing neither Rob nor I considered going into stand-up comedy because we'd now be laboring under the false impression that we're star material. A side comment, a joke, a play on words all elicit the students' laughter and grins. Twenty-four to thirty pairs of eager eyes follow us around the room. At first I thought it was just me, being the ham former students and friends called me. Then Robert confides that he feels really good about his teaching techniques, that everything he says and does is well received. We compare notes. His teaching style is different from mine; he runs a pretty tight ship, although he is flexible, gentle. I like to use music and games to get people talking. It doesn't seem to matter. There simply is no such thing as a discipline problem here. The kids are fascinated by us personally, our foreignness, our American connection, our window on an unseen world. Whatever we do or say, they watch, listen, and often laugh appreciatively. After the initial shy contacts, they decide we're not something to be feared. Foreign, yes. American, yes. But we do our best to be genuine and open with them, and they soon seem to place us somewhere between a grandparent and a pet, certainly not the stern *lausher* (teacher) they are used to.

Come to think of it, maybe that's not true. I haven't seen a pet since we came to China, no cats, no dogs. I asked a class last year if people sometimes eat dogs in China. They quickly denied it, but Sandra says they saw flayed dog carcasses for sale in at least one market.

Our new students are not new to one another, even though they're freshmen. They've had several weeks of military training together, a sort of boot camp, so they have a camaraderie that will last, I'm told, throughout their lives.

Rob and I begin with lessons, feeling our way to learn our students' level of challenge in the language. Stories of our family and lives fascinate them, and they hunger for tales of what it's like to be a college student in America. Since they are so curious about what Americans eat, we bring menus with pictures from our recent dash to America. The Denny's menu is particularly colorful, but we have several and design several lessons around them. The kids lose all shyness when I pass the menus out for them to study, pointing and chattering in Chinese.

"Wait a minute! This is an *English* class, so we *speak* English, even with one another, even if we're excited."

Many giggles. "Mrs. McKee, what is this meat-uh?"

"That's a hamburger. It's made of ground beef. A cow. That's an animal something like the water buffalo but not so tough. It's a big favorite in America."

"And this around this beef-uh? What is that-uh?" (Oh dear, I'm remembering now Rob's uphill battle describing the sandwich last year.)

"That's a hamburger bun. Bread. I'll bring some for you to taste next week." One brave student tells us he's been inside the McDonald's in downtown Ningbo and saw hamburgers but hasn't tasted one.

Finally, we begin role-playing. They're to pretend they're in a restaurant, three playing customers with one waitperson. Each group of four puts on a playlet for the class, ordering a meal. Some even phone ahead for reservations.

I sit down to enjoy the show. It startles me a little when they order Chinese-style, a number of dishes for all to share. They find the idea of someone choosing an entree and not sharing it ridiculous. My mind entertains wild images of meals with everyone sharing scrambled eggs, pot roast, hamburgers, strawberry shortcakes, and waffles.

I try to explain tipping. "It's an extra 'thank you' for service." Their eyes tell me that they have no frame of reference for such an idea. "Perhaps even as much as twenty per cent of the total bill." *No!* I begin to understand how really outrageous it all must seem when the first table tries to bargain for a lower price when the check comes!

"That will be $60.25 please," the waiter says with his pen poised over the imaginary bill.

"I'll give you only $15."

"Well, then, how about $40?"

"No, no!" I interrupt. "In America, in a restaurant, in fact just about anywhere, you don't bargain. You pay the amount asked for." A stunned silence falls over the classroom. Pay the asking price and then add twenty percent? Unthinkable!

I make good on my promise the next class and bring in slices of precious bread along with knives and forks. We draw out our restaurant play with dishes and Western eating utensils. Our Chinese colleagues are surprised that Rob and I can negotiate reasonably well with chopsticks in restaurants. We explain that California has many Chinese restaurants because many Asian people migrated to that part of the country. Now we offer our students a chance to try *our* eating implements, and they are eager to try. Each has a try at cutting bits of bread on a plate and spearing them either English style, fork in the left hand, or swapping it to the right, American-style. (A lot of wasted motion, we all agree.) There's a lot of clinking as knives and forks drop, much laughter, and curious faces as they taste bread, most for the first time. They conclude in Chinese and in English that chopsticks are a lot easier.

Thinking that we might as well share other new tastes with them, I bring peanut butter for them to taste on a cracker. Most like it. Next I offer potato chips. Rob and I were delighted to find them at Metro and often have a few at lunch. Generally Jenny drops by for a quick visit during lunch and wrinkles her nose at our potato chips. "Why do you always eat children's food?" she asks. Apparently potato chips are children's food to her. The students pronounce them good. Almost universally though, Chinese students nibble cheese and rejected it, but at least they can say they've had a taste of America.

Faces and personalities begin to emerge: Chen Li Bin with her dazzling dimples and cheerful if inaccurate English; Yang Xiao Hong, the only girl among them all who is a little overweight—very unusual in China. Her English is good, and she tries unusual phrases like "the flowers wave brightly" instead of the usual "the flowers are lovely" or "beautiful," catchall words, much overused.

I learn some of the meanings of their names. *Hong*, for example, means *red* and shows up frequently in names to honor, I presume, the red flag of Communist China. *Hua* means *flower*, and Ding Hua is such a pretty girl that her name suits her. Wang Zhao Xiang is an earnest young man with glasses who speaks carefully and smiles shyly when he's complimented. Yu Guan Geng and Yao Ping always sit together, handsome boys, intelligent and obviously good friends. Zhu Feng Feng, also known as Judy, steals my heart with her joyous English that tumbles all over itself, switching word order, tossing in Chinese words when she can't fetch the English equivalent, hunching over to laugh at herself and her enthusiasm. I wish more students would fling themselves into the language as she does.

My guitar enchants them. They *do* love to sing. I expand my repertoire and type up lyrics so they can sing with me. Their favorite is the love song from *Titanic*, which they sing with great fervor. "Near, far, wherever you are, I believe that the heart does go on. Once more you open the door, and you're here in my heart, and my heart will go on and on." What do they think as they sing? I feel a twinge in my heart as it dawns on me that one day I will leave all these tender young people. My heart and theirs will go on. Have I opened any doors?

Judy comes to our apartment late one afternoon lugging a guitar case. "My uncle has given me a guitar," she explains. "Would you please teach me to play it?" I explain that my skills are very limited, but I will show her the few chords I know. We begin, and I find she's very quick, and while her fingers are still rather clumsy, she understands music and will soon be able to take off on her own with her guitar.

I see her eying my piano keyboard. "Would you like to play it, Judy?"

"Yes, I can play a little." She sits down and plays a lovely piece. I'm astounded, since pianos are out of reach for most Chinese families.

"Where did you learn to play?"

"Oh, we have a piano in our house," she tells me. I put some music in front of her and she admits she can't read music but learned to play by ear. She plays another piece and finishes with a flourish. She's very talented. I ask if she'd like to learn to read music, and she says she'd like that very much. Earlier, Lucy showed me the simplified do-re-mi symbols she learned to read, which works fine for a single note, but she was thrilled to see that the scattering of black dots could designate whole chords and wanted to learn to read them also. So I add Judy as another music student.

Music is, of course, a language all its own and a direct conduit heart to heart. Several students want to learn the keyboard. I start lobbying the college to set up a music class. I'll be happy to teach piano to anyone who's interested. Is there a piano anywhere on the campus? I hit the bureaucratic stone wall. Much smiling and sucking of teeth. One day I *see* an old upright piano, partially covered with an ancient cloth and smothered in dust, in a dank corner of a cold, little-used room. The cover is locked. No, I'm told, no one knows anything about it. A key? Not possible. No one has a key. Days, weeks go by in a standoff, the college administrators telling me it's a fine idea for me to teach piano, and "soon, maybe" they will find some keyboards. Finally I admit defeat. No access to the ancient piano. The college won't buy even one or two keyboards for its students, so I set up a schedule for them at our apartment. As time goes by, I make paper keyboards so they can practice in their dorm rooms. Kids come for guitar lessons too, one or two at a time. I find they are passing the things they learn along to their friends because guitars show up in several dormitories. I reason that we speak English as I teach, so it's just an extension of the classroom. Furthermore, we have a whale of a good time!

Judy's infectious smile

CHINA'S 50TH BIRTHDAY

October 1st is a *huge* celebration in China, and this year is the 50th anniversary of their "liberation" when Mao Tse Tung hammered the warlords, Chiang Kai Shek and his Nationalists fled to Formosa, and modern China was born.

We watch the incredible parade in Beijing on TV. Quite a show! Some of our students wanted to come watch it and clued us in when it began. An entourage will come to watch a big soccer match on TV tomorrow evening. A rare five-day holiday honors the founding of modern China, but many students live too far away to go home, so we're operating a sort of open-door policy of our own. Rob and I grumble because nobody can tell us when our classes begin or when midterm and final exams are, but the Chinese are experts at putting on a flashy show! The parade is pretty impressive with its high-stepping troops, brilliant banners and well-rehearsed marching bands.

We were invited to a *huge* reception and dinner last night put on by the mayor of Ningbo for honored guests and "foreign experts" (that would be us!), to commemorate China's anniversary. We were stunned to see maybe forty or fifty Westerners among the hundreds of guests. We had no idea there were so many in and around the city.

Many were businessmen; a few others were educators. I've attended some very grand occasions in my life, but the impact on stepping into the glittering hotel ballroom was stunning. In the lobby guests met squads of the customary Chinese hostesses in red and gold brocade Suzie Wong dresses: Mandarin collar, body-skimming gowns with sly slits exposing gorgeous legs. The lobby was grand, but the ballroom shimmered in white and silver with touches of gold. Mirrors with extravagant displays of white lilies topped the round tables. Candles gleamed everywhere, and the chairs were swathed in white damask with graceful bows at the back.

We found our name cards. The gentleman on my right gave me his calling card, a time-honored gesture and a gracious way to introduce oneself. If he hands it with two hands, courtesy demands it be received with two hands. A whole ballet accompanies the introductory script. His card told me that he was the vice mayor of Ningbo. We bowed deeply to one another and made the expected small talk. I blush to admit that I smugly thought we must have caught the attention of the mayor's office somehow, no doubt for our outstanding teaching techniques. But alas! When the dignitaries were all introduced in Chinese and again in English to the assembled crowd, they stood and took a bow. There are about 137 vice mayors of Ningbo.

Maybe the menu would make up for our sudden dip in status. Tantalizing fragrances floated into the room, and we American carnivores felt *sure* we smelled beef, almost extinct in China. Faintly flowery scents and tangy spices made it hard to concentrate on polite conversation. By each plate (and we were served Western style with a complete, elegant place setting for each guest) was a lovely menu with a soft, Chinese scene painted on the cover. The left of the inside cover listed the food in graceful Chinese characters, and on the right side was someone's careful English translation: "Varieties Cold Dishes; Braised Shark's Fin With Mixed Vegetable; Baked Small Lobster In Butter; Sauteeed [Whoops! A few too many *e*'s here!] Beef In Holland Sauce; Deep Fried Pigeon; Deep Fried Two Delicacies [they don't tell us just what the Delicacies are]; Sauteed Chicken Dices(?) With Ginkgo; Deep Fried Butter Fish; Sauteed Lily Root With Celery; Yellow Croaker Soup With Salted Vegetable; Two Varieties Chinese Tit-bits [I won't even go there]; Desserts."

I was probably happier not identifying everything I put in my mouth, but it *was* delicious!

36

MORAG ARRIVES!

Help is here! Jenny says a new English teacher has been hired. From Scotland! We're thrilled to have the help and delighted to meet her. Morag McGilliam is her name. We can't help wondering if our students pick up differences in the pronunciation of certain words in English yet. They're already fighting an uphill battle to get it right according to our American version. Morag's lilt charms us, and we can't help smiling when she brings some music tapes to English Corner. Imagine a roomful of young Chinese blackhaired kids matching her brogue singing along with her, "Will ye go, lassie, go-o-o-o tae pick the heather on the hil-l-l?"

Morag is probably in her mid-forties, packed with energy, with a mane of tangled, rust-colored hair. She's a professional English as a Second Language teacher who taught in Germany. She speaks (with a wee bit of an accent) of her son in college in Scotland and a husband from whom she's been separated for some time. Rob and I still have all the English majors, but Morag gets several classes from other majors. Having her here, particularly with fresh ideas for the English Corner, is a great boost.

Neither Rob nor I had realized that we miss having someone (besides each other) with whom we can speak rapidly, unself-consciously, without selecting our words carefully. We can share nuances and small jokes with another native English-speaker that simply aren't possible with our Chinese friends and students.

The end of October brings cooler weather, more classes, and a pleasant routine. I can't imagine how, but our students know about Halloween. I drew only blank stares when I mentioned Disneyland. Try describing *that* to young adults who can't even imagine such a place! They know about Halloween, though. I briefly consider concocting a costume to wear to class since it's the 31st but decide I need to maintain at least a little decorum. We talk about Halloween in class, and I describe the fun and traditions of little children dressed up like storybook characters going from house to house begging for candy. The students' faces take on a faraway look as they imagine such a night. From their perspective it must seem outrageous, a little silly, and apparently wonderful because they pepper us for details.

At about 9:30 that night a loud thud at our door startles us. The hair on the back of my neck bristles, and sweat beads up all over my body. When Rob asks who it is, a witchy cackle answers. Morag's voice, though. I am visibly limp with relief when we open the door and find Morag in an outlandish witch's costume she's brewed up from a black fringed scarf, black skirt and pointed shoes. Hideous orange makeup smears her face, which features a hooked nose (Where did she get *that*?), a huge mascara mole, and a pointed black paper hat. She crouches over a Chinese twig broom straight out of *Hansel and Gretel*, and is enjoying her Halloween homage to America. We double over laughing, rummage in our precious store of candy kisses, and deal them out to her generously.

37

SHAKESPEARE BOY

Photographing our students worked so well last term that we repeat the process and take snapshots of each desk pair. They're amused and I think a little pleased that we want visual records of them. China is a country of community, not individuals, but the students are after all young people away from home for the first time. They're a little homesick but revel in discovering themselves all the same. I bring the prints in to show them, glued into manila folders with each student's number by the appropriate photo. I ask them to write their names beside their pictures using *Pinyin*, the Latin alphabet phonetic spelling, and to add the correct tonal marks above each syllable for me. They all know how to do that, and it helps me enormously to learn their names and pronounce them so they can recognize them.

I think I mentioned earlier that each class comes together at the beginning of its college stay and remains a unit for the three or four years of study. Students have no elective courses or the option to branch out and take a class outside the strict curriculum outlined for their major. They remain in the same classroom all day and teachers come to them. I'm pleased to count only twenty-five or twenty-six students in each group. The slightly smaller classes give us a little more breathing room for individual conversation.

All Chinese students are assigned to schools (or not!) based on test scores, but I wonder if they're also placed in class groups by achievement. I don't think so, since the level of English comprehension and ability seems to vary widely within a class. They're still getting to know each other and us, but personalities emerge quickly. There's Shen Zheng, a tall young man in class number 991, who insists on standing when I call his name. The others seem relieved when I explain that we hope to be informal and sit while we chat. I have trouble pronouncing Shen Zheng's name, especially the *zh* sound, which is something like getting your teeth ready to say *zh* but *really* saying *j*. He laughs and bobs his head, repeating the correct pronunciation for me. I think he's an artist because he doodles on his papers a lot and dresses in what I think he fancies is a Bohemian style. His English is fair.

All the students love to learn American slang. They think idioms are the key to advanced English, so we play with *pulling your leg* and *drop me a line*. Today I dropped *couch potato* on them. Baffled looks. On the whiteboard I draw a fat cartoon potato with arms, legs, and a laid-back expression on its face. Then I put it on a cartoon couch. We talk about the pervasive TV, a fixture even in homes without running water here, and many heads nod when they begin to realize what the expression means. When Shen Zheng understands he guffaws, then whispers to his seatmate Zhu Wei, who also laughs. Zhu Wei worries me. Of all the English majors, he is least able to participate. He doesn't understand what is said in class, and his responses are monosyllabic. His classmates try to help him. He's easygoing and friendly but seems to be in over his head. I'll see what I can do to help him.

I'm getting to know Qiu Zhi Fu. He comes from an extremely poor family, he tells me, but yearns to be a scholar. In English. He approaches me shyly one day and asks if I will help him study for a national English examination at the end of the year. We settle on two afternoons a week at our apartment. He shows me the study guide, a resource of past similar tests. I'm aghast at the difficult material and questions, tough even for a native English speaker, but Zhi Fu is determined. We begin studying together. Rob calls him "your Shakespeare boy." We read passages of Shakespeare and Milton and Walt Whitman, Zhi Fu sounding the words out painfully, then searching my face for the meaning. I try to simplify and explain, and we plod through the questions, many requiring essay answers. My hopes for him sag, and I know he's discouraged, but tenacity and "I will work very hard" are Chinese trademarks, so we move along. Slowly.

The class is especially heavy in girls. Yao Lan speaks fine English. Pronunciation is still a big problem, and I hate to interrupt the flow of conversation to correct, but often I simply don't understand. Since their high school English teachers never heard it spoken, I'm not too surprised. But Yao Lan is fairly easy to comprehend, and she has a lot to say. I want to encourage her, but others who are shyer need the spotlight too.

One Monday after class I approach Ruth, one of the new Chinese English teachers. Her responsibility is the new language lab, and I ask if she could show me around. She agrees and unlocks the door; we step inside. Pointing to a pile of cloth on the floor, she tells me to slip a pair of "socks" over my shoes to protect the equipment. About forty desks, each with earphones, face the front desk on the usual raised platform. The teacher's desk has a large cassette tape deck, each student's desk a small one. English majors come once a day to listen to some of the dullest tapes I've ever heard. Truly! The tapes have nothing to do with anything we're teaching or material the students get from the Chinese English teachers. They cannot speak into a mike and listen to themselves. They must try to stay awake listening to highly improbable conversations read by bored people who sound as if they come from various parts of England. Our students want to speak with an American accent, they tell us, and the English Department head, who was brought in for show at the beginning of the year for a few days from an important Shanghai university, told us he wants only *American* English taught.

"What do you do, Ruth?" I ask, "while the students are in here?"

"Nothing. I listen to tapes and can turn on different student's earphones to hear what they're hearing."

"Where do these tapes come from?"

Ruth pauses. "I don't know. They are required for our students."

38

RICE HARVEST AND CHEN YING CHUN

The weather is beginning to cool off, a huge relief after the brutal summer heat and humidity. Lately we've been treated to a slice of Chinese village life played out behind our apartment as the villagers process the rice harvest in the village square just beyond the canal. Every few days long sampans bring baskets of raw rice from the fields. The villagers spread it out onto the cement and hard-packed dirt and rake it out to dry for a day or so. Chickens and ducks waddle across it, and we wonder why everyone in China isn't sick! Apparently the rice is still in husks because the villagers sweep it up and pile it onto screen-topped bamboo tables. Five or six women winnow the rice as large fans underneath the tables blow the chaff away. They bundle up what remains, and a new batch is brought in. Everyone seems to know his/her assignment exactly. No one hurries. The long boats pole in, gliding to the bank just as the last batch is bundled up. It reminds me of a courtly dance, much rehearsed, so I imagine harvesting and winnowing haven't changed much in centuries.

The weather shift brings something else. Flies! We have fly swatters in every room, but we're battling a real infestation. We can't figure out where they come from since the windows are tight. We leave the patio door open with its deluxe fitted screen, so they can't get in there. The only place might be under the front door, so we put towels there. We must've killed fifty yesterday! We're surrounded by standing water full of refuse and floating garbage. Nasty little buggers! I hope they'll die off now that the weather is cooling.

I stopped on the way home from a class the other day to watch a fisherman drift his boat along the canal, checking his nets. I'd seen the long nets forming Vs in the canal, funneling the fish into a narrow channel. Could anyone actually *eat* a fish from this filthy water? Could a fish actually *live* in it? Apparently so, since the fisherman stood in his narrow boat, pulled up a long cylindrical net, and reached in to let several good-sized fish flop into his boat.

I've resumed my Chinese lessons. It's been almost three months since my last afternoon with Chen Ying Chun, and I've missed her. I believe she's glad to see us again too. Rob bows out, claiming his students need to practice their English anyhow, but my teeth are clenched and I'm determined to improve my Chinglish. He loves to joke with Ying Chun, and she obviously enjoys the fun. Her English is improving. I wonder if I'll ever get beyond cretin grunts. I'm in catch-up mode, and Ying Chun wants to gossip. "Tell me about your son's wedding." She wants to hear everything. We have pictures to share. She gazes at the lovely bride and examines her dress. "In China, brides traditionally wear red dresses, but now most brides want a Western white dress too. Often they have both." We've seen a few Chinese wedding shops in our wanderings where brides are fussed over and fancy hairstyles created. They evidently spend a lot of money on dresses and wedding preparations.

Ying Chun turns serious. "I would like to have a daughter." She has a son, maybe five years old. The only reaction I get when I ask about her husband is that her small nose wrinkles disdainfully. Of course, I know about the one-child policy in vastly overpopulated China. "What would happen if you and your husband had a second child?"

"Oh, we would be punished."

I push a little harder. "In what way?"

"No more money!" She shakes her head sadly, signaling the end of the conversation. For years people here have been controlled through their *danwei*, work group, which controls food coupons, permission to live in a particular city, even permission to have a job. They can't just move and work somewhere else or scrounge food. They had to have the proper credentials and coupons for all that in the past, though I understand life is not quite so harsh now. Young people *are* gaining more mobility, but wages and monetary support are closely controlled. Children are deeply loved here. They call an only son "the little emperor." They cherish daughters too I think, and the children seem to know they are loved, even though almost all go into child care, often all week, day and night, because both parents must work. Grandmother and Grandfather are the chief caregivers for the children at home. Young couples usually move in with the husband's parents when they marry (and much later than in America). It's a matter of economics. Housing isn't available, so families double up.

Ying Chun and I converse in a peculiar combination of English and Chinese. Now she wants me to buckle down and study Chinese by the book. My progress is slow, and I squirm to carry on a free conversation at the market or with new friends. She's firm, though, and we plod through the wretched books. We giggle as we study, and

I sometimes ask for special phrases for a particular need.

For her English we use a few of my textbooks, but mostly we chat. Like most Chinese, she can read English quite well, so if she doesn't understand something, I write it to clarify the meaning. I get a peek into her life as we talk.

Like most of the teachers at the new university, she has an apartment in a building in Ningbo set aside for Sunli teachers. She takes her little son to school every morning on her bicycle. He's one of the lucky ones who comes home to his mother and father at night. After dropping him off at school she bikes to the bus stop for the special bus that makes the one hour run from Ningbo to the school each morning. She repeats the process every night. The bus leaves the campus at four, which means she reaches the bus stop at five, grabs her bike, goes to the market for the day's dinner, then picks up her son and gets home at about six to cook supper. She's a petite woman with big round glasses. She pulls her hair back in a severe style, but like most young Chinese women always wears high heels and an attractive dress. Chinese women even ride bicycles with grace. During the summer months many wear a delicate white shawl to protect their shoulders and arms from the sun. The shawls and the flowing skirts flutter as the women skim serenely along in the mobs of bikes that crowd every Chinese street. I can easily picture Ying Chun negotiating the traffic on her bicycle every day.

The new dean of the sparkling Foreign Language Department invites us to dinner at a restaurant one night early in the term. He's on the staff of a Shanghai university, on loan to our school in name only. He is very nice, speaks excellent English, and taught two years in America. He wants to make big changes here but spends very little time on campus. He says he wants only American English taught, fortunate for us. Most of the language tapes available are British English, so pronunciation and spelling and even some syntax are different. He asks if we are willing to teach writing classes for English majors as well as our oral language classes. We're learning to play the *maybe* game Jenny plays so well with us.

We explain that we've been yearning for our own desks in the English office so that we can have office hours for students with difficulties. Is that possible? Yes, he's sure he can arrange it. And we would like an honors class for some of our former students no longer entitled to English classes but avid for challenging instruction in the language. Can that also be arranged? We say we're willing to work longer hours. Yes, he feels sure that can happen. So beginning next term we'll design a creative writing course (my field) and a business writing course (Rob's bailiwick).

39

SETTLING IN AND
CHRISTMAS SHOPPING

Sometimes I think I'm getting a grip on my role here, and both Rob and I begin to think we actually have something valuable to contribute. As soon as I relax, though, I see clearly that we receive a great deal more than we give. Our Chinese hosts are extremely gracious and solicitous of our welfare, but more than that, the students, now that they're over their fear of us, honor us with a devotion and trust I could not even have imagined nine months ago. My fears are not entirely gone. The memory of the violent explosion of hate after the US bombed the Chinese Embassy in Kosovo last May lies just below the surface. Certainly no one we know personally threatened us, and our students' forgiving response was astonishing. Still I can't forget that we're foreigners in a country recently given to ferocious brutality against its own people, eager to leap into the future while clinging to a monolithic and suspicious government. I do not dwell on such thoughts, but sometimes they creep unbidden into my heart.

In the still hours, a sudden weight of utter isolation crushes me. The separation from our family and friends, from the familiar, sometimes crashes down on me during the dark hours. I waited a long time for grandchildren. Now that we have nine-year-old Jordan, I see her bounce and grin in every Chinese child we pass. And I miss her! Wes, her father, went through a heartbreaking divorce when she was only one, so we spilled love and support on them during her earliest years. I see again his fumbling, male hands doing his best to braid her long, tawny hair. He tried to be cheerful as he took her to daycare years ago when we could not be there and he had to go to work. Most of the time, I bask in the attentions and needs of our students here, and I focus on the joys and successes of each day—but there are at times long, quiet hours at night.

It's October and time to think about Christmas shopping! A package takes about eight weeks to creep across the ocean, even though postage is incredibly high. I see a chance to stroll through the exotic marketplaces here and select unusual gifts for our children and for Jordan. Two problems: time is limited, and we haven't seen any exotic marketplaces.

In downtown Ningbo, stores present block after block of uninteresting displays of electrical parts, hardware, cheap clothing and umbrellas. Two or three department stores offer merchandise that tries to look upscale but is short on quality. Chuga has one or two variety stores beside the fruit and vegetable vendors and the hawkers of chunks of meat and live birds. The stores retain a Communist mentality, and clerks *literally* sleep with their heads on the counters over dusty displays of hardware, shoe soles, combs, or baby clothes. When they're awake, they neither know nor care about the products and spend their days in utter boredom. Enterprising entrepreneurs hustle on the streets but offer only cheap plastic kitchenware or garlic. None of it appeals to us as Christmas gifts. Our mailing deadline looms.

Finally, we find a lightweight Chinese checkers game for Jordan. Yes, they really *do* play Chinese checkers in China, and our students are good at it. We spend a whole afternoon in a department store, scouring the women's department for silk scarves. I learn the word for *silk*, and the clerks seem to understand my request, yet shake their heads regretfully, *Mei Yo* (Don't have it). Anything of good quality must be shipped out of the country since nothing in the stores is attractive. I finally spot some scarves that look like silk. A tag clearly says *silk* in English, so I point to the stack. An agitated conversation starts behind the counter, almost as if I've beat them at the game of hiding exactly what I want. I make my purchases and find some ties for the men—not thrilling, but I'm getting desperate. Now we face the hurdle of shipping the gifts.

We scrounge some boxes, and I buy some pretty wrapping paper and intriguing ribbons cleverly designed as only the Chinese could. If I pull on both ends, the ribbon balloons up into a perfect bow. Lucy, fortunately, knocks on the door just then. I'm ready to wrap some gifts and tape the box shut. "No, no, Mrs. McKee. You must not wrap anything. I will go with you to the post office. They will give you the proper box. They must inspect everything. Then they will watch you pack your box. Put it all into a bag."

After classes, we three set out on the bus with our bag of gifts for America. Lucy admires our selections and is happy to help us. She's sure we can't negotiate the Ningbo post office without her, and she's probably right. Our little post office in Chuga can't handle a package to the United States, she tells us. We change buses at the main terminal and bounce along in the double-decker into the heart of the city. We've seen the main post office on a busy corner many times but have never ventured inside. Today Lucy leads the advance.

There is slightly more order than in the Chuga branch. Shouting people gather at the windows and cluster around a raised kiosk at one end of the building. Lucy leads us to it, shouldering her way through the crowd and thrusting our bag of gifts over the high counter at the disdainful man behind it. He glances briefly at the contents, selects some boxes, and pushes everything back to Lucy. She leads us to one side of the counter where we edge between people busy packing things into uniformly-sized boxes. The man, on a perch slightly above us, keeps a watchful eye on what goes into the boxes. We may not put giftwrapped items inside, so I regretfully put our gifts in bare along with the gift wrap and fancy bows. They'll have to wrap their own Christmas gifts this year. We then return the boxes to the monitor, who expertly tapes them shut. The loss of privacy and the inspection would cause an outrage in America. Here it's just the usual way of doing business.

Addressing the packages challenges Lucy. She writes our return address in Chinese. I open my mouth to tell her she's written it in the wrong place, but she seems to know what she's doing. Then we write the addresses in English where Lucy indicates. She adds some Chinese in the upper left-hand corner. I shake my head and wonder how two cultures could be so completely opposite one another. Lucy leads us to a window for packages going outside China. We get our wallets out, and the sticker-shock is pretty big. But at least and at last our gifts are on their way.

It's strange to think of Christmas, not only because it's still two months away but also because Christmas is just another day here. Very few jolly Santa Claus posters appear in shop windows. Some have been there ever since we came last February. Santa has nothing to do with December 25th and is simply a marketing tool for the

Chinese. I begin planning a campaign of my own to have a Christmas party on campus and introduce to our students the person whose birthday we celebrate.

40

WEI WEI AND THE
ENGLISH LESSONS

Wei Wei is four. Maybe five. My head starts to whirl when a Chinese friend tries to explain how they calculate age. Some say a baby is already a year old when he's born. Since everyone turns one year older during the Chinese New Year celebration in January/February, determining actual age gets a bit muddled for me. At any rate, Wei Wei is a pistol. His black, intelligent eyes dart around a room, taking in everything like a clever crow. His hair is in a buzz cut, probably because no one can catch him to run a comb through it. His parents want me to teach him English. Zeng Jia Min, James, the pencil-slim man responsible for recruiting foreigners, particularly Americans, to do business or teach in the Ningbo area, is his father. We like James very much. He's been our trip planner and has traveled with us, proudly giving us an insider's view of China. I can't refuse his request. I want to ask why he doesn't ask LuJean to introduce him to English. She's been a pre-kindergarten teacher for years and has the know-how and patience for the job, but he's chosen me, so I need to be gracious.

I *do* plead with LuJean for some suggestions. She smiles sweetly and tells me to proceed just as I would with an American child: start with simple pictures of perhaps an animal and say the name. I remember a set of paper dolls of simple farm and barnyard animals previous American teachers left among our teaching supplies. "But, LuJean," I wail, "you know Wei Wei! He's a bundle of energy! How do I hold his attention?"

She smiles that kindergarten teacher smile and says, "You'll figure something out."

The evening arrives. Wei Wei, his father, his mother and Carr, James' sidekick who also accompanied us on several trips, arrive. Mrs. Carr (I don't know if Carr is his first or last name, and no one introduces his wife) along with their daughter introduced to us as Mary, all walk into our apartment. Mary is a little older than Wei Wei, I think. She goes almost immediately to my keyboard and sits to play a quite difficult piece. Her parents strain to contain their pride. Apparently I'm to teach Mary English too. Everyone sits down in our living room, and all eyes turn to me with a child on either side of me on the loveseat. Carr speaks no English; James' wife also shakes her head shyly. I pick up the stack of animal cutouts and offer them for Wei Wei to choose one. He pulls out and examines a pig. "Pig," I say and nod for him to try.

"Pig-uh," Mrs. Carr instantly offers.

"Pig-uh," Wei Wei repeats. This is going to be harder than I thought, what with audience participation, especially since that wretched trailing *uh* that follows the hard consonant sounds is a given.

I don't want to offend Mrs. Carr but again say clearly, "Pig."

"Pig-uh." Again Mrs. Carr encourages Wei Wei and Mary, who dutifully repeat, "Pig-uh." I say the Chinese word for pig which delights the children, and we try to outdo one another in pig noises. Mrs. Carr leans back, a bit startled.

Wei Wei looks a little puzzled at the next picture: a cow. I realize he's never seen one! Farm animals familiar to American children are not necessarily so to Chinese kids. I hurry past that one. "Chicken."

"Chee-ken," the children chime. Mrs. Carr is leery of our chicken imitations, so I think I've succeeded in scaring her off. We go through the stack, and I concentrate on five, hoping they can remember them for next time. It's enough. The proud parents bundle their precious children into their coats; they wrap up too for the winter chill and leave, apparently pleased with the first lesson since they set up a regular weekly time to show up.

As soon as they leave I make Robert *promise* to use his charm to deflect the parents' attention and keep them occupied while I work with the children. If I'm going to make any headway, I need to do it without the help of four eager parents, two who don't speak English and one who thinks she does.

James doesn't own a car. Very few Chinese do, but the better off rent cars for trips, often with a driver. Anyone well connected with the Party has the use of black cars for business, broadly defined. James is a Party man, I'm sure. He generally has a car and driver. One evening, though, the two families stun us when they roar up to our door on two huge motorcycles! They're outfitted in leather jackets, wives and kids stacked behind the men. It seems so out of character for them, but they grin and take off their helmets as they come in.

Sometimes we serve dinner to everyone before we buckle down to an English lesson. James has complained about the food he has to endure on recruiting trips to Canada or the United States. He has a delicate stomach but eats like a lumberjack when we travel together in China. All that makes me nervous the first time they come to dinner with us. He clearly thinks American food is poison, so I cast through my culinary repertoire to produce something palatable for James and company. I've learned that most Chinese like mashed potatoes, which are new to them. James surprises me again when he piles the butter onto a volcano of mashed potatoes. Another Chinese butter-lover! In fact, James mixes about equal parts butter and mashed potatoes! Chicken is a pretty safe bet, so I stir-fry chunks of chicken with various spices and vegetables.

I decide to go out on a limb and offer our hoarded lemon Jell-O with sliced bananas, certain to be new to their palates. The adults are polite about the Jell-O, but I make a hit with the children. The jiggling stuff has a certain play value. I bought a rather heavy, cake-like substance, maybe a distant cousin to our pound cake (remember that there are no private ovens in China, but some stores sell "cake"), and make a lemon sauce to drizzle over it for dessert. I breathe relief after our first meal when James, Carr, and their wives lick their plates clean. The kids ask for more too. They all tried using forks, but I have emergency chopsticks on hand, which they gratefully accept.

Rob does his assignment well, and I have a freer hand in working and playing with the little ones in one room, the adults deep in conversation in another. Mary has a sharp mind and watches my lips constantly. Wei Wei is more intrigued with what's in the room, so we name things together. He's always on the move, so we make up a game of hopping, skipping, and walking while we repeat the words. I'm not sure how much English they're learning, but I look forward to the evenings together.

James has invited us to come to Wei Wei's kindergarten to speak with his classmates. Of course, they don't speak English, but smiles are an international language, so one afternoon one of James' cars picks us up and whisks us into Ningbo. The classroom is neat and colorful, and the wiggly children sit at their small desks with their hands folded when we arrive. The teacher smiles nervously and comes to shake our hands. She doesn't speak any English either but has prepared the children to sing for us. We applaud their song, and then Rob and I begin working the room like Southern politicians getting out the vote. He starts on one side of the room, I on the other, leaning way over to shake tiny hands. We beam and say hello, waiting for the children to respond with the one word all Chinese seem to know: Hello! Excitement mounts and the little bodies bob up and down like Halloween apples in a barrel, waiting their turn. I watch Wei Wei out of the corner of my eye. He pretends indifference to our instant celebrity. When I get to him, I speak slowly and ask him to show everyone how to hop. Since his culture prizes the community above the individual, Wei Wei recognizes a rare moment to shine, and he *hops*! We encourage all the children to follow. Then I whisper to Wei Wei to skip and to say the word out loud in English. He beams and shouts the word and demonstrates. When the bedlam quiets, I tell Wei Wei to walk, and he orchestrates the diminuendo with skill and obvious pleasure. He spoke in English, and they understood!

41

THANKSGIVING AND CHRISTMAS

A strange thing happened today during one class. Not alarming. Just strange. As I was trying to give the kids a feel for when to use *a*, and when *the* feels better (tough for Chinese whose language has no articles), the classroom door thudded open, and a couple of men burst into the room with huge shoulder-mounted cameras. I'd noticed faces peering furtively through the window in the door but dismissed it. The men began taking pictures without saying a word to anyone. I decided to ignore them. They didn't stay long, and the students paid no attention. Sandra and Woody had mentioned that a TV crew once almost moved in with them for a day and filmed every move they made. It's hard to remember that we're such oddities here, foreigners, so I chalked the photo op up to Chinese curiosity. But it did feel strange. I guess the men assumed I couldn't understand them even if they did try to explain, but it would have been nice had they tried. They may've been surprised.

Morag has been feeling a little blue. We discover that yesterday was her 46th birthday, and she feels a bit lonely and forgotten. The university leaders gave her a cake and some flowers, but we think the day might be dreary, since she's arrived so recently. So we go with her to downtown Ningbo to have dinner and celebrate. She went to town the day before and befriended some young Chinese, promised she'd come back Saturday night. We load her birthday cake into a taxi, and off we go. Her new friends appear in the restaurant with flowers, and we karaoke "Happy birthday to *you-u-u-u*," eat meat dumplings, and drink apple juice and Pepsi.

Wine and alcohol are rarely served here. At first I thought our Chinese hosts had noticed that we don't drink alcohol and were being courteous. But a quick glance around most restaurants shows that it's not customary to drink alcohol with meals. I see rows of liquor bottles in stores but can truly say that we've never witnessed public drunkenness. Bars and nightclubs are few and far between. At any rate, Morag feels properly feted, and we have a delightful evening with people who enjoy trying out their school English on us.

Thanksgiving is approaching. Rob wants me to produce a traditional feast for some Chinese friends. Fine! I take pictures of a turkey to class and try to describe the bird to them. They go into paroxysms of laughter when I gobble! In other words, no such animal exists in China. Even a mutant chicken needn't worry about Thanksgiving, since an oven to roast it in is beyond the reach or imagination of a Chinese cook. My husband rhapsodizes about pumpkin pie, and I know there *are* pumpkins here somewhere because we've eaten some nasty little pumpkin balls on several occasions. Even if I *could* locate the ingredients, I'd have to bake the pie in the same non-existent oven.

Of course, Thanksgiving Day is just another Thursday class day here. Still we have five members of the university staff in for noon dinner, my standard stir-fried chicken with vegetables, mashed potatoes, fruit salad and bread. Mr. Wang, the school vice president who is also our neighbor, joins us for lunch along with Sam, another administrator, Chen Ying Chun, my Chinese teacher, Jenny, and Morag. Since it is Thanksgiving, I smile and insist they eat with forks. They do pretty well and seem to enjoy the food.

Other than having guests for lunch, it's a normal day of classes, grading papers, and preparing lessons. I find some pictures of early Thanksgivings and modern American families gathering around a table. I decide to bite the bullet and tell them the pilgrim story and why we call it Thanksgiving. "The courageous people who survived that first difficult winter almost starving in a lonely, new world wanted to thank the native people who shared and helped them find and plant food. They were grateful too to their God for helping them. They fled a government that forbade them from worshipping as they chose. They felt richly blessed by God and hopeful for the future." Sympathetic nods.

Occasionally, privately, a young boy or girl asks us, "Do you go to church in America?" or "What do you do there?" We try to answer carefully, so no one feels pressured.

One evening, Bonnie, a frequent visitor and classmate of Lucy's, asks, "Do you have a Bible?"

"Yes, Bonnie, we do. And we read it carefully and often. It means a lot to us."

She asks, "May I see it?" Rob squirms in his chair, recalling the cautions against proselyting in our agreement with the Chinese government. We knew we could bring one Bible into China for our personal use, which is certainly what ours is for. I bring it out of the bedroom. Bonnie holds it reverently, and beams up at me, "I too am a Christian. In my hometown there are many Christians."

Really? Are you able to meet often?"

"Not often," she says, "but it is getting better."

I'm afraid to pursue the conversation much further, fearful of getting Bonnie into trouble, but finish with, "Bible study is central to our lives and helps us many ways." She nods and hands the Bible back to me. Maybe that was when I decided to ask if we could plan a Christmas party for the kids.

"Jenny, we'd like to have a Christmas party for all of our students." She smiles her *maybe* smile but tells us that some students once asked to have a Christmas party and the college president said, "No, Christmas is not a Chinese holiday." The president is different now with perhaps a different answer.

CHRISTMAS PREPARATIONS AND THE BEIJING OPERA

As the Christmas season approaches, we're asked many questions. We point out first that it's a very important religious holiday.

"What do you do in America at Christmas?"

"Well, we give presents to loved ones and have parties and pretty decorations."

"Why?"

"It helps us remember an important time more than two thousand years ago, the birth of Jesus Christ, who we believe is the son of God." The kids are always excited to learn more about our customs, so we tell Christmas stories, including the biblical account of the birth of Christ. We back away from anything that sounds like preaching or even a discussion of Christianity. They told us at our training center to avoid religion and politics because there probably is at least one student in each class charged with reporting anything objectionable. Even in private conversations, we're cautious. We don't want to get anyone in trouble by even the appearance of recruiting. We sense, though, a real hunger in the young people for spiritual food. What a joke on me! I who shy away from discussing my religion with others *yearn* to pass the conviction and tender strength that I hold so dear along to them. And I cannot.

Jenny comes to our apartment at lunchtime to give us the news. We have permission to give a Christmas party. Rob and I are like two children planning a wingding. "But we need a tree! We've got to have a Christmas tree!"

"I can get a tree for you." Jenny! Her husband works in landscaping and can get us a tree.

"Wonderful! It must be a pine tree of some sort, Jenny, as tall as he can get. And a live tree in a pot would be marvelous. We could plant it outside after Christmas to remind everyone of the childish American teachers who threw a Christmas party in China."

Jenny seems to share our enthusiasm, and her husband, whom we've never met, complies. In a couple of days *two* pine trees, each about six feet tall, appear in front of our apartment. They're very heavy with huge root balls in massive ceramic pots. When they first appear, we're pretty busy with classes, and since lifting them is a formidable task for Rob alone, he arranges for two of his husky students to come at one in the afternoon to help him move them inside. I notice them outside our window as late as 12:30 p.m. and begin to get lunch together. I look out again around 12:50—and the trees are gone! After a search we find them standing in two holes, ready for planting but still in their pots. Apparently the landscapers found them and assumed they were to be planted outside. The landscapers, nowhere in sight, must have taken a lunch break. Just then the students show up, so we take the tree we want inside our apartment, and the students lug the other one to the room where we'll have the Christmas party. I wonder what will befuddle the gardeners more, trees appearing and disappearing mysteriously or seeing through the windows that the foreigners have taken them *inside*.

So we have two Christmas trees to decorate. Never mind that they're shaped a lot like light bulbs, ballooned at the top and tapered off toward the bottom. We must face the matter of decorations and lights. A search through Ningbo shops and department stores yields paltry results. We find little intended for Christmas ornaments but buy fanciful key rings and other things never meant to grace a Christmas tree. Lights! We must have tiny white lights. Robert volunteers to make a swing through Ningbo in search of lights one afternoon when I'm tied up in classes.

When he returns he has a long story to tell: "I went from shop to shop, flailing my arms and trying to draw pictures of what we want. Finally in a small electrical shop I pointed to several things, and they dragged out what they thought I wanted, but we just couldn't seem to make a match. One of the shopkeepers motioned for me to wait and went running out the door. Finally, a young Caucasian man came in and spoke Mandarin to the proprietor, then turned to me and asked in perfect English if he could help me. What a relief! I explained that I was looking for Christmas tree lights. He looked very puzzled and said, 'What are Christmas tree lights?' I thought I had fallen down Alice's rabbit hole. Anyway, I explained and he understood, making some comment about having heard of Christmas lights before. I asked where he was from and he said, 'Israel.' Wouldn't you know, I find what is probably the only Jewish expatriate businessman in Ningbo to translate information about a Christian holiday into Chinese. But he helped me get exactly what I wanted."

Now that we have lights and a few ornaments, it strikes me that our students can create fanciful and unique ornaments with paper and ribbon, so we organize ornament parties, and the excitement starts to bubble through the campus.

On the business side of our lives, Linda, acting head of the English Department, calls us in to follow up on the visiting department head's request that we tackle some writing classes next term. "You could design the classes any way you like. It will mean much reading and correcting for you, we understand, so we will give your eight hours a week of business students to Morag."

I calculate quickly in my head. Offering writing courses to all the English majors will mean not only at least twelve additional hours of teaching a week, but also meeting with them more often. The eye-burning hours of identical errors and illegible handwriting loom too. I hear Rob agree to the switch. Outside the office he's excited. "Susie, you could handle the more creative, artsy stuff, and I'll teach the business and more formal writing."

"Who grades the papers?"

"Well, we'll split it right down the middle," he offers. "I'll grade the letters I assign, and you take care of the essays."

"Now *there's* a fifty/fifty split!" Enthusiasm must be blocking his ears. He doesn't hear the dripping sarcasm, but the possibilities of melding written and spoken language and, best of all, having each section at least three hours a week is exhilarating to think about. There is even a textbook we can use if we choose. I flip through it and find some short, good stories. Best of all, there are copies for everybody. They can do homework.

We discuss asking for the new classroom with the computer and screen up front. Rob agreed to the longer hours too quickly, I think. He's a master bargainer for eggs and supplies, but he caved in too quickly this time. We return to the office and ask, explaining how we want to use the new technology. We need the large room with the computer for the first lecture/discussion when two classes meet together, then two smaller rooms for practical work. Much head-scratching and toothy air sucking by the administrators. Then it's agreed upon! We get our badge of honor—one black marker for the whiteboards in the new building.

"Where can we get a key to the computer room?" I ask as we're about to leave.

Shock and confusion. "Oh, no key! You must apply to Mrs. Wu. She will train you to use the computer system, and only she has a key. You must ask her to unlock the room before class." I begin plotting to woo Mrs. Wu to get a duplicate key, although I have no clue where that might be done in China.

Meanwhile, on Sunday evening Lucy and five of her classmates "kidnap" me and take me to a Chinese opera in the village right across the river. Rob and I have seen snippets of the Beijing or its cousin, the Shaoxing opera, on TV and giggled at the posturing, the wild costumes, and the outlandish mask-like makeup. I ask the students about the ancient form of entertainment and expect the half-hidden sneer I might get from an American adolescent. But "Oh, yes," one girl says, "I remember in my village when I was a little girl, one winter day the group of actors came. They always came when the field work was done, so we were eager for something to do. We all brought our chairs to watch the plays, sometimes the same one many times. We know the stories very well. It was a happy time in our childhood."

The girls urge Robert to join us, but he grins and shakes his head. That presents a thorny problem. Our organization cautions volunteers about going separate ways. Obviously, there's a safety issue. We get guidelines but have 40 or 50 year patterns of paired behavior. I *know* Robert is no fan of the opera, and the exaggerated posturing and high-pitched overacting will never lure him. My curiosity about the unfamiliar, on the other hand, tantalizes me. I *am*, after all, Eve's daughter.

I walk with Lucy and the girls across the quiet campus to the gate. We turn left, suddenly hugging the side of the frenetic street to get to the village only a few feet from our backdoor but across the stagnant canal. Fumes from the jerry-rigged trucks and buses choke us, and I feel like a pinball target for the bicycles and pedicabs swinging out impatiently to pass lumbering trucks. Over the traffic horns Lucy says, "It is really sad that these operas are disappearing in China. Now villages have TVs, so the village elders do not offer to pay the actors to come." It's completely dark, and even though we're bundled up against the sudden winter, the dank cold creeps through the soles of my hiking boots and into my legs. It's impossible to avoid the ice-crusted mud. At last we turn into the street that leads into the village. She admits she isn't really sure just how to get to the village square, and we have to stop twice to ask directions. This daughter of Eve begins to marvel at my elders' wisdom, and my shaking isn't entirely due to the cold. But soon we hear the gongs crashing and follow the noise. Stepping into that square was like following Alice through the looking glass.

A huge open-sided tent rises from the concrete. A carnival atmosphere percolates through the milling crowd. Hundreds of villagers have dragged bamboo chairs, and standees add to the crush. Children dart between aunties' legs. There is absolutely no place to squeeze in, yet Lucy does, pulling me behind her. She leans over to whisper something in the ear of a seated woman, who leaps to her feet and gestures that I'm to sit in her chair. I'm terribly embarrassed, but Lucy smiles and tugs me down. She backs away, and I'm left to see reenactments of timeless Chinese myths. Yes, the gaudy robes are threadbare; the whitened faces with garish eyes and drooping, fake beards poorly fitted to the actors are obvious. There are green faces, too, and purple, always with gargoyle eyes or improbable features painted on. I can't follow the stories, but the performers twirl, sometimes in fury, sometimes shrieking comical asides to the audience who are certainly in on the jokes. The people around me are either hugely entertained and absorbed in the musicians' onstage leaps and whangs or talk noisily through the performance with their neighbors.

All the while, the ancient lady next to me keeps up a running commentary in my left ear. Her face is a benevolent prune. It doesn't help my comprehension that she has no teeth, but she pats my arm, reassuring us both. I try my best Mandarin on her, but she pays little heed. Hours later on the way home, Lucy giggles and says that they speak a strange dialect in the village that even she can't understand, but she admits she enjoyed watching us. "The grandmother did not understand one word you said, nor did you understand her, did you, Mrs. McKee? It's okay."

Back in the warm apartment we huddle around the heater and try to describe the evening to Robert. The troupe stays almost a week, a loud clang announcing each evening's performance. The sounds echo across the water long into the night. From our bedroom window we can see a bit of backstage as the actors whirl down the steps of the stage or sit looking bored on low bamboo stools, waiting for their cues. Early one morning we hear urgent voices. Across the canal the whole acting group, maybe 30 or 40 people, stands beside the canal as huge poles (for the tent?) and boxes are packed into long sampans, and they depart for another village and another performance.

43

WINTER AND LING YA FEN'S PARTY

H umidity and condensation are simply facts of life here. Water literally drips down inside the windows, and black mold forms above our bed on the beautiful new walls. Clothes are often wet inside, and Rob's been known to take my hair dryer and blow it full blast inside his coat before he puts it on. Mildew and mold form on everything. The lovely wall hanging painting of a long-legged crane and the tip of a pine bough (all symbols of longevity) decorates the wall facing our front door. The Office of Foreign Affairs where James and his boss work gave it to Rob on his birthday last May. At first gray tendrils seemed to creep and lengthen in the image, but a tentative brush with my hand confirmed that mildew had invaded the fabric. I brush it and hang it in the sun regularly. It's *wet* here!

Winter has clamped down. The canal is iced over. Rob, in the diligent pursuit of his self-appointed laundry specialist duties, decides early in the morning to mop the tiled floor of the deck before hanging out the wash. He announces when he comes in that that wasn't the most thought-through thing he'd ever done. The deck is a sheet of ice, and he slid around on it hanging the clothes up. The icy wind zings through our bones and reminds us that our students don't have the warm coats we brought with us. On the campus, no rooms are heated except ours and a few administrative offices. My heart aches for the kids as they pile on sweaters and thin coats. Their hands, especially the girls', are cracked and blue from the cold, even with mittens. There is no place for them to get out of the cold except our apartment. With the Christmas tree and the cozy warmth, we're about the best game in town. I'd like to think our scintillating personalities draw them, but my growing comprehension of Mandarin tells me maybe that's not entirely true.

As Christmas nears, the students come more often in the evenings. Lucy shyly gives Rob and me scarves she knitted. Linda, a frequent visitor and classmate of Lucy's, brings a live plant I'm sure was the prototype for the plant in *Little Shop of Horrors*. I don't *think* it's a man-eater, but it certainly looks like one! Our students know Christmas is coming and that it's a family gathering time. While they don't understand what it's all about, they want to fill in our lonely spots as much as they can.

This evening Rob plays Chinese checkers with Lucy and Linda while I fix dinner. Bonnie arrives, and the girls play while Rob and I eat, since they ate in the dining hall. Another game begins with a lot of quiet strategy and laughter. As I clean up the kitchen I hear them say to one another in Chinese, "It's too early to go back to our room and go to bed and too late to go to the classroom to study. We'd rather stay here where it's warm and play." So Rob and I are not necessarily the human magnets I hoped. They ask permission to stay, and the box of Hershey's kisses on the coffee table cinches the deal. They giggle happily when I spill the beans and tell them I understood what they said.

The powerhouse lady (whom we've never met), the mover and shaker behind Sunli group, invites us to a pre-Christmas party in Ningbo. She's behind the changes at the college soon-to-be university. Since December 25th is just another day in China, we're surprised at the invitation's holiday emphasis. Ling Ya Fen and her board of directors are opening their first university level school with our college, but she heads up several primary and secondary schools. They are considered very advanced, like the one where we lived last summer. China is experimenting with private enterprise, and she definitely has the idea!

At the downtown restaurant we are amazed when we're escorted into the private dining room and see ten to twelve non-Chinese faces among the Chinese. We and Morag meet Americans, Australians, and Canadians who teach at the elementary schools and secondary school Miss Ling runs. She *bounds* over to us, hugs us enormously, chattering in rapid Mandarin. She speaks not a word of English though it is important in her curriculum. (She sent her son to Australia to study English.) Then she gives each teacher a Christmas-paper-wrapped gift and waits expectantly while we open them. We unwrap framed photos of ourselves teaching in the classroom! Then she speaks to Robert and me through an interpreter and says she loves the way we teach and the energy and expertise we bring to the job. She says she has seen a video of us in action (and stills, obviously). So *that* is what the mysterious visitors were doing in my class that day with their monster cameras. Rob and I discuss the surprise on the way home and guess it's better to send someone with a camera and let a group evaluate what he records than to send just one person to pass judgment on teaching skills.

We walk a fine line with our Christmas party plans. Because of the mounting interest, we get permission to have two parties, one for the English Corner participants and anyone on campus who wants to come, and one for the English majors. The English Corner party comes first, the Tuesday before Christmas. The second pine tree stands in one corner of the dingy room where groups gather for special occasions. We've swept the cobwebs away, and for days kids have come to create ornaments from foil paper and other bits we bring in. The tree's strung with our hard-won tiny white lights, and the magic of a Christmas tree shines from the children's faces as they gaze at the first one they've ever seen. I say *children* even though they are nineteen or twenty years old, but their eyes sparkle as children's eyes should at the wonder of the new sight.

The night of the party more than 120 students stream into the room. The bitter night cold seeps into the room but is soon forgotten with laughter at the mechanical Santa we stationed at the door to greet everyone with a tinny rendition of "Jingle Bells." Candles burn in the windowsills, and magazine pictures of Christmas trees and Christmas scenes decorate the flaking walls. The aroma of oranges and chocolates on the tables draws the guests further into the room. At a signal from Rob, I turn out the lights and turn the Christmas tree on. The students' joyful collective gasp is payment enough for the hours of preparing and decorating.

We hauled my keyboard from the apartment and start the evening teaching them Christmas carols. The only song everyone knows is "Jingle Bells," and everyone joins in lustily. We talk a little about Santa and teach them "Rudolf" but go on with stories of gifts, love, and unselfishness this time of the year. I think we can't possibly have the birthday party without telling them about the Guest of Honor, so we read the story of Jesus' birth and talk about His impact on mankind. Rob and I sing "Silent Night," and a few voices join ours. Then more voices. As more hesitant voices sing "Sleep in heavenly peace, sleep in heavenly peace," I wonder if my heart can contain the joy I feel. I discover I can be completely content here with these people and miss my own children and grandchild enormously at the same time.

But there are more plans for the evening. We asked the students ahead of time to bring one wrapped gift worth eight yuan (one dollar) or less and collected them as they came in. I imagine Rob stuffing them into a pillowcase in another room where we stashed a Santa suit for him. Woody Wall had the suit a previous American teacher brought and left behind. My good sport husband stuffs himself and a fat pillow into the suit. Sure enough! He bursts into the room *Ho-ho-hoing*, and the room turns into a kindergarten teacher's worst nightmare. Chinese reserve and restraint dissolve, and I'm afraid they'll mob him! He laughs and waves them back to their seats so he can give out the gifts. It takes him quite a while to go around to each kid, but they insist on a personal interview and titter happily with the trinkets, stuffed animals, and toys they unwrap. They're all eight-year-olds again, and even the macho boys fling their arms around their friends and anticipate their turn with Santa. Of course, they know it's Robert. He doesn't even bother with the ratty beard that comes with the suit since he has a neatly trimmed white home-grown one. But they all want to play the game. I sing some songs with them, and they enjoy the sweets. I'm afraid I've created a few chocoholics.

After everyone gets a gift, the high-pitched conversations and laughter bubble. It's one of the coldest nights so far, and even though we all have our winter coats on and the people load heats the room somewhat, we decide to launch Plan B. No one shows any signs of going back to the dorms. We put a country song on the tape recorder and tell them we're going to teach them an American western, *very* western, dance. We line them up and demonstrate some simple line dance steps. "Hands on your hips. Step behind, step, step. Clap. Turn. Pretend you're wearing a big cowboy hat and boots." Some ask more English-savvy friends for a translation, and then—roars of laughter. They catch on quickly, and after a few minutes 120 Chinese students are bobbing in unison and doing a perfect toe and heel. We warm up quickly. They ask to do it again and again.

Finally, even *they* are exhausted, and we all creep back to sleep and dream, I hope, happy dreams, sleeping in heavenly peace.

The Christmas party for the English majors is similar and just as successful. We added a twist, though, when we asked each section ahead of time to plan and present a little skit at the party. Their party comes a week after the English Corner party, so they know what's coming. The skits are imaginative, and even some of the shy kids step out and shine. A few of them tell me they've never gotten a real toy before. Their parents say birthdays are to be ignored, unimportant and expensive. To see the childlike wonder in their faces at the Christmas tree and their studied attention to the Christmas story put a permanent mark on my heart.

On Christmas Day (a class day) kids stream to the apartment after class, all afraid we're lonesome. And the Christmas cards they hand us or push under the door threaten to cover every inch of our place. We receive bouquets of flowers and a few other gifts too.

I smile and consider: we're supposed to teach *them* Christlike love by example, but they're teaching *us* what unconditional love really is.

Rob surrounded by students at our Christmas party

OUR OWN CHRISTMAS

We're finally alone. And it's Christmas night. Our students are all back in their dorm rooms or studying in the dim classrooms. It's just another night to them. I'm free to unwrap the memories and thoughts in my heart of our own family. The busyness of leading up to and pulling off the Christmas parties was a fine antidote. I fear the emptiness I'll feel when I think of Jordan's wide-eyed past Christmases. I suddenly feel every lap of the oceans between us and wonder just who the child is now when I yearn for our own children to surround us. But our family has outdone itself sending boxes, and there are tenderly wrapped gifts for us under our light bulb tree.

We light the Santa candle stumbled upon in a downtown store weeks ago. He's been lit for many evenings to the delight of many students. The tip of his red cap has burned down so that he glows from inside, which is exactly what Santa should do. I plug the tree lights in, and the magic springs to life, setting off the handmade foil ornaments, some expertly crafted, some munched with clumsy hands. We've had a fine meal, and now is the moment to open the gifts, mailed last October from America, all painstakingly chosen by our family. Weight is a mailing issue, so they measured the ounces against the pleasure they hoped each gift will bring. There are taste bud tingling treats, although the chocolates melted into a solid mass, and may have been frozen; we delight in packages of soup mixes, impossible-to-find-here spices (imagine sending spices to China!), macaroni and cheese mixes (oh boy!). One box is packed in popcorn, my favorite! It's about two months old, but I'm willing to try it. Bonnie knows my obsession. We unwrap football videos for Rob from Robin and Bob and more edible treats, then discover photos of Bonnie and Rod's new home. We study them carefully and note the spacious rooms for Bonnie, Rod and Wally-the-cat, proudly posed among the boxes, grinning at the camera. Precious magazines are here and glorious books from Wes and Bettina and audiotapes of *Prairie Home Companion*. Thought and love wrapped all invisibly, and my tears are really happy tears.

We both laugh when I unwrap a curling iron. We've jerry-rigged and struggled to make mine work. At probably $6.95, the marvel is a *most* precious possession here! Our children put together a calendar of the coming year with family photos on each month. Some are group montages of past family events; some are beloved faces beaming at us. A huge Hershey's candy kiss is one gift we'll either have to hide or parade around to our classes. The smaller version is the grease we sometimes use to encourage shy students to volunteer an opinion or an answer in class, tossing candy kisses to eager raised hands.

Rob and I exchange gifts. He's found an unusual large blood-red vase with contemporary ram's heads molded into it. Though I can't imagine how I'll get it back to the States, I adore it and vow to figure that out later. I found a cashmere sweater for him. At least, I *think* it's cashmere. The labels are all in Chinese. It's no made-for-export product, but it feels cloudlike and Rob seems pleased. It's a poignant Christmas we know we'll always remember, sweet and sad, heart-stretching. Happy Birthday, Jesus!

December 30th is the first day after the Christmas rush that we sit down, clean up after ourselves, and catch our breath. Even in a land that doesn't recognize Christmas I can still make dust whirl around the holiday. Rob and I discuss this and think it's because we tried to give the students a bit of the flavor of Christmas without interrupting the campus routine. So we were doing double duty.

The last day of the millennium turns almost balmy. Two thousand! It's hard even to say it. Letters and e-mails from home say gloomy soothsayers warn of huge computer crashes, airplanes flying endlessly, banks unable to open because software wasn't designed to handle the new numbers. China, as usual, glides patiently on. We take a walk in the afternoon, a nice way to end the year. The kids have the day off and many go home, so except for a few boys lethargically shooting baskets, we have the place pretty much to ourselves.

We take the Christmas tree down on New Year's Eve. Several days ago we invited our student/friends to select an ornament to take home. Little dangly toys, key chains, and student-made decorations disappear quickly, so there was little to take off. We pack the memory-laden white lights and the remaining decorations in a box for the next foreign teachers' Christmas. We hope we started a tradition that will take root and grow, not for the parties, gifts, and decorations, but for the potential future meaning for the students.

New Year's Eve we crawl into bed and watch some of the celebrations around China on TV. China is good at incredible, well-planned extravaganzas for almost any occasion, though nobody on our campus can keep the copy room open for business more than two hours a day. The munchkins seem to be napping or eating the rest of the time.

Some friends wrote recently to ask if it's a strain for us to be together constantly, working and playing. I guess we have a good marriage, a good friendship, which is, what a good marriage is. We're not apart very often here. We teach different classes, occasionally go shopping alone but not too often since we have to haul everything home in backpacks, so Rob gets pressed into service, which he cheerfully accepts. In the evenings, he grades papers or writes lesson plans while I chat with students in the living room or play Chinese checkers or give a piano lesson. We joke that typically I flit into the study like a grasshopper after everyone leaves and look over his shoulder and steal his lesson plans. Not a bad deal. I play while he works. We do have some time alone together, though. The kids respect our privacy, and we don't have visitors *every* night. Sometimes I tell the ones we know best to make themselves at home, usually to play the piano, while we fix dinner or grade papers.

We like to let students come practice their English informally, but we know they watch what we do always from the corners of their eyes. Occasionally Robert kisses my cheek, something no Chinese would ever do in public. We tell them we love each another and don't mind showing love and respect around friends. They giggle and the girls say they hope that their husbands will be as "romantic."

The question of our volunteer status pops up continually. "You do not receive pay for teaching?" Money and salary are certainly not taboo in China. Curious students asked us right from the start how much money we got for coming to China to teach them English. "None," we said. "We're retired and heard that students in China want to learn English from native speakers, so we came," They're stunned. They keep coming back to the question, unable to fathom the idea of volunteerism. We say their government is generous and provides the apartment. "We're still healthy, and we wanted to visit your country. It's nice to think that we can help with our language." The Chinese teachers don't earn much but certainly rely on a salary to exist. There are professional English teachers who travel from country to country for about what the local teachers make. Jenny tells us a couple from North Dakota will come here next term. He is a teacher, she says. His wife is not but will accompany him. It'll be great to have help with the workload and to have American company. I'm pretty sure they'll be paid a little.

A friend who lives in Maryland asked if he could send us anything to help us with life or teaching. We were using the only maps in the classrooms to show the kids exactly where California is. We noted with something of a jolt that the maps had China exactly in the center with the other countries slightly elongated and wrapped around the edges. Chinese love to point out that their country is shaped like a proud rooster. The United States looked a little skewed to me and the relationships of the continents to one another didn't match the geography in my head. So we asked Jim in Maryland to mail us a good world map. A sturdy tube arrived quickly—he must have paid a fortune to get it here!—and when we opened the huge map it was Christmas again.

Yes, there's North America right in the middle of the map, the rest of the world wrapped tidily around the edges. Maybe every nation designs its maps that way. It had never occurred to us before! But at least now we can locate California for our kids and laugh at all our provincial attitudes.

45

END OF WINTER SEMESTER

Just before this semester's final exams, several older girls—Stone, Bonnie and their roommates, last semester's students—invite us to their dorm room for an evening. Rob says, "Sue, I just wouldn't feel comfortable waltzing into the girls' dorm, even though they tell us 'Auntie' (the resident house-mother) says it would be fine." We've entertained the girls several times in our apartment, and it's sweet they want to reciprocate. Beside, my curiosity is piqued. I'd love to see how girls actually live here. So they send an escort party over after dinner and urge Rob to join us. He graciously declines and we set off to the dorm.

Winter has its icy fist around us again after a few almost-balmy days slip by. I clutch my parka around me and try to ignore the biting cold as the girls do. Stepping inside the dormitory doesn't offer much refuge. The wind can't find its way into the halls, but the cement walls and floor seem to magnify the damp cold. They lead me down a dark hallway and up some stairs. I try not to compare the Spartan setting with the warm dorms of my college memory, full of giggling girls, posters, music, brightly colored curtains, and the aroma of just-delivered pizza. We go into a long room, identical to others I peek into along the corridor. Four bunk beds stacked three high line one wall. Eleven girls share the room. There are no closets. They show me eleven small trunks, one for each girl's clothes and possessions. One scarred table with two chairs crowds the center of the room. Nothing on the walls. The one window at the end of the room is cracked, and the wind finds its way in, a stealthy and unwelcome guest. The bare light bulb in the ceiling struggles to light the gloom. I understand why they go to the dimly lit classrooms at night to study. But the smiles of the other nine roommates waiting to greet me warm the room considerably. They sit hunched together on the lower bunks, waiting, and bubble enthusiastically as they welcome me, offering one of the chairs and a bowl of oranges. They crowd around, all talking at once. Stone, the natural leader, says, "We would like to perform for you, Mrs. McKee, with very much pleasure." A girl I've seen only briefly before stands and begins playing a flute. She does a very creditable job with a haunting melody. We all applaud when she finishes. Another sings a Chinese pop song with gestures, mimicking the TV. Then they pass rice cakes around, pretty gluey to me but a treat for them. The fact that they perform so unselfconsciously strikes me. If someone can sing, or dance or recite, she's happy to share the gift.

The heavy stench from the bathrooms in the classroom building is missing here, since the girls have no indoor toilet but must duck outside to a structure meant for the purpose. There is only cold water in the sinks for washing bodies and clothes. Clotheslines dangle from every window, and the omnipresent laundry hanging out all the windows more than makes up for curtains. I ask about showers. Stone says, "Yes, sometimes we save our money and go across the street where a woman has a private business where you can pay for a warm shower. The boys laugh at us and tell us it's a waste of money to go there." I marvel again that they are so meticulously clean and manage their personal hygiene in the most primitive of circumstances.

The fall semester ends January 8th with two weeks of final examinations. Crunch time in China. The tension is palpable. We decide to test our International Business students with individual ten-minute oral interviews with all sixty or seventy students. It's a grueling business, but we're surprised when some of the more voluble students stumble in a one-on-one situation or we find sleepers able to carry on a pretty good conversation with a little encouragement. We give a token written final, but the oral conversations are the real test—and we don't reveal that until after we finish. We hoped to relieve the tension that is so much a part of their lives.

Lucy shows up almost every evening to chat or practice the piano. She graduates this year, and we're amazed at how completely unprepared for life the kids are. They'll face a very tough job market. In the past, students were assigned to jobs, like them or not, but that was the "Iron Rice Bowl." At least they got a meager supply of food guaranteed for life. Suddenly that is changing, and young people scramble for scarce jobs in the desirable big cities (better pay) or sink back into poverty in the villages. They have to search for jobs with no system that matches jobs with applicants and no training in preparing a resumé. Lucy tells me, "Most people have an uncle or a friend who has a place in his business. I have nothing. I am the first one in my whole village to go away to college. I was told I must study animal raising. I don't like it!" She screws her face up and brushes imaginary dirt from her dress. "I want to stay in Ningbo, not return to my village. I like to teach English." An idea strikes me and I decide to ask James, who encourages foreign teachers and businesspeople to come to Ningbo.

Surely he is in contact with many schools and knows of one or two that need a fresh, young Chinese English teacher. We've been helping James' little son Wei Wei, after all. I'm learning the art of *guanxi*, the Chinese equivalent of "I scratch your back; you scratch mine." We offer to write a letter of recommendation for Lucy, and she smiles her gratitude, though we wonder if anything we do or write will help her.

A three-week Spring Festival holiday is coming up, the biggest vacation of the school year. The place will be deserted. James asks if we'd like him to arrange a trip to northern China to see the ice-carving festival during the break. It's tempting, but we toss the idea around and decide it would be nice to just stay in our (warm!) apartment and explore territory closer to home. Several invitations to students' homes tempt us, and we thank them but feel the need to unwind and enjoy the quiet. Three whole weeks!

Jenny's worried about us. She will be off campus too. In fact, all the buildings will be locked. She's afraid the campus will be oppressive. Actually, we're a mite worried ourselves. The two other American teaching couples who've been in the area with us have completed their contracts and returned to the US. We love them and will feel quite alone without them. The Rileys returned to Reedley, a small orchard community outside Fresno. The Walls spent two full years here and were ready to return to Portland. Sunday meetings and shared dinners have ended, and no service couples are coming to replace them. We rarely got together except on Sundays, but we'll miss the moral support and cheerful phone calls. The new teachers from North Dakota will be a help but not the same. We're not sure what we'll do on Sundays. There is a fairly big Christian church in Shanghai, which foreigners may attend. That's a four-hour bus ride one way, a pretty long jaunt to church, though I'm sure we'll try it.

We're a bit forlorn, but we don't want to undertake a strenuous tourist trip.

Jenny frowns. "What will you do? It is very cold outside. I think you will be lonely. Would you like to learn *tai qi*?" I smother a smile. I've seen and admired mostly ancient Chinese men and woman on city streets, alone or in groups, sliding silently through the graceful motions and poses. Sometimes the old men have bird-cages alongside them on the sidewalk, letting the birds take the air as they go through the ritual movements with their comrades. I can't imagine Robert and me bending our American bodies so gracefully, but I glance over at him to read his reaction. "Okay," he grins. We believe we've signed up for one lesson to alleviate Jenny's guilt at leaving us alone.

At the appointed time we walk across the silent campus to the barn-like hall which passes for a gym. It's unlocked. We step inside, and the wind slams the door behind us. It's no warmer inside than out. A janitor comes in another door, glances at us, and retreats. We know a skeleton crew is taking care of things, but we don't know who our teacher will be. A slender girl bursts through the door and rushes over to greet us. She is Li Yi, whose merry, lively eyes seem too big for her round face, though it may not be size but rather vitality that makes them so important. Her smile tells us she's eager to please, but she shakes her head and admits she speaks but little English. Apparently she's a physical education teacher and has delayed her return to her parents' home in the mountains for personal reasons, I hope, and *not* in order to teach us *tai qi*. We learn that her specialty is the graceful ballet with the sword, which is hard to imagine since she's the antithesis of belligerence.

We begin. She demonstrates a few movements and nods for us to try them. We feel awkward, especially as we remember snickering at the broad, almost grotesque movements we've seen. We grew up in a culture that worships heart-thumping, competitive sports. *Tai qi* seemed sissified and simple. It soon becomes clear that it isn't simple, and we're working up a sweat! It challenges every muscle in the body, and the old brains have a hard time recalling which movement follows which. We watch her effortless ballet and try to match our twists and bends to hers. Not even close! But she keeps a straight face. Evidently her mind is deeply engaged as she moves. An hour and a half fly by. As we're putting our coats and hats back on, she smiles that radiant smile at us and says, in English, "Tomorrow? Same time?" Oh! We thought this was a one-shot deal. We discover that she's here for several more days, eager to accept the challenge. "Okay. Tomorrow. Same time."

Again the knockout smile the next morning and, "You remember?" The rising inflection in her gentle voice sings as she wonders what the foreign oafs have absorbed.

"Not so much. Please show us again." So she does, then glances over her shoulder to see if we're studying her movements. We are, but I despair of reproducing them. I'm amazed that Robert is willing to try. We begin again.

She begins every day with the question, "You remember?" She's probably a third our age and treats us with respect but also with the patience of a gentle parent. Occasionally a janitor looks in and some-times gathers others to watch the spectacle. We know that we look foolish, but we try our best to please the gentle, graceful girl. Finally, she confides she must leave the next day to go home. Rob asks to videotape her going through the movements she taught us to help us remember. She agrees, and we now have a video of her concentrating on her lovely dance. At the end, she looks at the camera and us and flashes her million dollar smile. We will remember.

46

LUNAR NEW YEAR

A huge bang! It's early evening, and I *know* it's the Chinese Lunar New Year's Eve, but every nerve in my body screams! I guess I haven't altogether overcome my initial fears. Fireworks. It's only fireworks. I think. Yes, off in the distance, flashes and sparkles fade in the sky. We bundle up and walk outside to get a better look and see big fireworks going off in at least six different spots not too far from campus, not small sparkler-type poofs but great blossoms of color high up in the air. Well, after all, the Chinese *invented* gunpowder, and fireworks, but we figure the Fourth of July makes better sense since it's warmer. After about half an hour we retreat inside and enjoy the spectacle from the windows.

So begins the Year of the Dragon. I wonder what it'll bring for us. In our son's life there are big changes. He's landed a new job in the foothills above Sacramento, promoting "non-linear editors" (specialty computers) to TV stations all over the world. He felt he was withering at the TV station in Fresno, where he worked since he graduated from college. Bettina, his bride, writes that the new job has put the sparkle back in his eyes. It doesn't hurt at all that they'll be close to fishing lakes and streams in the Lake Tahoe area, one of Wes' passions. We're lobbying to get all of our children to China at the end of our service this summer. Wes and Bettina probably won't be able to come because of the new job. Bonnie, Rod, Robin, and Bob hope to come for three weeks. A holiday trip to Shanghai whets our appetite to share this world with them.

Our adventure to Shanghai resulted from a whim. Rob read that we could travel by water overnight to Shanghai from Ningbo. We negotiated the various buses to the office where we bought advance tickets for the ship. I practiced my best Mandarin beforehand to ask for first class tickets, one way. We planned to take the four-hour bus trip to come home.

I stood in line, drawing the usual stares from the Chinese crowd. The line was unusually orderly for China, but when my turn at the window came, all order dissolved and curious faces pressed close to see what I wanted. I made my speech.

The wizened face behind the window stared at me, then muttered that they didn't *have* first class on the ship.

"Well, second class then please." She snatched my money, counted out change, and pushed two tickets through the cage to me. I must've looked as uneasy as I felt when I found Robert waiting for me.

"Did you get a first class room on the boat?"

"Uh, no. They don't have first class."

"Will we have a bed?"

"I don't know that either. I didn't know how to ask!" We spent the next two days picturing ourselves crowded amidships on pallets, pushing away chickens and squashing fleas all night.

We arrived at the dock with sandwiches in our backpacks and tried to be as inconspicuous as we could in the crush waiting to board the ship. If keeping your footing getting on and off a Chinese bus is an art, the lunge of humanity as the gate was opened for passengers to board was a trial by ordeal! I was afraid I'd stumble and lose my death grip on Rob's arm and he'd have to come back later to scrape up my scattered bones. Fortunately, that picture played out in my mind only. We got on deck as the crowd dashed to claim a spot in the general seating area below. We clutched our tickets and followed signs and arrows, hoping they would lead to a room corresponding to the number on our tickets. They did! We gratefully stepped into a tiny room with two bunk beds and an even more miniscule bathroom with rusty but functional plumbing. I sagged onto the bunk. The question remained whether the room was ours alone or if bunkmates would join us. It didn't really matter. We *wouldn't* be sitting up with three thousand fellow travelers.

We ate our sandwiches and an orange, then went up on deck to watch the sunset and the activity as we prepared to cast off. The waterfront in Ningbo is all business, not pretty at all. Rusty, working ships are tied up in muddy, grime-filled moorings in the river. The clunk and grind of our ship's engines warned us that we were about to set off on our adventure. We elbowed our way into a spot beside the rail to watch the riverside details slip away and disappear entirely into the dark. We're almost used to the stares and then the smile when we nod and smile to people who've never seen a foreigner before. A *Ni hau* (hello) from us usually catches them off guard, and they regain their manners and reply bobbing, "*Nimen hau, Ni hau Ni hau!*" The crowd by the rail thinned as people returned to the bowels of the ship to eat their rice cakes and settle in for the night. Rob and I walked through the dense humanity in the huge, steamy room below, grateful that whatever I said to the ticket lady got us a relatively private spot for the night.

A young man came into our stateroom late in the evening, just as startled to see us as we were to see him. He mumbled something, then disappeared. If he paid for a bed that night, he never used it. Maybe the thought of sharing it with two non-Chinese was too much for him.

We got up before dawn the next morning after a fairly restful night and went on deck to watch the ship enter Shanghai harbor. We saw dim lights in the fog up ahead; then misty ghosts passed that must've been other ships. Foghorns and faint city noises floated out to meet us. I rubbed the sleep from my eyes and realized that we were at the mouth of what foreigners call the Yangzte River. It has many names in Chinese and many moods, some deadly. As more pink light crept through the fog, we were aware of all sizes and shapes of ships bustling even at this hour: cruise ships, tough little tugs darting in and out, lumbering barges, sampans with laundry flapping, huge cargo ships loaded with steel or sea vans. Then the breathtaking sweep of the delicate spires of an ultramodern bridge introduced us to the inner harbor. We crept past the Bund, a stretch of large, mostly nineteenth century British-style buildings in full light by then. We weren't prepared to find eighteenth and nineteenth century Europe in China! It reminded us of the city's choppy history, the prize in a tug-of-war between European powers not so many years ago, forced open for trade against the Chinese's wishes. Enclaves of homes and buildings seem to breathe the rarified air of the French, British, and Americans who posted signs in Shanghai's parks: "No dogs or Chinese."

We soon found the hotel Woody and Sandra recommended from past trips to Shanghai and began absorbing the city. We covered a lot of miles on foot past narrow, winding alleys that looked how I imagined China should look. Then we'd burst into neon-lit streets with incredibly modern malls and neighborhoods of sky-reaching glass buildings, more Western than anything we'd seen in China. We rode buses, the metro, taxis, wandered through a tranquil garden, visited Sun Yat Sen's home made into a museum, marveled at the paper dragons, red banners and lanterns everywhere as China prepared to celebrate the Lunar New Year and the Year of the Dragon. We learned to flow with the crowds in the streets, letting the noise and bustle swirl around us. We haggled for dragon kites to send home, paying probably twice what the vendors hoped for.

On Sunday a taxi took us to the address we had for our church, a large home. We were unprepared for the forty or fifty people who streamed in with us. Everyone slipped off their shoes in the entry and put on socks from a basket there, Chinese style. The socks didn't do much to keep the chill off as we gathered in the living room, converted into a simple meeting room. Caucasian families greeted each other and welcomed us. They told us that usually about 100 people attend, but many were traveling during the holiday. There were a few Chinese in the crowd too. In spite of China's ostensible religious freedom, citizens may not attend church services, though they may attend social events. "Therefore," they laughed, "we have many social events." There was even a small organ at the front of the room. It felt like home to worship with a congregation, feeling the companionship of not only the Spirit of the Lord but of others who meet each days' challenges here in China.

We had three invitations to stay in homes overnight the next time we come to Shanghai! We accepted the offer of dinner after church at the home of the American Vice Consul and his delightful family. They had three teenage children who attended the American/British

School in Shanghai. They'd lived there for most of their lives, and spoke fine Mandarin, returning to the States every summer. With the other guests we guffawed and gasped at stories of the bungling and machinations that are a diplomat's daily life, miniscule slights often blown out of proportion into international incidents.

We reluctantly left the good company in Shanghai and returned to the eerily quiet campus. Even the usual twenty-four hour construction crews are silent. The nets of the many new basketball courts outside our windows blow in the wind, waiting for the raucous boys to return. The Year of the Dragon begins.

47

END OF LUNAR
NEW YEAR

urphy's Law functions in China just as well as in the United States. Everyone knows household problems, sulking electrical wires, and burping plumbing fixtures erupt on holidays, including the Lunar New Year. Rob discovers a puddle on the bathroom floor, which in The Swamp wouldn't have been remarkable, but is alarming in our pristine new apartment. He traces it to the on-demand water heater and more precisely to a flexible metal tube that has sprung a leak. Never mind that it's only about six months old; it obviously must be repaired or replaced. The "technicians" Jenny confidently sends to take care of such things are all away for the holiday. What she *doesn't* know is that in the new apartments they are usually looking at an appliance or a repair job completely foreign to them. They are masters of duct tape and rusty wire repair and can coax additional coughing out of an aging truck engine, but for household repairs they put on a suit and try to look knowledgeable. Which they're not.

We chuckle at the memory of the bathroom ceiling fan incident. Soon after we moved in we noticed that the fan didn't seem to be drawing at all. The room remained steamy after a shower, the windowless walls dripping even more than usual. Rob turned the fan on and held a tissue up that hung limply in his hand, oblivious to the fan's loud whirring directly above it. The technician was called in. He appeared, and Robert demonstrated. "You see? It doesn't draw air up at all."

Technician: "Okay okay" in English. Then in rapid Mandarin, "I'll be right back." He dashed out the front door, snatching the test-tissue from Rob's hand, and returned triumphant after about half an hour. "I've been to all of these new apartments. No problem here. All the bathroom fans work exactly the same." And he left.

So Robert climbed up, dismantled the fan, and pulled it down to find that it was installed so the flapper that opens the vent was put in upside down. He ripped the flapper off, reinstalled it, and we now have a functioning ceiling fan. Unless everybody else in the new apartments performs the same surgery, they will have weepy bathroom walls.

The crisis now is not so much that there are no technicians to call, but that most shops are closed and we haven't a clue where to look for a replacement for the ruptured tube. We confer and decide to search Chuga first. We wander through the narrow streets, stepping into any cubicle that looks as if it might carry plumbing supplies. We're surprised to find more shops open than there were a few days ago. Capitalist China is alive and well. If there are a few yuan to be earned, folks will open up their stores, even during a big holiday. We find what looks like tubing and Rob holds up the leaky tube. *Yo mei yo*? (Have or have not?) Mostly we get *Mei yo* with sadly shaking heads. Finally we connect with a helpful clerk, who rummages in a box of dusty parts and produces a very similar tube. Maybe we're in luck.

We dash through the vegetable market and scoop up some things we need. It's bustling today since food is the centerpiece of the days-long holiday. My nose twitches as the aromas of raw fish, eels, roasted duck, onions, acrid charcoal, and cold, wet concrete mingle in the air. Housewives push through the crowds purposefully, clutching live chickens or ducks by the feet. Rob says it's my imagination, but I'm *sure* the trapped animals single me out with their terrified eyes, pleading for a reprieve.

Clusters of balloons float in the gray sky. Hustlers smile at children who whine to their parents for just one balloon. Firecrackers are for sale everywhere; the salesmen are doing a thriving business. The excitement is contagious. On the little kamikaze bus home, people burst into song. We enjoy the jostling crowd but are glad to step off the bus and walk back to our silent apartment. The flexible tube fits perfectly. All is well.

For the most part the holiday is cold and cloudy, though today we wake to a blue sky. Well, we see patches of blue through the smog. And sunshine! We decide to take a walk and prowl through the village just over the canal. Except for my nighttime soiree with Lucy at the Shaoxing Opera performance, we've never set foot there, though our bedroom and patio look right across the brown canal into the main square. We bundle up and set off, hoping to be invisible, just to get a flavor of what the ancient cluster of homes is like.

A few desultory open-air "stores" across the highway offer to repair bike tires or sell dusty boxes of foodstuffs, but the village has no commercial area. The grimy, two-story concrete houses huddle across narrow, winding alleys seeming to touch across the street. Even the traditional ancient Chinese wing roof tiles are too much trouble. No color, grass, or flowers here. Weeds, potshards, and rocks fill any unused inch. Discouragement, even hopelessness, hangs in the air. No home has running water, but we hear TVs blaring from many of them. They must hoard the scant electricity for that purpose.

The communal outdoor squat toilets with no doors (who needs privacy?) reek. Chickens and ducks browsing in the piles of garbage waddle out of the way. I have yet to see a garbage truck or trash collection of any kind in China, other than the wizened man with the broom and cart on campus, who dumps the trash over the wall. The people who live here probably walk to the tidy fields surrounding their village to work each day. Not many come outside today, so we get our wish and pass quietly, trying to absorb the step back into old China.

Back on campus, we decide we'd like our English majors to take on research projects next semester. We combed the library, with its sad collection of books in English, but hope our students will have access to material in Chinese they can translate into English. Since we'll be teaching them both oral and written English, maybe we'll ask each student to select a country, write a report on it, then report to the class orally. "Let's not ask for dry facts about some place in the world but have them pretend they're going to travel there. What should they be sure to see there? How will they travel? What kind of strange food might they taste?" Rob's idea.

"Maybe we can open their eyes to the world outside China," I agree, "and spur them to ask some interesting questions." We decide to coordinate our lessons and plunge into writing lesson plans, braiding the writing course into oral assignments, all from scratch. No lesson plans or manuals, but no one to scowl or shake his head at us either.

"Okay, Susie, we'll be team-teaching the first part of the writing course."

Yipe! We have such different teaching styles. I wonder if this'll work. The students will be back on campus soon. We'll find out.

48

OUR FINAL
SEMESTER BEGINS

irst order of business as we begin teaching again is to corral Mrs. Wu, the key lady. She's deferential, polite, but firm. No key to the classroom outfitted with the audiovisual equipment. We drool through the window at the overhead projector and the retractable screen. "You must be trained in the use of the new computer," Mrs. Wu says.

"Okay. We will be happy to learn. When?"

"Soon." Pregnant pause.

I can out-inscrutable this Chinese lady. "We are free now. Can you teach us now?"

"No. Very busy now."

"When shall we return?" I'm annoying her.

She gazes around her tiny cubicle (a real emblem of power and authority, her own office!) searching for a way to get rid of me. "Tomorrow. Very difficult to learn. Take much time. You and Mr. McKee come together, yes?"

"Yes! What time shall we come?"

Now she's treed. She slams an appointment book open on her desk and studies it. It looks blank to me. "Two o' clock. Takes much time to learn."

"We'll be here tomorrow at two o'clock."

The fact is, it *is* very difficult to learn. The keys are, of course, printed in Chinese. Since neither Robert nor I took advantage of the computer craze in America, we're woefully bankrupt in computer skills, but our bulldog determination and my frantic note-taking with diagrams of the keyboard and English notations of the keys show Mrs. Wu that we're able to use this marvel of technology.

"Now, may we have a key to the room?"

"Oh no!" Mrs. Wu can't hide her horror. "I am only one to have key. Before each class you come find me, and I will unlock the class-room door."

"But we have a class that begins at eight o'clock in the morning."

"I will be here."

"But we need to prepare, to try different things and see which plan is best before the class." Another long pause.

"When will you do that?"

Rob takes a deep breath. "We would like to go into the classroom the night before class to prepare and be sure we're ready."

Mrs. Wu considers us carefully, measuring our trustworthiness. We try to look dependable. She wavers. "Yes, I will let you borrow the key the evening before. Please come to find me each time, then return the key to me after your class, yes?"

"Yes, Mrs. Wu. Thank you! We will be very careful." We have to repeat this exercise three times a week, the key ceremony. We later learn that only one other teacher has a class in the room once a week. I wonder if he has a key.

Again we have students visiting our apartment, bearing edible offerings from home. One of our favorite boys, King Lake, proudly announces he's brought us "delicious food from my hometown." That always makes us squirm since the definition of *delicious* is definitely cultural. We smile and appreciate their kind thoughts of us but hope we won't have to taste in the eager giver's presence the dried, pickled fish or nameless soggy homemade something someone's mother made for us. The glutinous rice wrapped in bamboo leaves takes the cake, so to speak. I'm determined to try one after Chris, who proudly tells us her grandmother made them for us, leaves. Robert shudders and won't watch me. It looks and tastes just like the dried glue stick in the Chuga post office smells. Maybe if I zap it in the microwave. Even worse.

Classes begin with a bang. We have long-term plans and goals for both our oral and writing classes. We hit them between the eyes with a big push to improve their comprehension and pronunciation. We give lots more homework and daily evidence of their use of English. We hit on the idea of requiring students to keep journals. In English. They like the idea of writing their thoughts, ideas, and feelings in a notebook. We tell them they are private; we're not actually going to *read* their journals, but we ask them to bring them every Friday and open them on their desks. While they're at work on other assignments, we circulate to glance at the journals to see that they are in fact writing at least a paragraph almost daily. That will have poignant and amusing results.

We see each class twice a week now, but they still need more exposure to English. We set up a listening lab, reading stories and conversations onto tapes for them to listen to.

Dick and Edie Betting have arrived from frigid North Dakota. They're warm and delightful folks. Dick is the retired English teacher, tall, with a sardonic grin. He came to China before for a summer session at Madam Ling Ya Fen's high school, and his curiosity was piqued for more. Edie is along for the ride. She will not teach, just wants to soak in the atmosphere and support her husband. They're nice old poops like us, laid back and pleasant. They live in an apartment in the other new building. They'll be here for only one semester. When we had them over for dinner, they admired our lovely hardwood floors. Their floors, it seems, aren't quite so attractive. Black goo oozes up between the buckling floorboards. Edie asked me what to do about the persistent mold that creeps up the walls. I showed her my bottle of bleach and made scrubbing motions. After they left Rob said, "I think we lucked out. They lavished more attention and money on this building because the university president and dignitaries live here." Ah, yes. Everyone's equal, but some are more equal than others, eh?

John McCrea joins us too on the English teaching staff. He's Irish but doesn't have much brogue. He's a professional ESL teacher, just come from Korea. He's taught in Malaysia and Germany as well. He's much more formal and proper. We're all to have a full load of classes for the semester, but Rob and I keep all the English majors. With Morag, our ranks have swelled to five foreign teachers.

Me in the classroom

49

THE BETTINGS
AND JOHN

Dick Betting, our new teaching colleague, has much more experience in teaching composition than I, so now that we're teaching writing, I ask him to give me the Cliff notes in thirty minutes or less. He grins and gives me some excellent pointers, even shows me how he sets up short exercises after which the students exchange papers, read, and grade one another. I have some teaching manuals and ask for his opinion of various approaches. His input and suggestions add sparkle to my lesson plans.

Edie, his wife, is good company. I'm afraid she'll go stir-crazy alone all day while we teach, but she seems content to read, putz around their apartment, and welcome Dick's students in the evenings, often feeding them too. She seems unflappable, which is a valuable trait in this country. When their wall hot water heater explodes, she takes it in stride. She jokes about the black goo oozing up between the buckling floorboards, and we compare notes on the village life we spy on from our back windows.

John McCrea, the Irishman, is polite but aloof. He's probably in his fifties. The six or seven strands of much-too-long hair he combs into position over his balding front pate shake loose sometimes and flop on the wrong side of his head like a duck's broken wing. He's very aware of his suddenly naked, tall forehead and tries to shrink as he finds a comb to reposition the thin locks. Everyone pretends not to notice. His superior air puts me off a little. Maybe Rob and I try too hard to adapt to our hosts, but John sets my teeth on edge when he is a dinner guest in a Chinese home or even in the teachers' cafeteria, knife and fork protruding from his shirt pocket. He lived and taught in Korea before he came here, but he likely avoided chopsticks there as well.

The English majors are excited at the prospect of choosing a country for an imaginary visit and researching it. They whisper, though, that there isn't much information in the library. Rob and I trusted that, while there isn't much in English, surely articles or books in Chinese give some inkling of other countries. Not so. The kids are not lazy. They don't have much research training, but they *want* to know more about the world. And they've drawn a blank. It's hard for us to comprehend the utter isolation these young people accept. It's the air they breathe. There's no local library they can go to; no one in their villages has traveled more than a few miles from home. Any information they have comes from the news doled out by the Communist Party. They see their benevolent leader on TV and hear how he faces down world leaders and stands for peace and freedom. Their pinhole picture of other nations filters through that lens. We felt we were on safe ground asking them to be armchair tourists, avoiding politics, but find they have no notion what we're talking about when we describe watching artists on the banks of the Seine or riding a donkey in Morocco.

We start a databank out of our home. We brought some travel magazines, and our predecessors left a collection of *National*

Geographics. I ask several friends to e-mail us brief overviews of countries they've visited. The response is stunning. We get several one- and two-page descriptions of travel in Switzerland, Italy, South Morocco, Thailand, Germany. Students browse through our personal bookshelf and gape in wonder at the color photos. Their childlike amazement at this sudden sunlit window on the world is touching. And sad. Are we doing them a favor by giving them a glimpse of other nations and the way others live? Or are we showing them planets entirely beyond their grasp? They are hopelessly in the dark about the outside world.

We asked the students to choose a destination that interested them. For example, many boys are frothing-at-the-mouth soccer fans, so they might like to visit Italy or Germany. "Don't just give us dull numbers of the population or ancient history. Tell us what kind of food they eat; what would be fun to see and do there; how do you think they're similar to the Chinese or how they might be different." They work in pairs for three weeks until time for the oral reports.

The reports are fun to listen to. I see foreign lands through fresh eyes and hearts. Of course, they have little information to work with, but typically romantic, they embroider the streets of Paris, and their eyes glisten as they tell about California's year-round sunshine or skiing in the Swiss Alps. They applaud one another's sometimes halting, first-ever try at speaking before a group. In English!

In our oral classes we try to divide the time between listening skills, just trying to comprehend the spoken word in English; practicing their own speaking, correcting their pronunciation; and relaxed conversation when they can try unfamiliar words and phrases. I tell the fable of the Three Wishes about the woodcutter who gets three wishes from a good fairy. He squanders them wishing for a good meal. I ask what each one would wish for.

"I would wish for much money to travel to interesting places."

"I would wish to study in America."

"I wish for no disease anywhere. Everyone healthy."

"Then," I smile, "What would all doctors and nurses do?" But I apologize. I threw cold water on a wonderful wish.

"I wish for healthy for my parents."

"I wish for *lunch*!" We meet the period just before lunch.

"I want to wish for a place, very quiet, with many trees, Very beautiful. Birds singing." (Come to think of it, I still haven't heard one birdsong in China!)

"I would like to wish to be as a small child again. My life very happy then." The toll of grades and pressure shows in that wish.

Some giggling girls confer. "We wish for good husbands. Maybe in five years."

"I wish for everyone in the world to have peace." Amen.

50

IN HANGZHOU

March 8th is Women's Day in China, a national holiday. No classes. To honor the day our university organizes a bus trip to Hangzhou, about an hour's drive away. Edie, Dick's wife, and I are invited to join all the female teachers. Sadly, Morag has decided to return to Scotland. I think she was just plain lonely here. She may have been happier at the Sunli high school, where there are several young, single teachers from Australia, Canada, and America. We enjoyed her, but an elderly twosome probably wasn't the social milieu she needed.

In Hangzhou Edie and I end up with a Chinese teacher new to the English department. May is her English name. She's somewhat older than most of the teachers, a thin lady with features rather sharper than most Chinese. She tells us she spent several years in America getting her master's degree, even married an American. "He returned with me to China because my elderly mother was very ill. He tried to adapt to life here, but the harsh conditions were too difficult for him. He went back to America." She says that wistfully but without a great deal of regret. She confides that she, on the other hand, couldn't eat the "slabs of meat" in America.

We three decide to take a cab to Hangzhou's famous West Lake area. Traffic bustles around the shops there. Paths with weeping willows surround the lake, which in some seasons is awash with lotus blossoms. Islands invite walkers in carefully crafted gardens

At the taxi stand a driver pesters us to hire him. May snaps at him to discourage him. Finally, we agree to let him drive us into town, and May negotiates the price. When he leads us back to his "taxi," it certainly doesn't *look* like one. He explains in rapid Mandarin that he's a driver for a manufacturer in town. It's his day off, and he's using the company car to pick up some extra money. Believe me when I say that entrepreneurship is alive and well in China. Edie and I are ready to bolt. May says it's customary in the growing economy. He tells May that he can get us into Mao Tse Tung's summer home, which is not open to tourists. He knows the guards. It's on one end of West Lake in a compound fenced off for communist officials' use. Were we interested? It would be only an extra ten yuan (about $1.25). May encourages us, says she's sure it will be safe.

After a short drive, we pull up to a tall gate guarded by severe, uniformed men. Through the wrought-iron fence we see abundant green, luxurious villas scattered among the manicured lawns, and a glimpse of West Lake. There's a whispered conference with the guard, who waves us through. The driver has spoken the truth. He tells us we can't get out of the car, but he'll drive slowly along the meandering road through the impressive landscape, past villas linked by roofed corridors, gardens and smaller lakes. We come to the end of West Lake where he points out a section of the lake that is also roped off. Fresh water pearls were once grown there to grind into the face powder Madam Mao liked so much. I ask if the palaces are still used. One big one looks like a very fine hotel. Apparently government officials still may use some of them, he tells us, but #1, Mao's place, is off-limits. That man, Mao Tse Tung, credited with liberating the common man from the warlords' heels and fighting off the invading Japanese, revered for freeing Chinese women and writing that "Women hold up half of the sky," lifted *himself* to a very comfortable spot above common men and women.

We've seen enough, so our chauffeur drives us to the public side of West Lake and drops us off. We wander along the tree-lined boulevard around the lake, but the mist and cold drizzle discourage a long stay. We find a place for lunch that has *tsao mien*, a local dish of noodles fried in a puddle of oil and tossed with veggies. It's likely American chow mein is modeled on the dish, but the similarity is hard to see. Or taste. These noodles are soft and pliable, probably lethal from the cooking oil, but delicious. We relax and munch and mull over the bizarre sights we've seen. Then May invites us to join her with some old friends she's about to meet nearby and spend the rest of the afternoon with them.

The friends are gracious and take us walking past tea shops where we gawk at old men who lean, arms and hands bare, over huge, heated vats of tea leaves, lifting and stirring the leaves with practiced hands. The various teas' aromas make my nostrils tingle. We gaze admiringly at young women in cake-decorating bakeries as they whip three-second roses out of mounds of frosting directly onto fancy wedding cakes. Finally, it's time to flag a cab to return to the meeting place and catch the bus home. It's been a marvelous day. I've peeked into the city's bustling life, seen fifty-year-old vestiges of the privileges of a communist leader who is hardly ever mentioned now, and sauntered through a gentler time with hope for China's future.

51

STAY IN CHINA?

Mr. Wang, the university vice president, invites us to go bowling with him again. I guess Robert didn't make too big a gaff by outbowling Mr. Wang on Rob's birthday. We get the feeling he wants to tell or ask us something while we enjoy the evening. He does. He urges us to sign on for at least another six months, maybe a year, at the university. He quickly adds, "We will pay for your plane ticket back to America for the summer. Then we would be honored to pay your way back to China in the fall for you to teach our students again. We are very pleased with your instruction." It's very flattering. We tell him we'll have to discuss it.

It's hard to believe we have only three months left of the eighteen-month agreement. Time has sped by. We joke to one another that it took us six months to figure out what in the world we were supposed to do, then six months to start doing it. We think we've become effective only during the last six months. We both have mixed feelings about the invitation to continue teaching here. On one hand, we want to get back to America and our family, especially after a particularly tough class. On the other, we both feel we've been blessed to know and love our students—especially after a successful class or a good experience with a student. Faced with the idea of walking away and never seeing them again, I want to bury my head in the sand.

Slowly, we realize independently that we should leave and not return in the fall. I push my sadness at the prospect of leaving the students away from my heart and concentrate on the joy of seeing our own kids and Jordan. Anyway, the decision's made, and we have to figure out how in the world to transport all of the Stuff we've collected back to the States.

The weather's turned beautiful, and everyone thinks winter is over and we're going to have some sunshine. As I recall from last year, the trend for the next month or two will alternate between clear and rainy days and progressively warmer temperatures. The ever-present smog makes even the sunny days gloomier.

We know many here yearn for something more in their lives, but don't know what that is. We may not speak of the Bible or its examples and teachings, though it gives us guidance and comfort. Then too, our students have become precious to us, especially as we watch the older ones struggle to graduate, searching for jobs in an overcrowded market. They hunger to stay in the Ningbo area so they can continue to study and use their education to find better paying jobs. If they can't find a job, they have to return to their villages, where disease and ignorance await them.

The Foreign Language Department (the new name for the English Department because the authorities hope to hire a Japanese teacher next year) has started publishing a monthly newsletter. Linda asked me to write an article for the first issue. I decided to write our response to the many asked, and sometimes unasked, questions we hear. This is what I wrote:

Why would we leave our family, friends and home to come to China to teach English and ask for no salary? Several people have asked us this question during our year here at Zhejiang Sunli University. My husband Robert McKee and I feel very fortunate that we've had a full and happy life in America teaching, traveling and rearing our family of three children. It was time to retire from our jobs; our 'kids' are all grown and married with busy, full lives of their own. We're both healthy and have always felt it was important to reach out to help others if we can, since we've received so much love and help in the past. We belong to an organization that sends volunteers all over the world. They make arrangements for and send people who are willing to help in many different kinds of ways. Some who are trained as doctors, dentists, and nurses go to areas where health care is needed. Some go in to help disaster victims with clothing and food. Many volunteer to help teach English in countries who request this. That's how we came to China. This sounded like something that we could both do with pleasure.

Of course, we miss our family, but our students here have been marvelous! The kindness, respect, and love that we have felt from each of them have made our stay such a delightful experience. We've had the privilege of traveling to many cities and towns in China, of visiting exquisite lakes and gardens, of walking through museums displaying art and historical treasures, but our deepest and warmest memories will be of each smiling, hardworking Chinese student, and the wonderful other teachers and friends here at this college. When we return to our home in America in July and must say, 'Zai jian' to these Chinese friends, we will be anxious to hug our own children, but we know that we will leave pieces of our hearts here in China.

52

JUDY AND DRIVER'S TRAINING

J udy, Zhu Feng Feng, has the widest grin. Of all of the 144 English majors, she has the most bounce. She wanted to learn to play the guitar and has made progress with it, coming to the apartment often for lessons and staying for supper. Her ability to play my keyboard amazes us, and she admits she has a piano at home, something quite rare in China. Several clues indicate that Judy comes from a home with more spendable income than most Chinese homes. She plunges daringly into the murky waters of the English language, the results usually a comical mix of Mandarin, sign language, and English. She knows I'm studying Mandarin and launches into an explanation in Chinese when she can't find the English phrase she wants. Sometimes that helps, but usually we both wind up laughing ourselves into tears and backing up to try again. She's what I would call a shy extrovert, clowning to cover tender feelings. But she is determined to savor every flavor life has to offer.

I asked her a few weeks ago if she'd be comfortable playing her guitar with me in class to accompany the kids while we all sing. She thought about it and then agreed to do it. Rob brought his class in one afternoon, and we had a singalong while Judy and I strummed.

She did very well, and it was fun to watch her blossom.

Rob and I are startled today walking across the main quadrangle to see about a half dozen "deuce-and-a-halfs" (the Chinese army equivalent to our army's two-and-a-half ton trucks) with the motors roaring. I think my *fight-or-flight* button must be stuck on *flight*. I'm a devout coward and instantly see visions of the communist army bearing down on our gentle students. "Wait a minute, Susie," Robert cautions. "Look! The wheels on those trucks are off the ground. They're jacked up. Let's go get a closer look." A closer look is about the *last* thing I have in mind! The noise is deafening, and the huge trucks quiver on shaky supports.

Either I remain rooted to the ground alone or I approach the behemoths with my knight. I go. In the driver's seat of each truck we recognize some students. Seated beside each student a man in a military uniform barks commands. Gears grind mercilessly. Metal against metal. The trucks shudder.

We scurry on to class, and I ask my students, "What is going on outside the old classroom building with the trucks?"

"Oh, those are brave students who are learning to drive. It is very expensive and very difficult." Driver's training! In huge military trucks! I guess they are what is available. The chances of any one of the kids ever actually driving an automobile are slim to none, but here they are.

Later in our apartment I mention this to Judy. She giggles and hides her mouth behind her hand, hunching over at the good joke. "Yes, I am one who takes the driver's training. I am the only one in all the English majors. Soon we will take the trucks out and really drive them on the road." I close my eyes and try to imagine Judy behind the wheel of one of those monster trucks, dodging the gnat-like bicycles, cars, and three-wheeled trucklets that infest the roads. I widen my eyes in mock horror, and Judy doubles over laughing at the prospect.

An update on the driver's training: Judy tells us, "Today I drive the truck and hit a tree. It is only a small tree." She doesn't seem at all upset, in fact, finds it pretty amusing. Maybe that attitude explains a lot about Chinese driving.

53

THE LEAP

I still have one class a week in the old classroom building. The accumulated chalk dust and grime somehow seem even more primitive when I dash in from the new white classrooms. In this room, the raised platform for the *lauscher*, or teacher, is badly deteriorated. Floor slats are chipped or missing, and the broken edges around the perimeter of the flooring form a jagged no man's land around the raised desk. After 45 minutes, the bell clangs the ten-minute *xiuxi* (pause) to give everyone a moment to run to the bathroom or stretch and get ready for the next 45-minute segment. I linger out in the hall chatting, so when the bell signals the end of *xiuxi*, I leap through the door and sail onto the platform, hoping to use the remaining time for conversation and instruction.

I miscalculate and stumble and crash onto the edge of the platform. A collective gasp rises from the students, their horrified faces turned to me, and I struggle to my feet to assure them that I'm all right. But I can't! The stabbing pain along my left shinbone sends waves of scarlet before my eyes. I open my mouth for an apologetic laugh but hear only a moan. It's me! Many kids are out of their seats, rushing to the front. Two boys help me up. With a deep breath I find

I can speak. "Thank you." (Take a breath.) "I'm okay." Luckily there's a tall stool for the teacher in this room. I perch on it gingerly and manage a thin smile. "Now that I have your attention~." Nervous laughter as they slip back to their seats. The throbbing in my leg becomes a dull companion, but I muddle through the rest of the class. I glance down at my foot after I take my post on the stool and am shocked to see that my white sock is now red. Hidden behind the desk, only I notice.

I don't remember getting back to the apartment. It was the last class of the day, and I expect Rob will be home soon too. In the bathroom I stare at my gray wool slacks, stained on the left leg, when Rob comes whistling in. "Rob, could you come in here and help me please?" We both stare as we peel back the slacks to see that my white long underwear looks as if it has been dipped in purple/red dye. Caked blood covers my leg. I guess the thermal underwear acted as a pressure bandage after I ripped my shin open on the edge of the rotted, splintered platform.

How to remove the clothing without starting the bleeding again? Rob is all business. "Let's soak your leg in the tub, peel the clothes off, and examine that gash. Susie, we may have to take you to the hospital." We both shudder at the memory of the desultory hospital staff but even more at the sloppy hygiene we saw there. "Actually, more bleeding might be good for it. There are probably germs from the ice age on that platform!" We know the tap water's not potable but hope it doesn't increase the possibility of infection. He scurries around for the bleach and the Neosporin. His military training and his experience with the Vietnamese Rangers reassure me. Then he whistles, "Wow! I think I can see your leg bone!" which makes me a little dizzy. After it's cleaned to his satisfaction, he slathers on cream and cinches the gash with American bandages. "I think that even with stitches you'll still have a scar there, but it should be okay now." Relief. My "doctor" agrees that the wound should heal satisfactorily.

I'm content to sit with my left leg up for the rest of the evening as I prepare for the next day's classes. I try to disguise the slight limp from the students, but they notice immediately. Their solicitousness is touching, but we move on with English.

Lucy invited us to go to downtown Ningbo this evening with her and some friends to see the Lantern Festival. People light red paper lanterns and join in a happy parade. It's been four days since my swan dive, and the throbbing in my leg has subsided, though my left foot is swollen, the heel and foot sorely bruised. Robert is alarmed, and I'm scared. We examine the leg for signs of infection radiating out from the original gash. Nervous jokes about amputation aren't funny. He assumes his firmest voice. "We are *not* going downtown on the bus to stand on our feet for hours. That'd be just stupid!" I agree.

Lucy's disappointed when she finds me propped up on the bed with my foot on two pillows. "I'm sorry, Lucy. It would be foolish for me to go tonight, although I would love to be there with you." She nods sadly and leaves.

A gentle tap on our door comes rather early the next morning. Lucy has a red lantern for me. Her worried face asks the question before she does. "How are you, Mrs. McKee?"

"I'm getting better every day, Lucy. Thank you. The lantern is lovely."

The swelling in my foot lasts about two weeks. We change the dressing and clean the wound, and I keep the foot elevated when I'm not in the classroom. No permanent damage—except to my dignity and grace.

Sundays are strange days for us now that our American teacher friends are gone. We looked forward to the spiritual and emotional boost of our prayer services together. Now we're alone, and Sunday in China is just another workday. The university doesn't have classes, but downtown bustles with activity, and students sway on the buses going to and from other schools. Rob and I try to keep the day sacred and focused on the Lord. We read the scriptures and take a good look at our lives and the blessings that cushion us. We don't want Sunday to be just another day, so we use it to write to family and friends. This Sunday we offer a particular thanks that I seem to have healed completely from my giant misstep, and I plan to spring a little more cautiously in the future.

One of the older classrooms

5 4

THE PAPER CUTTER

The dragon lady in the library no longer controls duplicating. She has vaporized, and a younger woman, sometimes with a helper, is in charge of making copies for the university staff. I think the copy machine in its own room in the new classroom building is new too. Teachers are still not allowed to touch it, but the new overseer is kinder than her predecessor. She inherited the white gloves, but she listens very carefully when I explain what we want done, then bobs her head in agreement and understanding. I am a little more confident with my Chinese copying vocabulary. We try not to overburden her, but much of what we do begins with a worksheet for each student. Often to save paper we set up what we want duplicated on a half sheet, then take the full sheets home and halve them. I have no clue what the word for paper cutter is; I do the charades thing, chopping at the paper with my hand to the new lady's amusement and befuddlement; we search every inch of the copy room for evidence of a paper cutter. No luck.

So Rob and I set out on the bus for Ningbo in quest of a paper cutter to buy and donate to the university. Not so easy. After scouring any store that looks as if it has office supplies and the couple of department stores that sell business machines, we find one. In fact, we find two. "We'd like to take them out of the box to see them please."

Worried discussion among the half dozen or so interested clerks clustered around us. "Sorry. Not possible." Oh no, here we go again. My vocabulary reaches its limits when we try to reason that we want to see the paper cutters only to compare them for our needs. "Both very good," we're told.

"Yes, I'm sure they are, but we need to *see* them, know exactly what size they are, how they operate." It strikes me very funny that a customer can't examine what he's to buy, but the furious bargaining to consummate a purchase is predictable choreography, maybe because in "established" stores, prices are clearly stamped and one is expected to pay without a whimper and without looking or handling anything. We finally manage to close the deal and lug the large paper cutter, its lethal cutting arm firmly clipped to its side, back on the bus.

We proudly present it to the copy lady who watches in utter fascination as we slice our copies in half in her room. Can it be she's never seen such a thing? I explain that this is for everyone to use. She can keep it there in the copy room. She giggles, and a high-pitched exchange I can't follow bubbles between her and her helper. I thrust it toward her, and she backs away. I nod and smile and hold it out so she can find a place to keep it. Reluctantly she takes it, and we leave, happy to add a "modern" convenience to the copy room.

The next time we come to make copies we see the paper cutter in its box way up on a high shelf. We expected, hoped even, to find it on the long table used for collating and stacking copies. We have to climb the ladder and drag it down to use it, then put it back. We note that dust gathers on it. Apparently, either we're the only ones who need to cut paper or the copy lady won't let anyone else touch it. Oh, well.

Robert and I have our own desks in one of the two English teachers' offices in the new building. We lobbied long and hard for them, and we keep office hours so shy students who won't drop by our apartment can come there if they need to. The concept is strange to them, though, and few come. We use the time to grade papers and chat with Anna and Sunny, who enjoy asking about America. Dick has a desk there too, so we're a jolly group.

I think I mentioned that Rob and I got one black marking pen apiece to use on the pristine whiteboards at the beginning of this semester. We've pretty much used them up, so we go to Linda, the acting English department head, to ask for more. "Not necessary," she tells us. "Come with me." We follow her to her office, stacked floor to ceiling with papers, dictionaries (each student gets a fat English-Chinese dictionary), and unknown impedimenta. In the corner she shows us a large black pot that reeks of ink, black ink splashed on the desk where it sits, puddles seeping into the new floor. Tongs encrusted with dried ink lie beside the inkpot. "See? You just hold the pen in the ink for a short time. Then it writes very well." Linda looks triumphant.

Robert, who cringes at anything gooey or messy, turns pale. In some ways, this surpasses the glue pot in the post offices. It doesn't smell quite so horrific, but the splash factor is worse. I dutifully clutch my worn-out pen with the encrusted tongs and dangle it gingerly into the pot. I look over at Robert's incredulous face and say, "Never mind, Honey. You go on back to the office. I'll do yours too." I know what he's thinking though. There'll be another trip downtown to buy as many black markers as we can find.

5 5

ROB'S EYES

Robert was warned before we left the US that he would probably need cataract surgery when we returned. He says his eyesight is deteriorating pretty badly now. And quickly! I tell him I'll be his "seeing-eye person" until we are back in America, and we try to ignore it. But I see he's worried. A spot in front of his eye just won't go away, he tells me quietly. Then Friday evening he closes his book and says, "I really can't read. I keep seeing something like strobe lights in the corners of my eye."

All kinds of alarms go off in my head. We're not dealing with just fuzzy eyesight. There's something seriously wrong. "How long have you been noticing that?"

"Uh, I don't know. Since yesterday. Maybe the day before."

I send an e-mail to Jim, a retired ear, eye, nose and throat doctor friend in Maryland. In this age of specialization I think he was only "doing noses" when he finished his practice, but I need instant education. We describe the symptoms to Jim and wait.

An answer comes back all in capital letters: "GET TO AN EYE SPECIALIST. IMMEDIATELY! POSSIBLE RETINAL DETACH-MENT. MUST BE TREATED IN A MATTER OF HOURS.

OTHERWISE IRREVERSIBLE BLINDNESS." There's absolutely no way that either of us will consent to invasive medical treatment here in China, so we e-mail Bonnie in California to pave the way for medical appointments there. We e-mail our organization support team in Hong Kong for advice. There is a representative based in Hong Kong. We met him only once when he and his wife flew here to see us. We send in a quarterly report, but that's the extent of our contact.

Rob is not willing to wait for bureaucratic flip-flop when he's in danger of losing his eyesight, so a phone call from Hong Kong early Saturday morning delights us. They've arranged for tickets for us to fly today to Hong Kong. We'll be met at the airport and whisked to an American trained Chinese ophthalmologist. Jenny is out of town, but we quickly pack a few things and dash onto the main road outside the campus—in a cold drizzle. We try to flag a cab to take us to the airport. I called Sam, who works with Jenny, to explain the situation and apologize but ask them to cover our classes. I have no idea when we'll be back. Usually the cabs swerve in front of oncoming traffic to pull up beside us if we are waiting for the bus, and we wave them away. Now when we desperately need one, there are none. I've forgotten the umbrella, so icy rain drizzles down my neck, but my shivering comes from deep inside where I sense I'm the one in charge right now. Rob is the take-charge guy in crisis situations, but he's a little numb with the possibility of onrushing blindness. A small yellow taxi almost whizzes past us, but we shout and wave our arms. It skids to a halt, does a U-turn, and the driver warily opens the door for two drenched foreigners. I carefully enunciate the phrase asking him to take us to the airport and hold my breath. He nods understanding, and the car leaps out into traffic.

The flight is a long ordeal. Hong Kong has recently gone back under Chinese control with much hoopla and celebration. Though part of mainland China now, Hong Kong's long customs lines and scowling security agents scrutinizing our passports and visas make us feel like we're entering another country. My husband seems quieter and whiter than usual.

A representative will meet us at Section C. If I were less worried I would have been in awe of the enormous new airport, set on an island built for it. High-speed trains run continuously, bringing passengers in from the airport's various wings. We stumble onto it, grateful for the signs in both English and Cantonese. It's clear that Hong Kong is much more international and cosmopolitan than the China we've just come from. I study faces on the train from all over the world. We're not such an oddity here. How will the rep know who we are in the crush?

Section C doesn't thin the crowd much, but we locate it and stand, trying to look conspicuous, succeeding only in looking pretty bewildered. Maybe that's why he locates us after only a few minutes, a big man with a smile that lights up even the mammoth skylit waiting room. He grabs the small suitcase from my hand and leads us toward yet more trains. He's a retired doctor he tells us; his assignment is to respond to the health problems of the area's volunteers. He questions Rob about his symptoms. "How long have you noticed the flashing lights? Do they ever disappear completely? Well, we've set up an appointment with an American-trained Chinese eye specialist. We'll take this train, which will zip us right into downtown Hong Kong, drop your things off at the hotel, then get you to Dr. Zhou."

I *feel* the weight slide from my shoulders, physically. I read once that we need to know really only two prayers. The first is difficult and takes years of effort and practice though it's just one word: *Help!* The second prayer is *Thank you*. I've been praying the first in my heart for two long days. I'm grateful to slip into the *thank you* mode.

Dr. Zhou is young, friendly, and professional. He examines Rob with equipment I've never seen before, dilates his eyes, then smiles and says that Rob's eyes are *not* threatening retinal detachment. The symptoms were clear and we were wise to err on caution's side, but Rob has posterior viscous detachment, which does not currently threaten to damage the eye but is worth watching.

"Thank you!"

56

HONG KONG

Hong Kong! The name reverberates with exotic images for me! Both of us are lightheaded with relief. I feel as if I've held my breath a very long time and have just stepped into crisp mountain air. I inhale deeply.

It's Sunday, and we take a taxi to the address where church services are held. The building in an upscale neighborhood. Here people practice religion openly. At least they *did* under the British. Now there's some ambivalence since Hong Kong has been returned to the Chinese government. On the surface everything stays the same. Many questions remain about Hong Kong's future.

We're welcomed into a large, pine-paneled chapel. The congregation, a mix of many cultures, is much larger than in Shanghai. We drink in the music and the spirit of the meeting and bottle the serenity and fellowship to take home with us.

The area volunteer representative and his wife tell us that their apartment is so tiny they can't change their *minds* in it. They cannot invite us to dinner there but would love to take us to a restaurant in town. "What kind of food would you like? We have it all here!"

Robert and I are bewildered. There's nothing but Chinese food in the mainland, except for the miserable McDonald's and Kentucky Fried Chicken franchises which the Chinese assume is what all Americans eat. "You mean you can find French or Italian cuisine here?"

"Sure, or Thai, Indonesian, Dutch. What do you want?"

Now I ask the Big Question: "Can you get a green salad? I haven't tasted lettuce since we left the States."

"Sure."

"I want to go there." They laugh and we settle on a favorite Italian restaurant.

Hong Kong contrasts sharply with Ningbo. The glass high-rise city vaguely recalls San Francisco. I had no idea Hong Kong was so hilly! Some sidewalks have built-in escalators! The Brit rule wrought unbelievable changes to the Chinese culture *we* know. On the way to the restaurant, Rob points out Hong Kong citizens queuing up politely for the bus. And the buses! Hundreds of double-decker buses and trolleys drive in orderly fashion on the "wrong" side of the street. No honking or darting up on sidewalks to pass another vehicle. No bicycles on the streets. Public transportation is so good and so cheap that bikes are neither necessary nor allowed on city streets. Most signs are in English as well as Cantonese instead of the Mandarin of mainland China. People on the streets are well dressed, very citified, all nationalities. The malls and sophisticated shops look trendy and expensive. As night settles over the city, neon blazes everywhere, rivaling my memories of Times Square.

At the restaurant I catch the aroma of roasting garlic, beef, peppery spices, vinegars, and my taste buds explode. But what I want is a *salad*. We're shown through the laughing crowd to a bright table and study the menu and the treasures listed there. "Can I trust the

Caesar salad? Is it okay to have that here?" Even if you could find lettuce in China, cleanliness would be the problem.

"Yes, the salad is safe here, Sue. Don't you want anything else?"

"I just can't think beyond a salad right now."

And so I have a salad. The crunchy, crisp, cold Romaine gently coated with olive oil and pungent Parmesan cheese and dripping with garlic and vinegar satisfies my soul. I polish off a hearty helping of lasagna as well.

The next day we're on our own. We wander through the downtown streets a bit, still amazed at the difference between the modern, bright, busy streets and gray Ningbo. We see many young Filipino nannies walking towheaded children in the park, likely the children of wealthy international business people. They must be rich to live in Hong Kong! A real estate agent who pops out of his shop when we stop to look at the ads in his window says a fairly decent flat runs a good $10,000 U.S. a month! We walk (and climb!) some side streets and see cement cubicles more like the China we know. A turn into a side street suddenly plunges us back into the China of many years ago, with the familiar sounds and smells of long-used toilets and garlic.

We pay a sampan to take us around the inner harbor where we peek at the thousands of houseboat sampans and the millions of people who eke out a living in the shadow of the glass skyscrapers. The day turns warm, so we strip off our winter coats as we watch the shrimp ladies peel the day's catch at the fish market. In the evening we're on our own for dinner and choose an intimate French restaurant. The exquisite rack of lamb, slim green beans, and, yes, another salad are the stuff of dreams to come.

The day develops a hitch, however. At the volunteer headquarters we learn that the government will not let us reenter China on the visas we have. "But if Hong Kong is part of China, how can they deny us entry? It's all the same country now!"

The young man, whose job at the office it is to iron out bureaucratic wrinkles, smiles at the outburst. He shakes his head and says, "It makes sense to the Chinese." He's Chinese.

"So what do we do now?" Rob asks.

"I suggest you call your university authorities. We cannot straighten this out from this end. They need to initiate the paperwork to get you back into China."

"How long will that take? It's fun to be here, but we're supposed to be teaching a full load of classes." He shrugs and rolls his eyes. Robert groans.

Through a crackling phone connection we finally get Jenny. Even through the noise I hear the worry in her voice. "Robert's eyes are all right, Jenny. A specialist checked them, and it's a minor problem, not the big one we were afraid of." I'm ashamed we waited almost twenty-four hours to call her when I hear her relief. Then we explain our dilemma. Jenny becomes all business. She assures us she will get moving to see what she can do about our visas.

Jenny is a quiet lady, but she knows the back alleys and twisted corridors of *guanxi*, the whole convoluted system of trading favors and back-scratching she must deal with quite often. It's a way of life in China—who you know and how much Party influence you have. We'll never know how, but the red tape is cut early this morning and we catch our plane back to Ningbo, clutching new visas that trigger only a bored nod from customs officials.

As a result of the hurry-up trip to Hong Kong, our classes were cancelled for most of the week. Now that we're back, we feel obliged to offer make-up classes, which means meeting with most of our kids four times (eight hours) a week instead of the normal two. It's a huge load but good for their English. We believe that we see improvement in their skill levels. Maybe it's our imagination or just hope, but we think we've seen improvement all semester long. They're just now at the point where they understand what's going on and grasp most of what we say. They *want* to learn. Teaching the highly motivated English majors is fun.

I meet with my "Shakespeare boy" almost every afternoon. Robert even has *me* calling him that. Qiu Zhi Fu comes in apologetically and speaks so softly that even sitting next to him I have a hard time hearing him. We wade through bits of Shakespeare, Milton, Pope, Hawthorne, with a sprinkling of others for about an hour from a study guide he brings. He reads aloud to me, then looks up pleading to know what the heck he's just read. I try to explain in simple words. It's March, and the examination he hopes to pass—a general exam given in Ningbo to any university student who wants to take it—is in April. I'm not sure what he plans to do with it, but I try not to show that I don't think he can pass it on the first try. He tells me he comes from a "very poor family in a very poor village." I met his father, also quite tall, thin almost to the point of emaciation, an older version of the boy. The father has the few long thin strands of a beard we see on pictures of old Chinese mandarins. He could not bring himself to meet my eyes when we met briefly on campus. His proud son introduced us and apologized that his father spoke no English. I figure this son loves his father and is proud of him but wants to lift himself to something beyond what village life offers. I don't know if Shakespeare will do it, but apparently he thinks it will.

57

CINDERELLA

Morning exercises begin sharply at 6:45 on clear days. All three thousand members of the student body are expected to show up at the soccer field. Rain cancels it. We're always up at that hour, but if we weren't, the loudspeaker barking out the numbers *Yi Er San Si Wu* would bounce us out of bed. The field is several buildings from our apartment, so we've never actually witnessed the calisthenics. Today we decide to walk over and admire the early morning activity. We have to hurry since it lasts only about ten minutes.

We feel as if we've joined some of Robert E. Lee's troops stumbling to Appomattox. Sleepy students, shirttails dangling, shuffle past us. No one speaks. If the overloud martial music annoys them as much as is does us, they don't show it. The heavy morning fog hangs on everything, though it doesn't muffle the canned music or the male voice that shifts gears and starts counting cadence.

I'd assumed an instructor of some kind showed up to direct the exercises, but no, no teachers in sight, and the lethargic exercisers strike Rob and me as funny. We wonder why they bother at all. Jumping Jacks look more like *standing* Jacks as the students shuffle

into line, glancing up at the loudspeaker indifferently. Occasionally
the "athletes" do a little playful pushing, but for the most part, the
kids don't even go through the motions. Most aren't even awake. The
cheerful voice on the speaker calls out the next drill, then launches
into the count again. Most pay no attention. After ten minutes, some
are still arriving when the finale is called and everyone starts moving
back toward the dining hall. They're slightly livelier. I won't be quite
so impressed now that I have *seen* the morning calisthenics as I was
before when I heard the loudspeaker leap to life.

Tonight everyone on campus is awake and invited to come to a
performance by the English Club. A group decided some time ago to
write and produce a play based on *Cinderella*. In English. I guess the
subject shows their level of sophistication. They'll have time enough
to become sardonic. We're surprised but accept their choice. They
do it all—script, rehearsals, costumes—completely on their own.
They want to surprise us, so we get to see only the final rehearsal.
They've prerecorded their voices and lip sync the actual performance. Since there's no auditorium on campus, they use the dining
hall. We sit on a bench and smile, truly impressed, as the rehearsal
progresses. During the ball scene, however, the boys, who've been
coerced into it, have no idea how to waltz and turn to us for help. We
give a brief dance lesson and smile as we put the boys' hands on the
girls. Since boys don't usually even *sit* beside girls in class, touching
them seems outrageous to them.

The dining hall is packed for the performance, the benches
sagging with the weight of too many sitters. There's not even
standing room as the expectant crowd shouts across the room to
locate friends. Boys perch in the windowsills with spotlights trained
on the makeshift curtain. The spring evening is warm, but the heat

from all the bodies and bright lights is stifling.

Chinese audiences are pretty rude, not just at the university, but also at the rare professional performances we've attended. The audience talks out loud, pops up and down, and clumps up and down the aisles nonstop. We hope the actors won't be unnerved. After a long wait, the show begins.

The beginning is a bit shaky, and since the voices are already on tape, comical miscues occur when an actor gestures too soon or too late for the voice. The audience shows no kindness and guffaws. The tape gets stuck several times and pauses embarrassingly until somebody fixes it.

But about midway through the story something magical happens. The girl who plays Cinderella has been almost mute all year in Rob's class, he says. She is painfully shy, and he's amazed that she accepted the part. The costumes are really quite extraordinary, and the evil stepmother and stepsisters are *very* evil. We realize the story is not familiar to the Chinese audience, and they are engrossed in the outcome. When the fairy godmother (Auntie in this version) appears to the weeping Cinderella, the students applaud.

There is an interminable wait before Cinderella appears in her ball gown. The audience shuffles, but when she steps out onto the stage, the shy girl is transformed! The kids must have rented the gown from a costume shop. She floats onstage, a vision in white floor-length organza. She glows, the audience gasps, and a fairytale comes to life! Her chin comes up and self-confidence marks every gesture. Her classmates see her with new eyes, and she knows it. The prince wears a fancy blue jacket with gold epaulets, and while he is appropriately dashing, it's all about Cinderella emerging from her chrysalis and we all know it.

A sustained round of applause rewards the play, and Robert and I pound our hands together until they're red. Afterward we linger to congratulate and hug all the actors. And this time they let us.

58

THE SEAFOOD FESTIVAL

Jenny arranges a van and a driver for a two-day trip to Tian Tai Shan (Mountain). Rob's read about this area and wants to go. We never told Jenny and did not expect her to plan the trip, but she insists. All part of her job. So we pack all five foreigners—Rob, me, Dick, Edie and John—into the van along with Jenny and bounce the three hours up to the mountain hotel, check in, then tour the Buddhist temple. In the privacy of our room Robert admits, "If I never see another Buddhist temple, it'll be just dandy with me."

For me the sharp smell of the incense, the tall tapers burning outside the temple, the flying wings and grotesque gargoyles on the roof beckon and repel at the same time. The bowing, nodding worshippers are mostly old people, in whom the communist fist could not crush tradition and religious faith. Food and drink offerings line the several altars over which popeyed Buddhas in garish colors and impossible poses loom. Serene Buddhas sometimes line the walls too, some tiny, some tremendous. Tourists swarm over the temple; laughing schoolchildren, families on holiday, people by the busload all enjoy the many buildings surrounding the main temple.

The next day we climb aboard another little kamikaze bus after Jenny noisily negotiates the price and begin an hour's white-knuckle dash around hairpin turns farther up the mountainside, careening along the one-lane, mostly dirt road, with the horn blazing. The rule is, he who honks first whizzes around the blind corner first. There is no guardrail. I try to enjoy the scenery. Jenny seems completely at ease, while the foreign cowards stop trying to look casual and concentrate on mentally willing the ride to end. I can say this now: it *is* worth the trip. We got back down safely. Maybe the death-defying ride enhances my visions of villages clinging to the mountainside, tiny terraced fields planted every inch around them. We walk through bamboo forests to crashing water-falls. At last I am seeing the stuff of Chinese paintings! People trudging along the road barely look up at us, as they continue as they have for millennia, just putting one foot in front of the other. We peek into compounds and tiny businesses where babies romp, tiny bare bottoms visible through split britches. I *am* glad we came.

Then another two-day trip (spring seems to be the time for travel) to a seaside town for a seafood festival sponsored by the Foreign Affairs Office in Ningbo. That's James and Carr. The trip is open to any foreigners working in the area, so we meet several new people, a total of twenty-two people in two vans. I wish we could just beam ourselves to our destination instead of enduring the insane Chinese driving! The constant weaving in and out of traffic and honking don't make for a relaxing ride. Everyone is gracious and kind, but when the professional drivers (of vans, buses, of all autos!) get behind the wheel, especially in pedestrian and bike traffic, it's a wonder they don't litter the roads with dead bodies.

The seafood festival is a first ever for the village, very old and quite lovely with lots of beach and unspoiled coastline. Although Ningbo is built at the confluence of three rivers not so far from the ocean, its waterfront is dirty and industrialized. As we approach the village, we inhale the fishy saltwater smell. There's a heavy overcast, smog or haze, but the air feels lighter.

We're treated like royalty here! An extravagant display of seafood, fanciful clamshells, and glass balls spill over satin draped tables in the hotel lobby. There's no time to rest because we have a tight schedule for the weekend. Rob and I try to keep a low profile as we travel, especially when it's just the two of us, so we're startled when a police escort of four cars, sirens blaring, surrounds our vans and whisks us from one place to another. It all begins to feel like a Woody Allen movie, although the villagers don't pay much attention to the hoopla.

The first night we screech to a restaurant where the city treats its foreign guests to a seafood banquet. Since seafood is pretty low on my list of favorite foods and I've learned in the past year that when the Chinese say *fresh* they mean *raw*, I'm not too excited about the prospect. Chinese hosts flank me right and left, urging me to try the small crabs and snails on the sampling dishes. I smile woodenly but manage to get enough vegetables and rice and do my peanut trick without offending anyone. I think. I look across the table and see that Robert has a few of the tiny green crabs on his plate. Remember that everyone picks up what he or she wants from the serving dishes with chopsticks and eats it. Bones or shells are spit right back onto the table. A small saucer by each diner in fancier restaurants is a nod to more modern table manners. Rob is about to pick up a crab with his chopsticks when it sticks its little head and legs out of the shell and marches across his saucer. Remember, *fresh* equals *live*. Quietly he covers it with another shell and pushes it aside. Even his adventurous palate can't handle that.

After the meal we journey (noisily!) along a boulevard lined with red silk lanterns. Beautiful! We come to a lovely park with a huge amphitheater and unload. There we watch an extravaganza perform-ance by brightly costumed dancers and musicians. Since we are the only foreigners, the TV and still cameras turn on us quite a bit. We try to be gracious with the sudden celebrity, but it's a bit unnerving. The show opens with massed drummers and cymbals, one of the most exciting things I've ever witnessed! The drums range from Volkswagen-sized to handheld tom-toms. The drummers wear scarlet and gold, and the precise beat thuds into my heartbeat. There must be a hundred of them on the stage! The noise is almost deafening but thrilling. Then maybe fifty men come onstage doing the dragon dance, darting in intricate patterns, waving the dragon's sinuous, silk body while the man carrying the head on a pole shakes and bobs it expertly. The throbbing drums and crashing cymbals are almost unbearable. Then they stop, and the silence drops us back into ourselves.

The next day we tour two factories in town. One makes high voltage transformers, another, auto parts. Everything is spotless. Workers smile. Long explanations praise the Party. We smile and nod. Where are the factories *out* of public view?

We go to a beach where several groups in costume perform intricate dances *en masse*. An older woman's group in fancy pajama-type costumes works out with drums strapped at their waists. Yet when we foreigners arrive, everything crumbles. The performers are so curious to talk with us that everything comes to a standstill while they ask to have their pictures taken with us. They even ask for autographs! Shy young children come up once they see we're accessible and ask their mothers to take a picture of us together or ask us to sign the books or papers they thrust into our hands. I hope it doesn't go to our heads.

59

OCCUPATIONS

O ur students can't believe their ears when, after complimenting them for the excellent reports on foreign countries, we tell them we have another oral report project for them—and this time on an individual basis. We move immediately into what we call the *occupation* block of instruction.

For four weeks Rob has been teaching business writing, including letters, memos, and reports. It's an uphill battle because the Chinese and American cultures approach business correspondence from diametrically opposed postures. The Chinese use circular, flowery language in business discussions, and Americans favor the direct frontal approach. The kids are aghast when Rob explains, "You open a business letter by stating its purpose directly."

"But, Mr. McKee, no polite compliments?"

"No. You compliment business associates by not wasting their time. You say exactly what you want or what you can give them." Stunned silence. Robert concludes his lecture on business letters, "Be concise! You can be polite and still be concise." He glowers, then grins, and they giggle nervously.

The students know that foreign trade moves commerce and money, and the language of that trade is English. They also know Robert has a master's degree in business, which is to them rather like clutching the Holy Grail. American business practices lead to comfortable lives for young people, lives undreamed of by their parents. They listen with heightened attention when Rob tells them what is expected in a good Western business letter, but cultural norms runs deep.

We split one writing exercise into sections after Rob's presentation and ask students to write five good topic sentences, then develop one into a cohesive paragraph. (Oh dear! I sound like an English teacher!) That is more challenging than one might think for a mind accustomed to circuitous oriental thinking. To get them to decide exactly what they want to say and then *say* it in a topic sentence is, shall we say, a cultural coup.

They want to sidle up, even to fictitious recipients, with questions about the receiver's health, shared memories, comments on China's growing role in the world market before bringing up the annoying nuisance of ordering a pencil or applying for a job. My red pen fades from lining out so much of the cocktail party chatter that opens their letters.

The matter is, in fact, serious business since when they graduate they will have to search for a job, something new in China, and the new import/export businesses springing up everywhere will need the English skills they're learning. They must also learn to present themselves to Westerners and to people who deal with Westerners. A command of English means good money, so this is not just a writing exercise.

We asked friends in the States to send us *Help Wanted* ads from city newspapers. The kids devour the business sections. All that they are sure of is that they want to succeed in *business*. They have no idea what that means or what one *does* in business. We read through the ads with them and copy those with the best job descriptions. Armed with the ads, we ask the students to select a job to apply for, and the writing classes work on resumés and application letters.

The students and the university administrators are excited about the idea since it's a practical application of education and something the students need, since so many international joint ventures are starting up here. They hire English speakers at salaries considerably higher than at most other jobs.

We're getting pretty good at operating the new audiovisual equipment. We've learned to do the doorkey two-step with Mrs. Wu so she doesn't lose face, but we use the room for preparation. I prepare cartoons and large word outlines for the opaque projector, and Rob creates discs in our home computer so one can display whole paragraphs, lists, charts, etc. while the other is lecturing. The kids are entranced with the information on the large screen. We tried to teach them to take notes but the concept is absolutely foreign to them.

The kids also keep personal journals in English. They have so little chance to use the language that the journals seem like a way to try to keep it flowing. I explain that writing almost every day helps them think in English, and I assure them again that we don't read their thoughts. While they work on some writing exercise in class, Rob and I circulate and initial the latest journal entry. We tell them not to worry about grammar or spelling. We don't want weather reports or lists of what they do every day; we encourage them to express feelings or explore ideas that interest them. I hope the journals can be springboards for later creative writing assignments.

I find, though, as I walk up and down the rows of desks initialing the journals, that poignant words and phrases jump out at me. Since they're writing in *my* native language and I'm a quick reader (and a snoop), I catch bits of their thoughts. Of course, some may *intend* their entries for my eyes: "Today Mrs. McKee's class very interesting. We laugh and learn about cheese food." But others say, "Grandfather very sick. My heart is sore. Tears wash my eyes when no one sees."

Occasionally I glance at an entry and the words and syntax say *Not student work*. A lazy, resourceful kid has copied a paragraph right from his workbook, thinking it *looks* like a journal entry. That's a conundrum. I don't want to blow my cover and reveal that I can really read much of what they write. I decide to approach the problem generally instead of individually. "I can tell by seeing a few of the words in some of your journals that you are copying the writing. Those are not your words and thoughts. Please do not cheat yourselves of the opportunity to learn." Some blushes, some tittering.

Actually the idea of plagiarism is hard for them. We're dumbfounded at first when they lift whole passages out of a book and hand it in as homework, swearing it's their own work when it so obviously is not. We have to soft-pedal though, since in their culture plagiarism is neither a word nor a problem. It's wise to copy and revere your elders. In addition, many Chinese teachers don't even read the homework handed in, just check it off as completed. I read at least 144 essays a week for the writing class; on maybe seven of them I write a note in red: Is this your own work?

Today I get a sheepish note:

"I'm very sorry for not doing my homework with carefully and single-hearted devotion. Last week, as a member of Student Council,

I'm busy doing my work. Last Tuesday evening there is a dance party at our college. Most of our member took part in it and also I organized this party with other members. I hadn't done my homework until last Tuesday afternoon. After lunch, when I heard that this homework must hand in, I did it immediately. But it didn't do myself. I copied it from our Extensive Reading Book. I'm very sorry for that. But I pledge that this condition will not happen again. Please forgive me. Not angry with me?"

No, "not angry with" you, Xu Dan Dan. I counted her excuse note as a better paragraph than what she had copied, graded her accordingly, and thanked her for her honesty and courage.

60

SOME ESSAYS

One block of instruction in the oral English classes is revealing. This class includes listening to a short magazine article entitled "*Is* honesty the best policy?" We like to let them listen to improve listening comprehension, then have them discuss the issue in small groups for conversation practice. We ask them to discuss: Is it OK to lie in certain circumstances? When? Why?

I circulate, listening, and hear that it's okay to lie to keep from hurting someone. Is it okay to lie to protect yourself? Disagreement. All agree that if a friend cheats on an important exam they would not tell the proctor but would warn the friend to stop. It's fascinating to hear how situational they think honesty is, even though all agree that it's commendable. Would American students come to the same conclusions? The exchanges are brisk, even heated. That's good. They're learning to express themselves in English.

It's quite a departure for them to discuss things openly in class. Typically English classes recite or listen to the teacher read or to sit in the language lab for an hour listening to tapes—pretty boring ones, at that.

I have introduced them to creative writing. Since I read all the papers, Rob's as well as mine, I don't know Leon very well but his essay on time enchants me:

So far as we know, time is endless, immense and wideless. It is the tool that people used to count the speeding seconds, minutes and days.

We grow up from childhood–teenages-adult, the periods of these are made up of 'time,' so we've spent thousands of months, millions of minutes, billions of seconds. Because of the time, we can learn from the books, from people, from the society and we can keep our memories and the experiences about success and failed.

We can't live without 'time' and we also have to use the time efficiently. If we'd left the 'time,' I can't believe what the world will be turned to. That must a messing and confused place and all the people must had trapped into big troubles. How to use the time efficiently? Time is precious; we should master it, not the slave of it. And we must keep it in our own hand. It is a big treasure; we should do and must do something for both ourselves and the society.

We must study hard and learn more so we will not regret it that we've spent the meanless time and floated. The days, like floating water, it will never come back again. If we didn't do so, when we are old, there will be nothing left in your memories and to the generation. What a shame, isn't it? On the other hand, if you'd made your efforts and can't be remembered and famed like Einstein, Lincoln, Shakespeare, it's enough. Yes, it's enough, because you've done the work hard and all by yourself. So don't waste time; don't regret the lost; don't worried about the future. Fix a short aim; try to do your best. There is a saying: 'The more you did, the more you get.'

I smile at the charming syntax and the words he's created. I marvel at the tough assignment he's tackled and his noble conclusions. It's so Chinese, I don't even know how to "correct" it. Then I try to imagine tackling anything like this essay in Mandarin and stand in awe at his success.

My Xu Dan Dan writes:

It's sunset now. The sun receives his last rays, and hides himself at the foot of the mountain. The earth becomes gray, and has no vitality. It leaves us sad and desolate. After a busy day, people feel tired, and come back home for a short rest. They begin to hustle about preparing supper. Later, gathering darkness arrives.

Do their veins just flow with poetry?

61

YANGTZE RIVER

May Day. The first of May traditionally is the day when the Communists roll out their latest military hardware and rattle some sabers. We think it has become more a holiday honoring workers, even in China. Formerly a one-day holiday, this year we have seven days off. That is unusual in China, but the economy is improving to such an extent that workers are accumulating income for the first time. The work-seven-days-a-week culture leaves no time to spend that income. Tourism is becoming big business, but the Chinese need free time to be tourists themselves and feed the industry. That, Chinese friends tell us, is why we have an unheard of stretch of holiday this year.

Since we just went to the seafood festival, we decide to stay on campus to rest and plan the final push to the end of the semester. A fortunate decision, we learn, because the Chinese happily saturate hotels, transportation, and restaurants. We, on the other hand, spend some very relaxing days here. Many students can't afford to go home, so we have open house several days and play Chinese checkers, teach them Junior Scrabble, and take long walks together.

The downside is that the university administrators decide we must make up the Thursday and Friday classes we missed on the Saturday and Sunday the students get back to campus. We don't ask why anymore. We just do it. Maybe we've been here too long. I teach my kids to say *Bummer!*

Later in the month we go on a three-day cruise on the Yangtze River, organized again by James and Carr. We call this the "cultural phase" of our contract. We hope to grasp a better understanding of these people, and we want to show the Chinese that we honor their culture.

We're especially interested in seeing the world's largest dam being built for flood control and hydroelectric power in the flood prone Three Gorges area, where the Yangtze River winds through tall cliffs on either side, fabled for the beautiful fishing villages that dot the hills. When the dam is completed, the area will be flooded and immeasurable changes will take place, including relocating more than a million people! We want to see the area before it disappears.

The cruise is neither the nightmare it *could* have been (i.e. a dirty non-air-conditioned room, hordes of noisy tourists) nor the gorgeous vision of the Chinese tourist brochures, but something in between. About 100 tourists join us on a very clean ship set up to handle about 160 passengers. The food is good, the room comfortable with a private bathroom. The showerhead squirts in *every* direction, but hey! We're in there for a *shower*.

The narrow fishing boats, sampans, in which the fishermen live entrance me: tiny, just enough room for one man to crawl under the rounded, bamboo shelter and sleep. The miniscule boats brave the Yangtze's turbulent waves, which threaten to splinter them even on a calm day. The mighty Yangtze (the Yankee name for the Changliang, the Chinese name for one length of the tremendous river) has many stories. Ships have foundered on its tricky rocks; whole villages swamped and swept away; temples built to appease the gods and hold the floods back. Still it slashes through China, leading us back through time as we travel deeper into the reaches of the pitiless river.

A dam to control floods would normally be a fine thing. Yet on the cliffs on either side of the river we see painted white lines showing where engineers believe the waters will rise when the dam is in place. No one is quite sure! Whole cities must be moved; ancestral burial grounds, fertile farmland, homes, and temples will be under water. Some engineers raise the problem of silting at the damsite which might cause more flooding. James amazes us by saying in a conversational tone, "One big worry is that the Americans will bomb the dam."

"Why in the world would anyone *think* of doing that, James?" He shrugs and smiles, lifts his eyebrows, cocks his head.

The ship docks several times during the two-and-a-half days we're aboard, and all the passengers load onto buses that rumble through cities to trams that take us to hilltops to walk through temples (Rob's favorite!) and take in the view; or take smaller boats up tributaries to see more villages and fishermen up close, and marvel at the life they scratch out of rocky desolation. At one dock pairs of men, jockeying for passengers to ride in their sedan chairs up the rocky stairs to the village above, meet us. There are a few takers, all Chinese. As we huff up the stairs, the slim men dogtrot up the stairs shouldering the two bamboo poles, using the bouncing cadence to haul their passengers up the mountainside. That's the way royalty traveled in the past. I could not, would not let myself be carried that way.

Our two Chinese friends see to it that we see all the sights in the big port cities too: temples (Robert smiles politely), and the Yellow

Crane pagoda in Wuhan, a lovely four hundred year old structure. The damsite is so big it's hard to comprehend. Construction equipment grinds everywhere. We watch some smaller locks under construction and see models of the completed locks and dam. Certainly an engineering marvel, but I'm ambivalent about the whole thing.

We come back home tired but thrilled at the experience.

62

FREESIA AND
WINDING DOWN

The freesia bulbs Bonnie sent me for my birthday in April are languishing. Such a sweet gesture. She knows how I adore the aromatic flowers, but I don't have her green thumb. Somehow bringing them to life in gray China symbolizes my time here. I enlist King Lake and his girlfriend. Ornamental horticulture is their field of study, and he at least is confident he can nurse the unfamiliar flowers to health.

He brings the bulbs back to me planted in small pots, and we all watch my kitchen window for tips of green. At last! After tender nursing (King Lake gently scolds me if the soil's too dry or too wet), tiny shoots brave the light. One stalk grows until it leans against the window like a kangaroo with a broken tail. I stick chopsticks in the soil and tie it up straight. (Is there some deep symbolism here?) Soon they're not long enough, so I replace the chopsticks with one of the plastic rods used to pull the curtains closed. Like a gangly teenager the freesia stalk keeps reaching for the sky. Then on a glorious sunny day, I walk into the kitchen to see yellow blossoms dangling playfully on the leggy stem, and the aroma is spectacular!

The blossoms last only a few days, then fade. King Lake is thrilled and relieved. As our time in China dwindles I try not to compare the fragile flower and our service too much.

Besides, the weather's turned golden and pleasant, and we enjoy it. We're also looking forward to our children's visit to China in June. We plan various scenarios with them, explaining that we'll teach and give final exams right up through July. They can get three weeks away from work and home, and will follow an itinerary Rob has worked out. Then when our work here is done, we'll join them for their final week.

Meanwhile, I dodge the thought of leaving the students and never seeing them again. Too I silently wonder how I'll fit in when we step off the plane in America. The past year and a half has been life-changing for us. In my grasshopper fashion, I keep my head on lesson plans and on enjoying moments at the piano with Lucy, Judy, or the other students. I chalk up a breakthrough when my Shakespeare boy grasps the humanity of Shakespeare's Hamlet, kibitz when Rob matches wits with a student determined to whip him at Chinese checkers. I look across the canal and acknowledge the dignity of the villagers who must wash their clothes in dirty water. I have taught only English. I have learned much more.

If I get too romantic about the culture, something brings me up short. For example, I ask my kids to write a biographical sketch in writing class. Their Chinese-written workbook suggests a few famous people: Abraham Lincoln, Albert Einstein, Mao Tse Tung. I am not surprised that most choose Mao. After all, they were drilled on his thoughts early in school. He's very rarely mentioned or quoted now. They study Deng Xiao Ping's thoughts in class.

Interestingly, the Chinese we know certainly know about the

Cultural Revolution, even mention it from time to time, usually to shake their heads and tell how hard it was for their parents. The essays I plod through still sing Mao's praises, lockstep, and say almost without exception, "Chairman Mao made a mistake in his later years, but the good things outweigh the bad." Oh, well, a couple of million people starved because he refused to admit a *mistake* or two. To them, Tiananmen Square is just a big space dedicated to the glory of China reborn. The world associates the name with tanks crushing a student uprising, but not here.

A friend in the States asks our view of China's military threat to the world. Of course, we are two atoms here with absolutely no political expertise. I will say, however, that I never would have believed a whole nation could be kept in such utter and complete isolation from world events. I gather that young people in big cities now tap into the Internet and watch world TV news, but the people we meet accept what China's government-run news agency feeds them without question. There are no probing reporters' questions or contradictory opinions. We see China's military might on TV, and I don't doubt that incredible sums of money go for training and hardware. Reports here insist that it's all defensive.

I joke with Robert that deploying karaoke machines on the battlefield would divert a Chinese army. The troops would lunge for the microphones and croon, forgetting about the battle! Actually, I believe China hopes to dominate with economic muscle and the sheer power of its people numbers, out-producing and outselling the world.

Are they an economic threat? The market here is immense, labor plentiful and cheap, and the Chinese people have tasted economic blood. They very much want a slice of the world pie for themselves. Mom-and-pop businesses crop up everywhere as peasants struggle to grab the money blowing in the wind. The government pretends not to notice the grass roots capitalism.

Labor's cheap. While Robert mutters at almost-new pipes that rust and *everything* that leaks, while we rejoice at finding Scotch tape at last—though the Chinese-made version is too tough to cut or tear—we realize that Japan too at one time struggled to enter the larger world market. Quality control is lousy here, but China will get it right.

Buildings are being torn down and rebuilt everywhere we look, but the boom is often a façade. We notice that new apartment buildings we passed on the bus when we first arrived are still vacant and beginning to crumble a year and a half later. Can no one afford them? Is it a case of overbuilding?

Shanghai particularly has areas of modern glass skyscrapers and chic malls, classy hotels and upscale homes, where old Mandarin family compounds once stood. It's no longer considered risky for foreign businesses to invest in China's future, and the government is doing everything it can to attract them.

Would a Chinese military adventure serve those purposes? I don't think so.

63

FINAL EXAMS

Our assignment in China is winding down. For their final exam, we ask our writing students to select their five best essays and letters and hand in a portfolio. The oral final is a ten-minute individual job interview. We worked for weeks teaching resumé writing, job application letters, and language related to job searches, so asking them to pretend they're interviewing with a company looking for people with English skills seems logical.

Some kids, however, tell us that a few classmates are petrified at the idea of spending ten minutes in a closed room with either Robert or me. Speaking English! Judy giggles, hunches her shoulders in her usual glee. "Some of my friends in Mr. McKee's class are very afraid."

"Oh, Judy, why would they be afraid of him?"

"They know he is kind," she assures me, "but he speaks very quickly, and they are afraid when they are alone with him, with no one to whisper what he says, that they cannot understand him."

"Well, Judy, they *are* English majors. After a whole year of listening to him in class, it's time for them to have a real conversation. Alone. In English. He'll be gentle. I promise."

So we block out the hours to sit in our classrooms and assign interview times for all our 144 students. We suggest they dress in business clothes and practice the Western skills we taught them, like promptness, shaking hands, and looking another person in the eye as they speak. For some it's excruciating. We gave them a list of the questions that we'll choose from, so they have a good idea what's coming.

We begin the interviews. I try to be businesslike, not too soft and squishy, as if we're meeting for the first time. I come to the classroom door and greet each student, shake hands, and offer a chair. Most fall into the game with grace. I try to speak normally, neither too slow nor too fast, and to be encouraging. Most rise to the occasion and do a fine job. Some surprise me with their comments and discussion. They've obviously prepared. A few twitch in their chairs, and I try not to watch the sweat bead on their faces.

Rob comes back the first day very impressed with one of his girls. "Susie, I'd have hired her in a heartbeat on the spot. She was dressed in a very attractive suit, came in the door and put her hand out, and we had an excellent conversation. She did just great!"

I'm *not* looking forward to Zhu Wei's turn. Of all of the English majors, only one truly hasn't a clue what's said in class. Zhu Wei. He's a tall adolescent with an apologetic smile that reminds you of a whipped puppy. The boy who sits next to him helps him in class, I know. I've taken Zhu Wei aside after class and explained the simplest way I can that he needs to hand in his homework. I offer to help him. He hangs his head and mutters, "My English very poor. Very poor."

'Yes, Zhu Wei, but if you try to do the work I will help you. Your English will improve."

"Sorry. My English very poor." How in the world did he pass the college entrance tests? And how did he land in the English Department? I suspect some good old *guanxi* at work here. Somebody owed somebody a favor.

The interview is painful. I smile and lean forward, leading him to respond a little. He knows he can't speak or understand English. I agonize about giving him a failing grade but am reassured by Anna and other Chinese English teachers that even with my failing grade, he will pass along with his classmates.

A letter recently informed us that the "project fund" our sponsors set aside for the three-year teaching commitment to this college has some residue. We are to decide how to spend it to reinforce our instruction here after we leave. It's a lot of money by Chinese standards, several hundred dollars. We suggest our organization put it back in the pot and apply it to an orphanage or the elderly or some needy group, but they say it must go for some sort of legacy here at the college. What should we do? We trade ideas for days, then decide that the students need listening skills most. They have only a few very dull audiotapes of listening exercises with storiettes and then questions to test comprehension.

We decide to expand our tiny personal library of audiotapes in English that go along with small textbooks and donate them to the university library. We tell the ancient library director our idea and ask if he can handle an influx of books-on-tape in English and make them easily accessible to the students. We know the Chinese custom of locking anything new or valuable up, so we want reassurance that the books and tapes will circulate. At once he protests that if he lends them to students, they might be damaged or lost.

"Perhaps, but if they are gathering dust in the library, no one learns English or enjoys hearing the stories." We *think* we have his word, so we set out for the big Ningbo bookstore that handles some limited English material.

We take Jenny because we bring our tape recorder with us. We want to listen to bits of each tape because experience has taught us that many are poorly recorded or are in British English or are just plain boring. The storekeeper offers mild resistance, but when he realizes how much we intend to spend he takes us to a small listening room and gives us a steady stream of tapes and books. After we choose several dozen sets, no others interest us. We decide to shop in Shanghai on the way home or even buy some in America to ship back to the university until we spend every penny. I smile to think of Judy, King Lake, Robbie, Stone, and all the others reading and listening to *Black Beauty, Heidi, Romeo and Juliet, Pride and Prejudice*— simplified of course!

During the last two weeks of June, all students have final exams, and we go to a series of goobye parties, dinners and visits offered by the students. Nightly and sometimes daily activities with lots of warm, fuzzy comments are fun but exhausting. We try to discourage gifts, since we have only two suitcases to carry our belongings. We tell the kids we know they're generous and want to give us something but suggest a card or just a smile would be best. Beside, we know their resources are stretched beyond all reason. They *do* listen to us. Sort of. We accept a few lovely carved wooden fans, a tiny brass vase, a wall hanging, but an audiotape one of Rob's classes made touches us most. The students on the tape tell us how much they appreciate our time with them. Shy little Cinderella sings a charming song. They all join in a group song. One of my classes gives me an old-fashioned autograph book in which each kid has written us a thoughtful note. Another gives us a photo album with a snapshot of each student.

Qiu Zhi Fu, Shakespeare Boy, comes to tell us he was notified he did not pass the exam. He shakes his head, bows slightly, and says, "I will study very hard, and next year it will be better. I will miss my best teacher though."

We get permission to give our former students a party, and we have a hilarious time teaching them another line dance. Rob and I finally collapse into chairs, and they continue swinging to the very American western music. We order a large cake for each class of English majors and spend our last day with them singing, playing games, and trying not to remember that our time together will end. Soon.

Chris, the high school girl who bikes to our apartment most Saturdays, appears a few days before we're to leave with something on her mind. "My mother says it is okay if I come to America with you," she finally blurts. We've never met her mother and are flabbergasted to realize she's serious! "She says she knows you are kind and that I will be happy there."

We are stunned, speechless. The impossibility, the passport, the visa, flight arrangements, all rise in my mouth, but her trusting, yearning eyes stop me. I take her hands in mine and ask her how old she is.

"Fifteen." Maybe fourteen.

As gently as I can I tell her she needs to finish high school. "America *seems* like a golden place to you, Chris, and in many ways it is, but you would miss your friends and family terribly. No one speaks Chinese where we live. Everything would be very strange to you. If you are still interested in going to the United States when you are older, you can write us and we'll try to help you. It is very difficult to get all the paperwork and permission." The hope drains from her eyes. I want to weep. I had no idea she entertained such a possibility. I hug her and tell her she is a daughter of China and will bloom here where she was planted. Maybe we will help her arrange a trip to America one day. Will that ever be possible?

The campus empties quickly. Kids call and wave to one another as they dash for the buses. We've said our goodbyes, and I've wept quietly, sometimes openly.

Suddenly it's real. This place, so forbidding when we arrived eighteen months ago, became our home. The same students who feared us so the first day in class and for days thereafter make a point of coming to us and we hear more than once, "Please remember, Mr. and Mrs. McKee, you have sons and daughters in China now too." They know that we're anxious to see our own children again and our Jordan, but they're quite right. They have big chunks of my heart that will always stay in China.

64

POSTSCRIPT

I t's a good thing our attention has been splintered the past two weeks. If I hadn't been involved helping our own kids discover China, seeing our students disappear from my life would be too much. Rob helped our family plan and made suggestions, even sent ticket stubs to them to make sure the cabby in Beijing knew exactly which part of the Great Wall they wanted to see or the name of a restaurant we recommended in Xian.

They made it to Beijing, exhausted of course, but rebounded and soaked up all the things tourists must see and do there. They took the train west to Datong and Xian, reversing our trail the summer before. They couldn't get a *soft sleeper*, however, and had to endure an unending night in a sweaty *hard sleeper* with Chinese bunkmates who smoked continuously. It turned into a party, though, when Bob, our son-in-law, who couldn't *tell* them to knock off the cigarettes since he spoke not one word of Chinese, mocked a karate chop at the offending smoke. The young men were at first startled, then burst into laughter, put out the cigarettes, and taught them to count in Chinese. They also shared tips on how to buy good, cheap dumplings at the train stations.

They're having the time of their lives, and we're counting the hours until they join us here. Jenny has arranged for a car and driver to take us to Shanghai to pick them up Tuesday evening.

She told us some time ago that we are invited as honored guests of the mayor of Ningbo to a banquet, though she didn't know just when. We forgot all about it in the whirl of the students' leaving. We're pulling our thoughts together to go to southern China with our family, then return to America.

Jenny appears. "The mayor's dinner. It is Tuesday night."

"Well, Jenny," Rob says, "we just will have to miss it!"

She turns white. "Robert, you must come. You are a much-honored guest. You and Susan."

"Jenny, that's the *one* night we can't come! You know our children will get to Shanghai that night." He and I quickly confer. Maybe one of us can go in the car while the other attends the banquet.

Jenny will hear none of that. "You must *both* be there." She's adamant. She suggests, though, that one of the Chinese English teachers could meet the plane, take our family to dinner, then bring them to our apartment. Eventually we reluctantly agree, but we're both hugely disappointed. They'll be looking for *our* faces in that airport after one whole year, and we certainly ache to see theirs.

But we go to the banquet, a very posh affair in a five-star hotel. The mayor and mayorlets drone long speeches; huge bouquets of flowers are presented to Robert and to me, along with large engraved plaques in English and Chinese, praising Ningbo's "leap into the future" and our contribution. Other business people and a sprinkling of teachers are also honored. The usual willowy girls in the traditional *Qi Pao* (Suzie Wong dresses) stand at the speaker's elbow, deftly handing him flowers or plaques on cue. As soon as we can exit gracefully, we catch a cab back to the campus. One remarkable thing we appreciate about formal dinners and ceremonies in China is that when it's over, the master of ceremonies says so! "That is all now."

We hope Robin, Bob, Bonnie, and Rod will be waiting for us at home. No. No one. Well, it's a four-hour drive from Shanghai. They'll stop for dinner, so it's hard to gauge exactly when to expect them. We wait. The hours creep by as we pretend to read or busy ourselves with nonsense. Rob knows I'm beginning to imagine a bloody accident on the road with no way to contact us.

Around midnight car doors slam and jolly bantering reaches us. We throw the front door open at last, and the foursome falls into our arms laughing. Mr. Zhang, the Chinese English teacher we know only formally, stands back beaming paternally. The kids' words tumble all over one another as they tell us about their flight and then seeing Mr. Zhang with a sign with their names waiting for them at the airport. He took them to a restaurant where they spent *hours* sampling every Chinese delicacy he could order. We thank him profusely, pay for the meal, and he bows his farewell.

It suddenly seems like a dream. Both my worlds come together! The kids are excited to see where we've been living and teaching the past year and a half. We wish our students were still on campus so our children could see what we cherish most about our time here.

At last we get everyone bedded down for the night. We'll all be here for only one day and tomorrow night. Then we fly south to the gumdrop mountains of Guilin and Huangshan, Yellow Mountain. We're told this is one of the loveliest spots in the world. We'll see.

Lucy and Judy have remained on campus to meet our children. Anna, my butter-loving Chinese English teacher friend, and Ying Chun, my patient Mandarin teacher, and Jenny will join us all for a tour of downtown Ningbo and dinner at our favorite restaurant. I shake my head as my two lives merge. They're all enjoying one another. The jokes and laughter bubble. I feel as if I'm somehow floating up above, not quite here.

Bob and Rod tell everyone about the train episode, and Judy and Lucy giggle happily at the mental picture of the Chinese passengers tossing out their cigarettes and spending the rest of the night teaching Americans a few words in Chinese. Anna and Ying Chun quiz Robin and Bonnie for their impressions of China so far. All our loved ones are getting to know one another. Rob jokes with our sons-in-law that he'll buy their dinner here if they'll pick up the tab for us all sometime back home. We are eleven diners, and the bill for a several-course meal is about eighteen dollars!

Lucy has landed a job, not as an English teacher, but with a manufacturing company in Ningbo. She was hired, I'm sure, for her English skills since they need people who can speak with and fax foreign dealers. We hope her dream of working in Ningbo comes true. Judy will return to Sunli in the fall to continue her studies. She thinks she wants to be a tour guide and use her English to share her homeland with foreigners. She'd be grand at it! We all pretend that goodbye is only temporary, but the distance between our countries is huge, especially for them. Travel outside China is almost impossible. But we hug them as we stand outside the restaurant and say we'll return to China one day or they'll come to America.

Anna hopes her friend in Akron secures a teaching assistantship for her so she can go to America and work on her master's degree at last. Ohio is a long way from California, but at least it's the same country. Ying Chun shakes her head almost defiantly, saying she could never come to America to see us. "You will have to return to

China, Robert and Susan." And Jenny? She's more a world trav-
eler. She's been to Canada and Europe. Perhaps we will welcome
her to California some day soon. These pipedreams keep me from
sinking into a deep funk. The precious links are too important to
me to believe they'll just dissolve. And they represent many more
students and friends who have indeed become our "sons and
daughters in China."

65

TRAVELS WITH
OUR KIDS

Fortunately, I can't dwell on separating from our Chinese friends. The next morning we must be up early, packed and ready to hop an airplane to take the six of us to explore southern China, all new to us. Rob's done his homework, and Jenny has offered her advice. We're ready to fly into Guilin, quite a gathering point for tourists, so Jenny suggests we stay in a smaller town outside the city.

Rob and I in the lead, our little flock dashes across the square in Guilin, teeming with humanity, to snag the rickety bus. The village where we'll be staying for a few days looks little changed from centuries of rice farming. It's a Mecca for young backpacking tourists from all over the world, but the villagers have changed only slightly to accommodate them.

After a good night's rest we locate a shop, rent bicycles, and set out for the countryside, hoping to wander among the famous mountains that rise suddenly, peak in rounded tops, and drop off just as suddenly. Like gumdrops. Every Chinese ink drawing or painting shapes mountains that way, and as far as I know, they exist only in China. Here.

Bonnie and Rodney are our Granola kids, biking enthusiasts, athletes, so they sprint out on their own. Robin and Bob poke along with us old folks on our bikes. We all try to ignore the heat, but sweat drizzles into my eyes as we pedal along narrow roads through incredibly lovely countryside. Water buffalo plod through rice paddies just as they do in a thousand watercolors.

Our goal is Moon Mountain, and we spot a rock formation with a peekaboo hole at the top just ahead. Maybe that's supposed to be the moon. We pull up gasping at a tiny restaurant with three tables under a vine-covered trellis. The shade looks wonderful, and if the little shack actually serves food and something cool to drink, that's an added bonus. It does! A creek gurgles near the patio, and we hope the bottles of cool water they serve us weren't filled there, though at this point it really doesn't matter. A light meal refreshes us, so we cross the road, stash our bikes, and start hiking up Moon Mountain.

Magically about a dozen young kids carrying Styrofoam coolers filled with water bottles surround us. They call out the two English words they know—Cold water?—and hold up three fingers. Three yuan, about 37 cents. We smile and show them our water bottles. Surely they'll disappear as we climb.

Whew! The steps carved into the mountain are extremely steep! We pull our hats a little lower and wipe the sweat from our eyes. I sneak a peek at everyone, hoping someone will flinch and suggest we enjoy the view from here. No one does.

We begin the climb slowly, the parade of water sellers chatters happily and bounds around us. They show no sign of dropping back to find paying customers. We're grateful for a bit of shade, since at every turn, an even steeper path reveals itself. Rob and I call for a rest stop and select a rock to sit on. My face is scarlet from the heat and the climb. The smiling water sellers surround us at once and fan us with large leaves. It does feel good. I look up the path to see Robin and Bob have three or four young fanners each. We grin weakly and figure we should buy the kids' water just to keep them with us. We go on up the mountain, taking rest stops, drinking our water, and thanking our young sidekicks.

We take forty-five tough minutes to reach the top. The reward is a sparkling view of the villages and rice paddies below. I ask the children to point out their school. They do, and we buy at least one bottle of water from each child. They haven't even broken a sweat, and we're panting. No one else is climbing, so we're all alone up here with a dozen giggling Chinese village children.

When we get together with Bonnie and Rod later we learn they've made some friends too. Rod stopped when he noticed a bicycle repair shop at the side of the dirt road. He's a real bike enthusiast and wanted to inspect the shed with a few tires and bits of bicycles. Bonnie went on for a while until she realized he wasn't behind her. She doubled back to find Rod squatting on the dirt floor with a wizened old man, using hand signals to ask about tools and bicycle parts. The family invited them to their meager lunch cooked right there on the floor of the shop, which they accepted. Bonnie ended up holding a wriggly baby while mama and papa cooked and grandpa entertained them.

One evening we board a small ship in the river to watch the fabled cormorant fishermen. I'd read about the unique technique, and we all wanted to see it done. The ship pulls away from the dock at dusk. After dark, we wonder what we're actually going to see. Silently, a narrow raft pulls up and ties up to our ship. The old man on the raft, only about four or five rounded planks wide, reaches up and lights the lantern on a pole up at his prow, unties the line, then poles away from our ship. He wears only a sort of a loincloth, and while his body shows his age, the sinews I see look like steel. He doesn't glance up at the people looking down from the railing at him but concentrates on his fishing. A few feet from us he releases a large bird that almost immediately disappears underwater. The cormorant must be tethered to the boat somehow, but I can't make it out. It bobs to the surface, then dives again. Every once in a while the fisherman gathers the bird up and holds it over a basket on the boat. The bird's neck is banded so it can't swallow the fish that it catches. After each third or fifth fish, the fisherman relaxes the band so the cormorant can swallow some of its catch. The other fish go into the fisherman's basket on board. The almost ghostly ballet in the shadows the bobbing lantern throws on the water needs only the plaintive sound of an oboe accompaniment.

From Guilin we go to Huangshan or Yellow Mountain for a breath of cool air. We ride the cable car up the tall mountain, taking small backpacks for a one night stay. This is fabled to be the loveliest spot in all of China, and we gulp the cool air greedily as we take in the sweep of rock and pine vistas. We scramble around with hundreds of other tourists, mostly Chinese, to take photos at various gorgeous spots. A pleasant meal in the hotel dining room and a good night's sleep bring us to the high spot of everyone's stay here: sunrise on the mountain. The rooms include heavy coats (Chinese army leftovers, I think) so guests can go out before the sunrise to wait for the glorious colors. Breathtaking, though watching the sunrise with hundreds of voluble tourists vying for photo ops leaves something to be desired.

When the views have filled our eyes and souls, we pack up and begin our hike back down the mountain. The customary visit: Ride up, walk down. How hard can it be?

Steps are carved into the mountain, and the path curves and bends its way past lovely spots. A few hardy souls are coming up the stairs, and we make way for them. Sinewy men pass us carrying up and down the path everything the hotel uses: clean linens, food, trash, repair materials, doors, dishes. Absolutely *everything* must be carried up and down the mountainside. We gasp from the exertion, and we're going *down*, carrying almost nothing!

During a rest break, a man going uphill stops and sets down his bamboo pole and the pots on either end. We ask if we might heft his load. He nods approval, and Robert, who's very strong, can barely lift it off the ground. Rod tries and gets a little further. They are impressed by the grit and strength of the men, who tell us they typically make three trips a day. They're not permitted to use the cable car. All of the building materials for the hotel were carried up too. An hour later we arrive at the bottom, grateful and with a profound respect for Chinese workers.

We go on to enjoy a few days together in Shanghai, and then suddenly our kids are gone. We put them on the plane for America and return to our apartment to clean up and finish packing before we catch a plane back to the States.

66

TIME TO GO

Our apartment seems drearily empty. Our children filled it with life briefly. Our exhausting but exhilarating time together seems almost like a dream now. The rooms echo with the voices of our students as well. The whole campus is quiet, classes finished for the year. A few students, staff and groundspeople are around, but the stillness in unnerving.

We clean the apartment for the next teachers, hoping they'll feel the attachment and satisfaction we do. There were tears here too, and discouragement, even fear. We're sad that our sponsors have decided not to replace us with more volunteers. They think we're too isolated. Professional teachers will take our place here at Sunli.

And we begin to pack. We have much too much for two suitcases, so we winnow our treasures. I leave my coats with Jenny for students who need them; I leave my piano keyboard too for Jenny, who wants her son to learn to play. I already gave my guitar to a student who couldn't afford one of her own.

We come to the two elaborate bronze plaques—heavy and cumbersome—that we got at the mayor's reception. Maybe we should take only one home. They're identical. But how do we dispose of one without offending our hosts? If we put it in the one small wastebasket outside the door, someone will discover it and trace it to us. Our names are engraved on them. Rob wants to take it apart and dispose of the pieces in various places. That seems like a waste of valuable time and energy at this point. It's getting late, and my eye lights on the sluggish canal out back. "Let's just heave it into the canal. As filthy as that water is, it'll never be found." Robert reluctantly agrees.

By this time it's dark, but we peer around the corners like a Peter Sellers movie before we toss it into the drink. It makes a healthy splash in the middle of the canal. We go back inside to finish squeezing eighteen months' worth of clothing and memories into four suitcases.

We're not quite finished when we step outside to catch our breath. As we stand beside the door Rob says, "Isn't that something glinting out there in the canal? It couldn't be the plaque, could it?!" We squint through the murky darkness at something glowing in the moonlight in the middle of the canal. "Doggone! Who'd have thought it would *float*?" We're stunned! We *can't* leave it there floating in the garbage and flotsam, sure to be noticed. It would be the ultimate insult. But how in the world can we get it back? By now it's midnight. We're beyond tired, but we've got to retrieve that plaque.

Rob rummages through the apartment and comes up with some twine. He ties a rock on the end of it and tosses it into the water beyond the plaque, hoping to snag it back to our side. Now we're *really* characters in a Peter Sellers movie, desperately hoping no one comes along wondering what in the world the strange foreigners are up to *now* and at this hour of the night. Finally, the floating plaque bobs closer to the bank, but it's still about six feet below us. How do we get it up here? Another rummage produces an empty box. Rob ties string at the four corners, painstakingly lowers the box to scoop the plaque up—but the box *floats* and will not scoop under the plaque. This is getting really personal! He reels the soggy box in and punches holes in it, careful not to touch anything that's been in that unholy water. This time it works! The cardboard works slowly under the plaque, (space-walking astronauts use similar skills, I'm sure!) and Rob slowly raises his cargo up to our level. It's on the ground! Neither of us wants to touch it after its bath in the filthy water, so Rob wraps it in newspaper and dismantles the thing—he reminds me, looking up from under his eyebrows, that was his original plan— and stashes the pieces in several trashcans around the campus. It's well after 2:00 a.m.

Who would've thought it would *float*?

We're on the plane back to America. Jenny saw us off at the ultra-modern Shanghai airport. We even managed to hug her and think she will miss us too. Sadness at leaving the students we grew to love in China tempers our joy at returning home. We know we're deeply changed. Are they? Have we done any good? We couldn't share any of the joys and teachings of our faith with them. Perhaps we helped some improve their English, and that alone may mean a better life. We speak quietly, wondering what we left behind. I weep silently, knowing I'm leaving part of my heart.

I begin to flip through the autograph book a class gave me as a farewell gift. Each student wrote something of his or her feelings in it. I didn't have time to read them all before we left. A page falls open:

How time flies! The world is becoming so beautiful and our lives are getting so rich and colorful just because of you and Mr. McKee's existence.

One year has passed since we met last year. Looking back upon the days we spent together what I learnt from you was not only a foreign language but also being a human.

Our Chinese have such an old saying: 'There is no banquet lasting forever.' One year is short. Ten years is still not long enough. I heartily wish the time would stop, the day on which you will leave us wouldn't come for all my life. The leaving time always pitiful, but let's be happy now, though probably we can't see each other. Still we can communicate with one another. You and Mr. McKee's impressions have been carved on my heart.

From you that we learnt the most Americans' personalities— so gracious and generous.

From you I learnt the culture, customs and habbits of the U.S.A.

Especially from you I realized the greatest value of a person— devotion.

The atmosphere of your class is always so active that everyone of us is soaking in it.

The seas may run dry and the rocks may crumble, but the friendship between us will remain loyal for ever!

Good luck to you and your family and all the gracious people on earth.

Best wishes for my dearest teachers – Mr. and Mrs. McKee.

Yours truly,
Wang Zhao Xiang

67

SEVEN YEARS LATER

After seven years would China still feel gray? The dank April night our plane landed in Shanghai's driving rain was a gloomy beginning to our return. A weary ticket agent droned that our continuing flight to Ningbo had been cancelled more than a month ago. No one had bothered to notify us, so we were marooned in a soggy, unsympathetic city. Except that one kind woman pitied two desolate travelers hunched under backpacks and suitcases huddling in a metro station for shelter from the rain. My *putonhua*—Chinese language—limited at best, was encrusted with rust. Her English "Can I help you?" offered a rush of relief. A wiley cabbie had taken us in half an hour earlier, refused to turn on his meter, saying he would take us to a hotel we'd asked for at a fee the equivalent of about $50. We *knew* that he was gleeful to have entrapped two dripping, desperate foreigners. We weren't that desperate so insisted on his stopping and opening the trunk to retrieve our luggage. To his surprise (as he offered to lower his price to $35) we got out of the cab and waved him away, leaving us – a dripping white-haired couple standing in the pelting rain in a dark, completely unfamiliar city. That's when we stumbled into the nearby metro station. We told our story to the kind Chinese lady, who snorted in disgust that Shanghai was trying to regulate its unscrupulous cab drivers and apologized. She said that ride should cost no more than 30 yuan (about $3.75), and insisted on going out into the rain herself to find an honest cabbie who would take us to the hotel.

A night of uneasy rest. Even exhaustion brought only spotty sleep. We'd forgotten about the hard Chinese mattresses. But we managed to get to the train station the next morning by eight o'clock and bought tickets for the next train to Ningbo. We were disappointed that the earliest train we could catch didn't leave until 11:30. Later we learned that we were lucky to have gotten some of the last tickets for a *seat* on the train. Tickets for standees were sold later and the aisles of the train were filled with people rocking along for the four hour ride to Ningbo and points in between. Many clutched frayed, plastic bags of belongings. A young Chinese mother jiggled her baby on her lap and fed him slices of watermelon across the aisle from us. Rob and I sat abreast facing two peasant women who studied our faces then put their heads down on the small metal table between us and went to sleep. They both had tattered bags wedged on the floor, so we all had only a small, circumscribed area for our feet.

Through the grime on the window I watched the huge, identical apartment buildings and industrial complexes of Shanghai slide by. Gray? Mostly, but there were splashes of color here and there in this robust, gangly city of China. We even spotted a bit of blue sky after the downpour of the night before. I wondered if we'd made a mistake in making this trip—something of a sentimental journey. Can you really go back again? Should you? Our former students were all dispersed, busy with jobs or more schooling in various places. We'd kept up e-mails and letters with a few of them.

Lucy had e-mailed us some time ago that she was getting married. She'd sent us pictures and invited us to her wedding. We'd smiled and felt touched that she had included us in her plans for her wedding day. As Rob and I discussed the possibility of our return to China, the journey's improbability began to shift toward "Why not?!" I e-mailed Lucy that yes, we would be delighted to come. The phone beside our bed jolted us awake at something like 4:00 one morning shortly after that. It was Lucy's excited voice—so thrilled that we were really coming. She'd forgotten about the time difference.

So here we were click-clacking on the final leg of the step into our past. Cityscapes faded into rice ponds, villages, muddy fields and orchards. Unmistakable Hangzhou loomed in the window. It's about halfway between Shanghai and Ningbo. The distinctive rectangular turret on top of many apartment buildings is this city's trademark. Walks around Hangzhou's serene Westlake in the center of the city were pleasant hours for me seven years ago. We wondered if we'd see changes in this mighty dragon of a nation.

Betty's smile was a *most* welcomed sight at the station in Ningbo. She had been one of Robert's students and now worked as an assistant in Jenny's office dealing with foreign teachers and students at the college where we had taught. We had known that Jenny, our key contact at school, would just have returned from a university trip to South Africa and Mexico the day before we were to arrive. She had written that Betty would meet us. I'd phoned from Shanghai to tell her of the change in arrival plans so she had a taxi waiting at the Ningbo train station to take us to our hotel. Betty, the shy student was now a competent, self-confident young woman, who seemed genuinely pleased to be able to help us. Her English was much improved. She got us to our hotel and graciously said goodbye as we tried to get our bearings. After a few deep breaths I called Lucy, who had written that she would take us to dinner the evening we arrived to introduce us to her future husband and her sister.

Petite Lucy still sparkled and even submitted to being hugged by both Rob and me when she stepped into our hotel room. She kept repeating, "I'm so happy that you came!" Her radiance wiped away the greedy taxi driver, the soggy feet, the sleepless nights, and the jolting train ride. We followed her down to the hotel lobby where she introduced her younger sister Jill, who spoke a little English and her groom DunDun, who did not. We were a jolly group in the private room at a nearby restaurant. The eel, squid, all the fishy things Ningbo residents love that I'd tried to dodge when we lived here, were paraded proudly onto our table. With my chopsticks I surreptitiously selected vegetables and nuts from the delicacies offered.

"How old are you now, Lucy?" I really wanted to know. This question would've been rude by American standards, but is simply a polite point of interest in China.

"Twenty-nine Chinese age. Twenty-eight Western. Do you think I look young?"

"Of course. You look spectacular!"

She had a good job now with a shoe export company. Her English was valuable to the company since they dealt with several nations outside China. Her gentle management skills shone through then as she outlined the plans for her wedding day two days away. She had an appointment to have her hair and makeup done at 7:00 a.m. on that morning. We should be ready to be picked up at 8:00 after which our car and a caravan of three other cars would pick her up and begin the two-hour drive to her home village. Jill would ride with us. We would be driven to her brother's house, where her mother lived with her brother, sister-in-law and their three-month-old baby girl. We, along with about 100 relatives and friends, would go to a small restaurant there for lunch, then the caravan would return to Ningbo for the reception at the hotel where they would entertain an additional 150 guests, friends from Ningbo that evening. I think she was relieved when we told her that we had plans with Jenny and college friends to tour the new campus for the next two days. She still had "many things to do."

Jenny assured us on the phone that she was rested from her trip and we agreed to meet her at nine the next morning. Her hairstyle was a little longer than she'd worn it seven years ago, but she strode through the door with that same open smile, and no nonsense manner. Both Rob and I wrapped her in a bear hug before her Chinese evasion of public display of affection could set in. I felt she was genuinely thrilled to see us again too. We sat in our hotel room and swapped memories before we climbed into a cab for the trip to the new school campus that was just ugly concrete and brick shells when we left. Both Rob and I were immediately smitten by the cleaner streets and new buildings of the city of now about three million people, Jenny said. The thousands of three-wheeled bicycle pedicabs that had choked the city streets had vanished. "No longer allowed in Ningbo," Jenny told us, "but they may still ride in the villages." In their place were occasional similar bicycle-driven trash collectors, armed with short brooms. Men and women swept up trash and dumped it into the bins on the backs of their three-wheeled bikes early each morning and evening. We saw them lined up one evening near our hotel waiting to dump their day's take into large trash mashers. This was a huge leap forward from the debris-clogged streets that we remember. Tall buildings too had shot up in the seven years since we'd walked these streets. Instead of rows of narrow, makeshift shops hawking bolts or umbrellas, now gleaming glass windows of highrise department stores displayed Armani suits, Gucci bags, and millions of cell phones.

Even the metamorphosis in the city didn't prepare us for the stunning buildings and grounds of Sunli University's new campus. My awe at Chinese diligence and accomplishment ballooned. Where I remembered mud-spattered chunks of cement and naked steel columns when we passed the new campus site on the way to the airport to leave seven years ago now rose brick and glass dorms and classroom buildings with grass, flowers and graceful trees lining the paths between them. Jenny grinned as the cab dropped us off at the arched gate and we began our walk to her office. Photographs simply hadn't prepared us for the reality of this dream-come-true for the movers and shakers in this corner of the world. A few curious students glanced at us as they passed, but we were clearly not the new zoo acquisitions we'd been so few years ago. Jenny told us they now had twelve foreign teachers on campus. We toured the impressive library with its whole section of English language books, some still multiple copies of slightly outdated manuals, an eclectic mix of technical books and literature. I would love to've spent hours there, but Jenny and the smiling library deputy who accompanied us paced (respectfully) while Rob and I browsed through the stacks. Another smaller reference library juts out into a manmade lake created in the center of the campus. "It's like a ship," Jenny joked as we circled the huge picture windows overlooking the lake. We didn't try to hide our amazement at the facilities and progress that we saw.

The pièce de résistance was the English department, technically the Foreign Language Department, since they now offer Japanese instruction as well. Jenny walked us to an airy multistoried building and introduced us to Professor Wang, the head of the English department. He told us that he'd arrived a month or so after we left, and said many nice things that he'd heard over the years about us. He must've seen the eagerness in our eyes as he asked if we'd like to sit in on a class. Of course we did. The Chinese English teacher, a friendly faced man in his mid-thirties, welcomed us into his class and explained that they were in the middle of a debate on the six-party talks about Korea. Holy smoke! We'd felt exultant if we could've gotten our students to express an opinion on the pollution problems of the Far East. Mr. Wang, Jenny, Rob and I tried to fade into the background quickly though we knew we were a huge elephant in the classroom. After some embarrassed giggles the girl at the front continued her appraisal of the world situation albeit from China's point of view. After my delight at the fine level of English I heard, I couldn't help marveling at the desks and chairs—movable!—and the center cluster of desks with computer screens for the kids to access the Internet. In fact it looked as if all the desks had Internet access capability. As the girl finished her presentation another girl asked for questions. Hands went up. Hands went *up!* How we'd worked to encourage our timid students to raise their hands! Several questioned the speaker's conclusions and facts, very politely, in halting but fine English. We sat through three more presentations, all equally well researched and clearly expressed. Later I found that both Robert and I were quietly worried that we'd be asked to express our opinions on the hot political topic, and frankly we didn't feel well enough informed or qualified on the subject. At the class conclusion their teacher asked if we'd like to say something. We both stood and congratulated them on their excellent grasp of English and wished

that world leaders might reason and listen as well as they. In the hall
we thanked and expressed our admiration to both the teacher and to
Mr. Wang. As we continued our tour of the sprawling campus I
couldn't lose the image of my former dingy, chalk-choked classroom
with the rotting wooden platform. More than that I saw my first
terrified students as they tried to wrap their tongues around bewildering sounds for an individual—me—from a world far removed
from theirs. We had all stretched to meet one another on friendlier
ground, but now these kids seemed self-assured, competent even
cocky in their new-found English. I could only hope that these
students of today retain the gentle trust and devotion that we
received from their older brothers and sisters.

Jenny agreed to show us the old campus, now a junior college,
where we had taught. It took a ride in the school car and we almost
didn't recognize it when we drove up to the gate. New buildings
stood where fields of weeds had grown. We walked back to our apartment building—such a glowing refuge for us years ago. Our
apartment—a jewel in the crown of the college then—had been
converted into an infirmary. A little sad to see it chopped up, but
comforting to think that students found help here when illness or
problems loomed. Our gorgeous wood floors were gone, covered
over with more utilitarian tile. Mildew had taken its toll. The
formerly white, gleaming interior and exterior walls were wearing
the gray patina of China. The administrator who joined us from this
campus proudly pointed out the old classroom building, (where the
ancient classrooms of my first memories were) which was swathed in
green netting and swarming with workmen. This was to be
completely redone and ready for next term, she said. Again I
marveled at China's ability to put its head down and crash through

any impediment to its progress. So many changes in so few years.

We talked about the appearance of a booming economy with Jenny later that evening as we trudged up the five flights of cement steps to her apartment for dinner with her husband and fourteen-year-old son. (Elevators are still non-existent in apartment buildings here.) Yes, Jenny said, salaries had improved; food and other costs had gone up, but generally people were pretty well off. They proudly drove us to their new apartment they hoped to have ready by next year. Yes, they had a car, an older VW, which they planned to replace after their home costs were taken care of maybe next year. Their new apartment, smelling of plaster and new paint, was, thankfully, on the first floor. They even had a patch of yard in the back. It was a lovely two-bedroom apartment with indirect lighting in the living room, a balcony off the master bedroom, a dining room, and a modern kitchen. They'd had a room excavated behind the garage for a ping-pong table. Jenny's husband teaches in the horticulture department now at the same school, so they both must be making comfortable salaries to be able to buy this. Their son Ya Ya, the rascally seven-year-old we remembered, was shy now, but said he remembered us. When we tried to engage him in English, which he was studying in school, he'd turn his big, black eyes up to his mother and say, "Shenme shuo?" (What did they say?) But his grin told us that he liked having these peculiar Americans in his home since we brought his beloved Pepsi and his mother bought a package of rolls for our dinner, a rarity for them. Jenny's husband did the meal preparation for us, steaming a white fish, placing a tray of small shrimp boiled in their shells on the table, stir-frying together some "green vegetable" with nuts, and bringing out a dish of young bamboo shoots prepared with soya sauce. We ate and talked, with Jenny in the middle since neither Ya Ya nor her husband spoke English, and my Chinese was stumbling as it resurfaced. The marvelous Chinese expression, "Ting bu dong" kept coming to mind—literally—"hear, don't understand."

Anna, our good Chinese friend who had taught English with us years ago, then had managed to get a visa to come to America to complete her Master's Degree, was back in Ningbo. We loved having lunch with her and walking to Moon Lake, an artificial lake and park in central Ningbo. Again we were smitten with the enlarged park that was bristling with red and white azaleas. We strolled along paths in new green open space. As we waited to cross one busy intersection a woman on a moped stopped to speak with Anna. We assumed she was asking directions as the conversation went on for several minutes. As we crossed the street Anna told us that this woman had a job like Jenny's at another college and wanted to know if we were interested in teaching oral English there. We smiled and remembered that both Jenny and Mr. Wang had gently urged us to return to Sunli University when we told them how impressed we were with the growth there. "You don't have to stay for years. Only one term would be fine." Apparently there is still a great hunger for native English speakers in China.

The weather forecast for Saturday, Lucy's wedding day, had suggested the chance of rain, so we were glad to wake up to clear skies. We'd shipped over to Jenny a box with our dress clothes and our wedding gift, to avoid having to carry extra baggage. I had had the surreal experience in America of trudging through stores probing for an appropriate gift for Lucy and her groom. Every tag I turned over read: Made in China, so I finally gave up. I had one of my watercolors framed with plexiglass to make shipment surer and wrapped it in lovely bath towels (Made in India). Rob and I were up early; he grunted but pulled on his dress shoes, the wedding-and-funeral-blue-suit and tie. I'd had my red and yellow print, best dress pressed and buckled on my high heels so we were ready by 8:00 AM. Jill was right on time to pick us up. She introduced our driver, one of DunDun's good friends. The other cars were parked too outside our hotel. It seemed that all the occupants were on their cell phones, including the groom who had the bridal bouquet in a deathgrip. Obviously he'd been given this responsibility. After some milling around we all set off for the brief ride to pick up the bride. DunDun had on a suit with a rose boutonnière. The other young men were wearing suits too, but I mentioned to Rob while Jill was outside the car that I was a little startled that she was wearing jeans. Maybe she plans to change when we get to their village, he suggested.

A CD was playing in our car, I'm sure for our benefit, of semi-classical music. As if on Hollywood cue, Lucy hurried up to the cars scooping up her hooped white gown with her veil floating behind her as our music burst full volume into the wedding march. Rob had his video camera so he was out of the car taping the whole exercise. He explained to Lucy, who looked like a porcelain doll, that he would film everything and make a DVD for them of their wedding day and that pleased her. We had been designated as lead car apparently since we led the four cars, the bridal couple in the last car. Ningbo's highrise offices and apartment buildings thinned as we darted through traffic. Rob observed that the Chinese drivers' first rule—the need to be in *front* of everyone else—hadn't changed. Lane lines and darting into oncoming traffic are unimportant impediments to Rule One. We tried to relax as we slid by industrial complexes, then villages and tea bush covered hills. Our mood music was at top volume still and it became obvious that they had only one CD that was to be repeated as the wedding march rolled around four or five times in the two hour drive. There was much conferencing by cell phone and a few stops to regroup. Finally they stopped to decorate the cars. Pink rosebuds in clear suction cups were placed all over the cars, with two large bouquets fore and aft on the bridal car. We slowly pulled into a village, then onto a narrow alley that turned into a dirt dead end surrounded by apartments. The car doors swung open. We had arrived. We followed behind Jill and the young men up the steps to Lucy's brother's apartment. Lucy introduced me to her smiling mother and waved toward the three dozen people milling around the place, "These are friends and relatives. We will now have a rest." We were led into a bedroom where we perched on the bed's edge and watched the people traffic swirl around us. I was permitted to hold Lucy's sleeping three-month-old niece for a while, which I adored. Then we were told we should have something to eat in the kitchen. Wait! Weren't we getting ready to go to the restaurant for lunch? Bowls of steaming *jauzi*—dumplings— in soup waited at the table. We sat with Jill, one other lady and an elderly gentleman who beamed at us. I asked if he were a relative. No, a neighbor. As far as I could tell, we five were the only ones eating. There was evidence that a crowd had been entertaining themselves there for quite some time since the tile floor was littered with seed shells, bits of food and paper. And, again, all the women were in jeans, including Lucy's mother.

Lucy reappeared, this time in a flaming red and gold *qi pao*, the traditional Chinese wedding dress, and announced that it was time to walk to the restaurant. We all trailed down the stairs, across the dirt yard stumbling over a few stones, then out onto the dirt street the short distance to the small restaurant. I admired Lucy's ability to negotiate the rocks and dirt in her tiny high heels and elegant gown without breaking stride. The place was already crowded with her guests who gave her a raucous greeting as we were led to a private dining room upstairs. The bride, groom, Jill, the young men who'd driven the cars and we were all that could fit into that room. The other tables crowded into the downstairs. Food began arriving as the bride and groom took up the custom of going to each guest to pour his or her drink, (bottles of Pepsi, 7-Up, beer and wine were on the tables) and taking a sip with them. Smoking among the men seemed universal, so the groom was armed with cigarettes which he offered to each male guest.

Lucy had explained to us that it was a custom for wedding guests to request stunts of the bride and groom as they circulated among the tables, so we occasionally heard eruptions of laughter from downstairs as DunDun was asked to carry Lucy around the table or rub their noses together. Meanwhile I was focused on appearing to eat from the mounds of delicacies that kept arriving on our table—clear strips of squid, pink shrimp with accusing eyes and spider-like feelers, fish swathed in aromatic herbs, but with head and tail poised as if caught mid-squiggle in the river, and—this was a new one—a soft-shelled turtle, black and posed in a sticky goo that sure looked like swamp ooze to me. I desperately searched for some vegetables or my old stand-by—peanuts—but saw only a new dish brought steaming to the table—an orange-brown pouch—an animal's bladder or stomach (?) which my table companions pounced upon tearing sections off with their chopsticks. Could I please just have a peanut butter and jelly sandwich? I've always thought of myself as an adventurous foodie, but some internal brakes skidded on, and I played with my food, grateful that others were laughing and enjoying their own meal. I noticed that Rob too was peeling his shrimp slowly and sorting through the selections. He did try the turtle, which he later told me was tough and elastic.

After lunch we repeated the walk through town returning to brother's apartment for another "rest." Lucy changed back into her white gown and veil, while family and friends hauled wedding gifts, great bags of bedding and plants decorated with candy, into the trunks of the cars. Then the car caravan took off again, amid bursts of firecrackers that the neighbors set off as a sendoff. Jill explained that they had to pass around candy to the friends and neighbors as tradition dictated so they would be allowed to pass. Lucy's mother remained behind, not joining us for the Ningbo reception. Lucy explained that she would entertain relatives who'd traveled to their village there that evening.

That night at the hotel Lucy and DunDun hosted a gala reception for another crowd, their Ningbo friends. This time DunDun's parents and sisters were there. The banquet room was swathed in pink organza and white lilies. The only thing that might've been a wedding ceremony that Rob and I could detect was a brief time at the microphone by DunDun, then his father, then Lucy's former boss before dinner began. We were later told that the actual formal papers are signed at a government office possibly even a year earlier.

Since Lucy was a year older than our own students, there was only one boy at the wedding, who had had Rob for English for half a year, who came up to shake our hands at the reception. Our own students had scattered. Judy was living and working in New Zealand. We'd lost touch with King Lake and Barbara. But the tender memories of all of them simmered as we looked around the ballroom and saw the young couples, some with a child bubbling in the happiness of the celebration.

We could go home now. Our "sons and daughters in China" are moving on like floating water (!) with rich, full lives. Our own lives have been deeply enriched by knowing them.

Lucy on her wedding day

Gallery

Susan McKee's artwork, memories following their days in China.

人類登上火

Robert Selecting Eggs   *Ink and collage 16" X 20"*

Chinese Fishermen   *Ink and collage 16" X 20"*

Chinese English Students   *Ink and collage16" X 20"*

In A Chinese Sampan   *Acrylic and collage 30" X 36"*

Chuga, A Village Street Scene   *Acrylic and collage 25" X 30"*

Bridge In A Chinese Village   *Collage 25" X 30"*

On A Shaoxing Canal   *Acrylic and collage 25" X 30"*

Chinese Canal *Watercolor 10" X 12"*

Peeking Duck On A Bus   *Oil on paper 22" X 28"*

Chinese Fishing Nets   *Watercolor 10" X 12"*

Faithful Chinese In A Buddhist Temple   *Ink and collage 16" X 20"*

S usan McKee has spent a lifetime bouncing around the world with a military family. This rolling stone is finally gathering some moss with her husband, Robert, in San Luis Obispo, a charming town near the coast of central California. Their three grown children live nearby so spoiling grandchildren is a favorite pastime.